Historical Archaeology

Volume 49, Number 1   2015

Journal of
The Society for Historical Archaeology

CHRISTOPHER N. MATTHEWS, Editor

Montclair State University
1 Normal Avenue
Montclair, New Jersey 07042

IN ASSOCIATION WITH REBECCA ALLEN, ASSOCIATE EDITOR

Published by
THE SOCIETY FOR HISTORICAL ARCHAEOLOGY

Historical Archaeology is indexed in the following publications: *Abstracts of Anthropology*; *America: History and Life*; *Anthropological Literature*; *Art and Archaeology Technical Abstracts*; *Arts and Humanities Index*; *British Archaeological Abstracts*; *Current Contents/Arts and Humanities*; *Historical Abstracts*; *Humanities Index*; and *International Bibliography of the Social Sciences*.

Copyediting by
Richard G. Schaefer

Composition by
OneTouchPoint/Ginny's Printing
Austin, Texas

Contents
Volume 49, No. 1, 2015

CONTRIBUTORS

INTRODUCTION

ARTICLES

CONTRIBUTORS

MARJORIE AKIN, 20212 HARVARD WAY, RIVERSIDE, CA 92507-6621.

REBECCA ALLEN, ENVIRONMENTAL SCIENCE ASSOCIATES, 2600 CAPITOL AVENUE, SUITE 200, SACRAMENTO, CA 95816.

JAMES C. BARD, 1500 SW PARK AVENUE, NO. 424, PORTLAND, OR 97201.

R. SCOTT BAXTER, ENVIRONMENTAL SCIENCE ASSOCIATES, 2600 CAPITOL AVENUE, SUITE 200, SACRAMENTO, CA 95816.

PAUL G. CHACE, PAUL G. CHACE & ASSOCIATES, 2665 KUANA LOA DRIVE, ESCONDIDO, CA 92029.

GORDON H. CHANG, DEPARTMENT OF HISTORY, BUILDING 200, STANFORD UNIVERSITY, STANFORD, CA 94305.

SUE FAWN CHUNG, DEPARTMENT OF HISTORY, UNIVERSITY OF NEVADA, LAS VEGAS, 4505 MARYLAND PARKWAY, BOX 5020, LAS VEGAS, NV 89154-5020.

JOHN JOSEPH CRANDALL, DEPARTMENT OF ANTHROPOLOGY, UNIVERSITY OF NEVADA, LAS VEGAS, 4505 S MARYLAND PARKWAY, MAILSTOP 455003, LAS VEGAS, NV 89154-5003.

KELLY J. DIXON, DEPARTMENT OF ANTHROPOLOGY, UNIVERSITY OF MONTANA, 32 CAMPUS DRIVE, MISSOULA, MT 59812.

SHELLEY FISHER FISHKIN, DEPARTMENT OF ENGLISH, BUILDING 460, STANFORD UNIVERSITY, STANFORD, CA 94305.

LYNN FURNIS, 14382 FLOMAR DRIVE, WHITTIER, CA 90603.

RYAN PATRICK HARROD, DEPARTMENT OF ANTHROPOLOGY, UNIVERSITY OF ALASKA ANCHORAGE, 3211 PROVIDENCE DRIVE, ANCHORAGE, AK 99508.

SARAH CHRISTINE HEFFNER, PAR ENVIRONMENTAL SERVICES, INC., 1906 21ST STREET, SACRAMENTO, CA 95811.

J. RYAN KENNEDY, DEPARTMENT OF ANTHROPOLOGY, INDIANA UNIVERSITY, STUDENT BUILDING 130, 701 EAST KIRKWOOD AVENUE, BLOOMINGTON, IN 47405-7100.

MARY L. MANIERY, PAR ENVIRONMENTAL SERVICES, PO BOX 160756, SACRAMENTO, CA 95816.

JOHN MOLENDA, DEPARTMENT OF ANTHROPOLOGY, COLUMBIA UNIVERSITY, NEW YORK, NY 10027.

MICHAEL R. POLK, SAGEBRUSH CONSULTANTS, 3670 QUINCY AVENUE, SUITE 203, OGDEN, UT 84403.

ADRIAN PRAETZELLIS, DEPARTMENT OF ANTHROPOLOGY, SONOMA STATE UNIVERSITY, ROHNERT PARK, CA 94928.

MARY PRAETZELLIS, ANTHROPOLOGICAL STUDIES CENTER, BUILDING 29, SONOMA STATE UNIVERSITY, ROHNERT PARK, CA 94928.

CHARLOTTE K. SUNSERI, DEPARTMENT OF ANTHROPOLOGY, SAN JOSE STATE UNIVERSITY, CLARK HALL, SUITE 469, ONE WASHINGTON SQUARE, SAN JOSE, CA 95192-0113.

TIMOTHY R. URBANIAK, MONTANA STATE UNIVERSITY–BILLINGS, ARCHAEOLOGY FIELD TEAM AND DRAFTING AND DESIGN PROGRAM, 1500 UNIVERSITY DRIVE, BILLINGS, MT 59101.

BARBARA L. VOSS, DEPARTMENT OF ANTHROPOLOGY, STANFORD UNIVERSITY, 450 SERRA MALL, MAIN QUAD, BUILDING 50, STANFORD, CA 94305-2034.

GARY J. WEISZ, 11715 W. PINE STREET, SANDPOINT, ID 83864.

Gordon H. Chang (张少书)
Shelley Fisher Fishkin (雪莉·菲什金)

Fragments of the Past: Archaeology, History, and the Chinese Railroad Workers of North America
过去的碎片：考古、历史与北美地区的中国铁路工人

ABSTRACT

Although the labor of the Chinese workers who built the first transcontinental railroad (and other railroads in the western part of the country) was pivotal to the development of the United States, these workers have never received the scholarly attention they deserve. The incredibly rich work of archaeologists who have studied the thousands of pieces of material culture gathered along western rail lines promises to open vibrant new dimensions of historical recovery of this key chapter in the intertwined social, economic, and political histories of China and the United States.

尽管修建第一条横贯大陆铁路（以及其它美国西部铁路）的中国工人为美国的发展立下了汗马功劳，他们在学术界从未获得与其成就相称的关注。考古学家现已就西部铁路沿线上搜集的数以千计的文物进行了研究。他们丰富的研究成果必将为中美两国之间错综复杂的社会、经济、政治历史中这一关键篇章开启生动的、崭新的历史维度。

In 1865 the Central Pacific Railroad Company introduced large numbers of Chinese workers on the western portion of the first transcontinental railway across North America. Four years later, largely because of their toil, Leland Stanford drove the famous "golden spike" at Promontory Summit, Utah, to complete the line. The labor of these Chinese workers, who eventually numbered between 10,000 and 12,000 at any one moment, was key to creating the immense wealth that Leland Stanford used to found Stanford University and was pivotal in the development of the United States, particularly the West. These workers have never received the scholarly attention they deserve: that Chinese worked on the railroad is common knowledge, but little is known about any dimension of their lives and experiences.

The given historical interpretation of the construction and completion of the transcontinental line is immensely deficient and one-sided in several ways. It is traditionally told as a story of national triumph and achievement, and as the culmination of "manifest destiny," the ordained linking of the two coasts of North America and the physical connection of the nation; it is celebrated as the first step in healing the divisive wounds of the Civil War. The historical accounts of that achievement over the last hundred years have usually continued to play on these facets of the story. The contributions of the Chinese railroad workers are noted, but not fully appreciated, or omitted entirely. Whether an historical account celebrates the line as an accomplishment of the risk taking and acumen of the "Big Four" (the directors of the Central Pacific Railroad) or views it as an emblem of their Gilded Age financial machinations, the contributions of the Chinese railroad workers are overshadowed by the story of businessmen who benefited from their labor.

Challenging the narratives that focus on national triumph and the business elite is very difficult. It is always tough to "speak truth to power," even when writing history. But beyond the ideological, the task is immense simply because the extant documentary record overwhelmingly favors the elites. The Big Four left voluminous personal archives (correspondence, diaries, and financial records) that tell the story from their points of view. The enormous (almost endless) paper archives of the railroad companies reflect managements' points of view. From the Chinese workers, however, there is virtually nothing left today—not one letter, diary, memoir, or even a brief note. For the past century, researchers have searched for such material, but in vain. Nothing has yet been found in English or Chinese, in the United States or in China. Recovering their lived experiences and history beyond meager outlines has been a colossal, and frustrating, endeavor.

Here is the challenge: how do we as scholars give voice to the voiceless? How do we understand lived experience if we have nothing from the actors themselves? Is it possible to employ new methodologies of interpretation, beyond

Historical Archaeology, 2015, 49(1):1–3.
Permission to reprint required.

the traditionally historical, to recover and interpret the past? These questions lie at the core of the Chinese Railroad Workers in North America Project at Stanford University. The project was launched in 2012, with generous seed money from the president of Stanford, to reconstruct the lives and experiences of the Chinese men whose labor on the first transcontinental railroad helped shape the physical and social landscape of the American West (in addition to being the basis of the fortune that allowed Leland Stanford to found Stanford University). Recognizing that this key chapter of the past cannot be adequately addressed by scholars working in any one field, or on one side of the Pacific, the project brings together over 150 U.S. scholars in archaeology, anthropology, American studies, cultural studies, ethnic studies, history, literature, overseas Chinese studies, political science, and other fields. Between 2012 and 2014 the project has sponsored or cosponsored conferences at Stanford, in Taipei, and in Guangzhou. The fruits of this interdisciplinary and transnational collaboration will be publications in English and Chinese, and an open-access digital archive of primary materials.

For the past several years, we of the Chinese Railroad Workers in North America Project have been engaged in the most thorough interdisciplinary search for source material ever undertaken. We have accumulated the largest collection of contemporary reports and first-person accounts of the building of the western portion of the transcontinental line and are continuing to search for those elusive documents from the Chinese workers themselves. We also are exploring new ways to try to reconstruct that lost history; this includes drawing on the incredibly rich work of archaeologists who have conducted field research and studied objects from the Chinese railroad workers who lived throughout the American West. This archaeological work on the thousands of pieces of material culture gathered along western rail lines has been one of the most exciting developments in the research of the Chinese Railroad Workers in North America Project and promises to open vibrant new dimensions of historical recovery.

The articles in this special issue of *Historical Archaeology* are outstanding examples of the promise of the work that North American archaeologists have conducted over the

past several decades. The work that these archaeologists have done, largely completed independently of each other, is opening new vistas on Chinese immigrant life and railroad work in 19th-century North America, richly complementing textual materials. It is a truism that archaeologists dig down, that every excavation is by definition site-specific. In the case of the Chinese who worked on the first transcontinental railroad, however, one population literally moved along the roadbeds they were grading and the tracks they were laying across vast distances. Many of those individuals later moved on to work on rail lines elsewhere in the country—particularly in the American West—leaving material residues of their lives and their world wherever they went. Archaeologists at different sites may have been examining artifacts from some of the same individuals. At the very least, they were exploring material objects associated with individuals from many of the same towns and villages in China. This landmark issue brings together, in conversation for the first time, the research of archaeologists who have worked on often far-flung Chinese sites along the Central Pacific Railroad and other rail lines in the United States.

Each of the articles offers unique and careful study of a specific physical site, such as Summit Camp, or of a particular dimension of work and daily life on the line. The reader learns about foodways, health care, leisure activity, and ways of living and dying. Taken together, the studies help us as scholars to begin to learn even more. They offer tantalizing insights into social organization, interactions among Chinese and non-Chinese populations, and the conditions of life in a moving work environment. We can also begin to engage in comparative analysis; that is, we can begin to make some sense of rural vs. urban life; life in the American West vs. life in other locations where Chinese workers toiled, such as in the Canadian Rockies; life in the Sierras in the winter vs. life in the summer and in the desert. The picture of Chinese railroad worker life begins to become textured and dimensional, and moves beyond the simple and general.

Moreover, these essays from archaeologists are engaging those of us from other disciplines, such as traditional historical study and cultural studies, and encouraging us to see the past in new ways. We are challenged to employ new ways of thinking and forms of evidence to develop interpretation in our writing and even in our ability to "visualize" the past through the use of mapping and other digital humanities approaches. All this is most exciting and promising. This issue is not so much an "end" product, but the announcement of a beginning of efforts in inter-disciplinary collaboration.

It is also the beginning of a conversation that will be carried on across the country and across the Pacific. Placing the Chinese in the foreground of a narrative requires a rethinking of important contexts and vantage points long dominant in the telling of American national history. The story of the Chinese workers, an essential element of the railroad itself, is necessarily a story of trans-Pacific connections, of the intertwined social, economic, and political histories of China and the United States. It is a story of the Chinese diaspora and the overseas Chinese. It is also a story of ethnic America, a foundational experi-ence in Asian American history. These different narratives and interpretive contexts must all be considered to construct a fuller, richer, and more comprehensive understanding of the history. This collaborative project engages and speaks to many important bodies of literature far beyond those of "the railroad" alone.

What next? These essays will encourage and advance interaction with other scholars around the world, especially in Asia. Already, scores of colleagues in Asia are exploring this topic on their own, and these essays will no doubt inspire many of them to work with scholars based in the U.S. to examine this rich record of material culture. What perspectives and information they will contribute to the understanding of potsherds originating in southern China, gaming pieces, spiritual objects, food remnants, apparel, construc-tion and work skills, and beyond, one can only begin to speculate.

Acknowledgments

We would like to express our gratitude to Professor Barbara Voss for her leadership in organizing the archaeology component of the Chinese Railroad Workers in North America Project at Stanford, and to the editors of *Historical Archaeology* for the opportunity to develop this special issue.

GORDON H. CHANG
DEPARTMENT OF HISTORY
BUILDING 200
STANFORD UNIVERSITY
STANFORD, CA 94305

SHELLEY FISHER FISHKIN
DEPARTMENT OF ENGLISH
BUILDING 460
STANFORD UNIVERSITY
STANFORD, CA 94305

Barbara L. Voss (芭芭拉・沃斯)

The Historical Experience of Labor: Archaeological Contributions to Interdisciplinary Research on Chinese Railroad Workers
劳工的历史经验：考古学对于中国铁路工人之跨学科研究的贡献

ABSTRACT

Since the 1960s, archaeologists have studied the work camps of Chinese immigrant and Chinese American laborers who built the railroads of the American West. The artifacts, sites, and landscapes provide a rich source of empirical information about the historical experiences of Chinese railroad workers. Especially in light of the rarity of documents authored by the workers themselves, archaeology can provide direct evidence of habitation, culinary practices, health care, social relations, and economic networks. As archaeologists expand collaboration with each other and with scholars in other fields, interpretations of archaeological research move beyond site-specific description into analyses that trace the changing experiences of workers as they entered new environments and new landscapes. The materiality of daily life at railroad work camps is interconnected with the risks the workers endured and the wealth that their labor generated for railroad owners and investors.

自1960年代以来，考古学家已经研究了修建美国西部铁路的中国移民与美国华裔劳工的劳工营。这些文物、现场以及景观为我们提供了有关中国铁路工人之历史经验的丰富实证材料。尤其在工人们自身书写的文件相对匮乏的情况下，考古学能为他们的居住，饮食，健康，社会关系与经济网络提供直接的证据。随着考古学家拓展彼此协作，以及他们与其它学科学者之间合作，考古学研究的诠释范围已经超出了对特定现场的描述：如今，我们已能够追踪分析工人们在进入新的环境与景观后所发生的经验变化。铁路劳工营的日常物质生活与工人们所承受的风险，以及他们为铁路拥有者和投资者所创造的财富，都是相互关联的。

Introduction

The story has been repeated in history books since shortly after the completion of the first transcontinental railroad: in 1865, Leland Stanford and E. B. Crocker, investors in the Central Pacific Railroad, complained about the scarcity of white labor in California. Crocker proposed that Chinese laborers would be hardworking and reliable; both he and Stanford had ample prior experience hiring Chinese immigrants to work in their homes and on previous business ventures (Howard 1962:227; Williams 1988:96). Railroad construction superintendent J. H. Strobridge balked but relented when faced with rumors of labor organizing among Irish immigrants. As Crocker's testimony to the Pacific Railway Commission later recounted: "Finally he [Strobridge] took in fifty Chinamen, and a while after that he took in fifty more. Then, they did so well that he took fifty more, and he got more and more until we finally got all we could use, until at one time I think we had ten or twelve thousand" (Clark 1931:214; Griswold 1962:109−111; Howard 1962:227−228; Chiu 1967:46; Kraus 1969a:43; Saxton 1971:60−66; Mayer and Vose 1975:28; Tsai 1986; Williams 1988:96−97; Ambrose 2000:149−152; I. Chang 2003:56); see also Heath (1927).

The 10,000 to 12,000 Chinese who labored on the first transcontinental railroad were the largest corporate wage-labor force in the 19th-century Americas. Some historians argue that the actual number was much higher, at least 14,000 and perhaps 23,000 (Griswold 1962; Mayer and Vose 1975; Tsai 1986; Chew 2004). Working alongside an estimated 2,000 additional non-Chinese workers—mostly European immigrants, but also European Americans, African Americans, and Native Americans—the Chinese laborers on the first transcontinental railroad were recruited first from within California and possibly Nevada. Most were young men who had earlier worked in mining, logging, road building, and other trades. Some may have worked on earlier railroads, as small numbers of Chinese immigrants were employed on railroad construction on the Central California Railroad as it passed by Marysville in 1858, and on the San Jose−San Francisco Railroad constructed in the early 1860s (Barth 1964:117−120; Chiu 1967; Chinn et al. 1969:43; Bain 1999:209). But, for most, railroad construction was a new line of work.

Historical Archaeology, 2015, 49(1):4−24.
Permission to reprint required.

Soon the potential pool of new Chinese immigrant laborers in California was exhausted, and beginning in March 1865 the Central Pacific Railroad contracted with Cornelius Koopmanschap, a Dutch sea captain, to recruit thousands of new workers directly from villages in southern China (Griswold 1962:17).

Construction Superintendent Strobridge and the acting chief engineer, Samuel S. Montague, marveled in late 1865 at how quickly Chinese workers became "skillful in the performance of their duty. Many of them are becoming very expert in drilling, blasting, and other departments of rock work" (Heath 1927:12). Through these skills, Chinese workers on the first transcontinental railroad were responsible for some of the most significant civil engineering feats in the 19th-century United States: carving roadbeds out of cliff faces at the Cape Horn passage and blasting tunnels through Sierra Nevada bedrock. Their experienced and efficient labor was also central to the epic feat of laying 10 mi. and 56 ft. of track in a single day on 28 April 1869. At the driving of the Last Spike (Figure 1) on 10 May 1869, E. B. Crocker remarked to the assembled crowd: "In the midst of our rejoicing at this event, I wish to call to your minds that the early completion of this railroad we have built has been in great measure due to that poor, despised class of laborers called the Chinese—to the fidelity and industry they have shown" (Griswold 1962:322).

Chinese immigrant and Chinese American workers continued to build and operate the railroads of the American West for several decades following the completion of the first transcontinental in 1869. Yet for all of their significant accomplishments, there is very little known about their own perspectives and experiences. To be sure, Chinese railroad workers were described (often in racially charged language) by newspaper journalists, and the owners and managers of the Central Pacific Railroad described Chinese workers in reports, letters, and congressional testimony (U.S. Congress 1877; Hoffmann 1879; Heath 1927; Kraus 1969a, 1969b; Williams 1988; Bain 1999:222,237). But, in the archives the voices of the workers themselves are silent. With few exceptions (Chew 2004), the Central Pacific Railroad did not record the names of the individual Chinese workers, instead "working and paying them by the wholesale" (Kraus 1969a:51,54, 1969b:204,221; Williams 1988:97–98; Huang 2006:90). Journalists of the time and historian Hubert Howe Bancroft's researchers interviewed only white supervisors and workers (Kraus 1969a; Deverell 1994). Chinese workers were not called to testify in the court proceedings and congressional hearings that unfolded in the wake of the completion of the Central Pacific Railroad, including the 1876–1877 congressional investigation of Chinese immigration and the 1887 investigations of the United States Pacific Railway Commission (1887).

FIGURE 1. The Last Spike. William T. Garrett Foundry, San Francisco, 1869. (1998.115, Iris & B. Gerald Cantor Center for Visual Arts at Stanford University; gift of David Hewes.)

Additionally, to date, no personal writings, letters, or diaries of Chinese railroad construction workers on the first transcontinental have been found, although concerted international efforts are underway to locate such traces (Chang and Fishkin, this issue). Unlike the correspondence of white railroad workers, letters sent home by Chinese workers to villages in Guangdong and Hong Kong did not end up in regional historical society archives in the United States. In China, the many wars, revolutions, and cultural upheavals throughout the 20th century also led to the widespread destruction of family and town archives.

As a consequence, the same few descriptions of Chinese railroad workers on the Central Pacific Railroad are repeated again and again in history books and on public monuments. They note that Chinese railroad workers were hired and managed in gangs of 12 to 20 people, each of which had its own cook and a headman who handled accounts. They describe how Chinese workers were responsible for their own board and ate a diet that included imported Chinese staples, such as dried shellfish, fish, fruits, vegetables, and seaweed, as well as locally sourced rice, pork, poultry, and tea. They recount that Chinese railroad workers bathed daily, changing into clean clothes after work, and preferred to build their own dugouts and stone shelters rather than use company-provided tents. The Chinese railroad workers, it is recounted, kept to themselves and, other than gambling, enjoyed few vices.

Yet nearly all of these widely repeated descriptions are derived from a handful of primary sources. For example, Nordhoff's (1874) *California*, which is widely quoted in the historical accounts of Chinese railroad workers on the first transcontinental, actually describes a small crew of Chinese railroad workers in the Central Valley of California nearly a decade later. Another widely quoted source is a three-paragraph description of the "First Chinese" by Heath (1927), an employee of the Southern Pacific Railroad public relations department, published in the corporate newsletter *Southern Pacific Bulletin*. This, however, was written nearly 60 years after the fact. Similarly, journalists' accounts from short publicity junkets to view railroad construction are also frequently reprinted by historians as generalized

descriptions of the lives of Chinese workers. In this context, historical archaeology—always an important source of information about "those of little note" (Scott 1994)—emerges as a critical body of evidence that can provide direct access to the lived experiences of the tens of thousands of Chinese immigrants who labored to build the railroads that transformed 19th-century North America.

Archaeology and the Chinese Railroad Workers in North America Project

In 2012, Gordon H. Chang and Shelley Fisher Fishkin formed the Chinese Railroad Workers in North America Project (CRWNAP) to "give a voice to the Chinese migrants whose labor on the Transcontinental Railroad helped to shape the physical and social landscape of the American West" (Chinese Railroad Workers in North America Project 2012). Gordon H. Chang (2001, 2008), an historian who has been central to the development of interdisciplinary Asian American studies, and Fishkin (2005), an American-studies scholar who, among other accomplishments, is widely credited with developing transnational American studies, articulated a clear vision for an interdisciplinary, international research collaboration that would open new perspectives on a topic that is paradoxically emblematic of American history, yet often represented through stereotypes and misinformation (Chang and Fishkin, this issue) (Figure 2).

New Directions, New Challenges

Chang contacted me in February 2012 to ask if I knew whether archaeologists had ever studied Chinese railroad workers, and, if so, whether I and other archaeologists might be interested in joining in this effort. Over the next few months, I met several times with Chang, Fishkin, and other researchers on the CRWNAP to explore possibilities for archaeological collaboration. I also met with scholarly delegations from Guangdong, China, the home province of most 19th-century Chinese immigrants to North America, including those who worked on the railroads. These conversations identified several priorities for archaeological involvement, along with several core challenges.

FIGURE 2. Public commemorations of Chinese railroad workers on the first transcontinental railroad: (a) *The Chinese Coolie*, Kenneth H. Fox, 1972, Auburn, California; and (b) detail of mural *Shadows Past*, J. Bowers Foxey, 2012, Colfax, California. (Photos by author, 2012.)

For the CRWNAP, the research priority for archaeology was clear. In the absence of direct written evidence from the workers themselves, could archaeology be used to reconstruct the historical experience of Chinese laborers who built the first transcontinental and many of the other railroads in the American West? What was daily existence like? How was it the same or different on particular segments of the railroad? What was the workers' sensory experience—what did they see, smell, touch, hear, and taste? What did they eat, and how did they cook their food? What was their housing like, their bedding, and any furniture they might have had? How did they manage sanitation? What health challenges did they face, and how did they care for themselves in this new environment? What leisure activities did they enjoy?

Along with the potential for archaeology to reconstruct historical experience, CRWNAP scholars posed a number of questions related to demography and social life. What was the social organization of work camps? Were women and children present in the railroad work camps, even though they are not documented in historical records? What was the relationship between Chinese and non-Chinese laborers? Can anything be learned about the relationship between railroad workers and their home villages in China?

Still another set of questions focused on material culture and economics. How were the goods found on railroad worker camp sites procured? What was brought from China, and how were imported goods obtained and distributed? Did Chinese railroad workers participate in local and regional economies? Did they produce their own objects from local materials and eat food gathered from the local environment?

These research priorities are all questions that archaeology is well positioned to address. Where people lived, what objects they used in daily life, how they interacted with their environment and each other, and how they cared for their bodies and nourished themselves are central themes in archaeological research. They are also questions that move the historical archaeology of Chinese railroad workers in new directions. As discussed at greater length below, much prior archaeological research on

Chinese railroad workers has been largely descriptive. Studies that have moved beyond description to interpretation often focused on questions of assimilation and acculturation. In contrast, the questions posed by the CRWNAP challenge archaeologists to reconstruct the experience of Chinese railroad workers from the workers' own vantage point, a deeply contextual, inside-out perspective.

Chang, Fishkin, and I also noted several challenges in bringing archaeology into this interdisciplinary, transnational collaboration. First, there are problems of translation. Few North American archaeologists speak or read Chinese, and consequently historical archaeology has not engaged very much with Chinese-language archives and scholarship. Similarly, the historical archaeology of Chinese immigrants and Chinese Americans is exclusively published in English. The CRWNAP's translation programs are addressing the former; the publication of this thematic issue with titles and abstracts translated into Chinese is a small first step toward remedying the latter. Beyond language, there is the issue of disciplinary translation. The jargon and conventions of historical archaeology are largely opaque to those outside the field. The practice of thinking with places and objects is unfamiliar to those who are trained in the analysis of texts. Bridging these disciplinary differences requires sustained communication, as non-archaeologists learn about the practice of archaeology, and we archaeologists reframe our research in ways more compatible with humanities-centered scholarship.

The second challenge is methodological. Archaeology is inherently place-based, and most archaeological research on 19th-century railroad workers is site specific. Yet the construction and operation of 19th-century railroads was inherently about expanding and transforming mobility. How can the place-based strengths of archaeology contribute to this study of movement? Similarly, one of archaeology's core methodological strengths is the study of change over time. Railroad construction occurred rapidly, and work camps were short term, some occupied for only a day. What can archaeology bring to the study of such ephemeral sites? These place- and time-based methodological issues challenge us as archaeologists to think beyond our site-specific research and ask how we can collaborate better with each other to study the highly mobile historical populations of the 19th-century American West.

The third challenge concerns access. The majority of historical archaeology studies are presented in "gray literature": site records, cultural resource management reports, government agency studies, environmental impact studies, technical reports, and unpublished theses. Most of these documents are stored in regional or government agency repositories; many contain privileged information and are not accessible to other researchers or the public. Consequently, even though a large body of scholarship on the archaeology of Chinese railroad workers already exists, it has been nearly impossible for non-archaeologists to access this research. This thematic issue of *Historical Archaeology* is an important step toward bringing this research into broader circulation and dissemination.

**Into Action: Forming
the Archaeology Network**

To address these challenges and begin work on the research priorities identified by the CRWNAP, Chang, Fishkin, and I decided to establish a network to facilitate communication with and among archaeologists studying railroad contexts. To date, more than 90 archaeologists have joined the Archaeology Network of the Chinese Railroad Workers in North America Project. The first face-to-face meeting occurred as an informal gathering at the 2013 annual meeting of the Society for California Archaeology. Since then, regular conference meet-ups have occurred at annual meetings of the Society for American Archaeology, the Society for Historical Archaeology, the American Anthropological Association, the Association of Asian American Studies, and the Northwest Anthropological Conference, as well as subsequent annual meetings of the Society for California Archaeology.

In October 2013, the CRWNAP hosted a workshop at the Stanford Archaeology Center to begin the process of collaboration between archaeologists and other CRWNAP scholars (Figure 3). Over 65 people attended: roughly 40 archaeologists representing diverse government, cultural resource management, museum, and academic affiliations; about 20 other CRWNAP

scholars representing history, literature, visual studies, cultural studies, urban studies, geography, American studies, Asian American studies, and digital humanities; and several descendants of railroad workers. A key priority that workshop participants identified is to make archaeological research on Chinese railroad workers more accessible to other scholars and to the public, both here and in China. This thematic issue of *Historical Archaeology* is one concrete step in that direction, more than doubling the number of published articles and book chapters on the subject. For public outreach, Rebecca Allen, Mary Maniery, and Sarah Heffner are developing an interpretive book centered on artifacts found on Chinese railroad worker sites. To facilitate access to gray literature, Christopher Merritt coordinates an archaeology bibliography for the CRWNAP: <http://web.stanford.edu/group/chineserailroad/cgi-bin/wordpress/researchmaterials/archaeology/>. Members of the Archaeology Network are also working with state offices of historic preservation and federal and state agencies to develop protocols for redacting privileged information from other gray literature sources so that those too can be publically released. Eventually, all these materials will be incorporated into a digital archive being developed by the CRWNAP.

The workshop also identified new directions for research. While individual railroad worker sites have been identified and studied (discussed below), comprehensive archaeological survey is rare, and only small segments of historical railroad alignments have been studied. New surveys along some segments of the first transcontinental railroad are underway (Molenda, this issue; Polk, this issue), and additional projects are in the planning stages. Alongside new field research, workshop participants emphasized the importance of analyzing existing understudied collections (Baxter and Allen, this issue; Molenda, this issue), as well as intersite analysis of reported data to address broader themes (Akin et al., this issue; Harrod and Crandall, this issue; Heffner, this issue; Kennedy, this issue; Urbaniak and Dixon, this issue). Finally, participants noted that many railroad worker sites are endangered by erosion, development, illegal artifact hunting, and vandalism, and discussed the importance of protecting these sites through nominations to the National Register of Historic Places (Baxter and Allen, this issue).

FIGURE 3. October 2013 workshop of the Archaeology Network of the Chinese Railroad Workers in North America Project. (Photo courtesy Chinese Railroad Workers in North America Project, 2013.)

Under Chang and Fishkin's leadership, Archaeology Network scholars are forging transnational connections with scholars in China and other Asian countries. In September 2014, representatives of the Archaeology Network participated in a CRWNAP delegation to Sun Yat-sen University in Guangzhou. As historical archaeology is still an emerging field in Asia, the strongest connections at present are with researchers in folk culture, overseas Chinese history, architecture, and geography. Looking ahead, future interdisciplinary conferences and workshops are planned, both in the United States and China; the CRWNAP is also developing digital humanities platforms for international collaboration.

The History of Archaeological Research on Chinese Railroad Workers in North America

The rich history of archaeological research on Chinese railroad workers in North America has much to contribute to this shared effort. Formal investigations of Chinese railroad work camps began in the 1960s, although undoubtedly sites and artifacts had been studied prior to this by railroad historians, avocational archaeologists, and collectors. This coincided with the formalization of historical archaeology as a professional and academic discipline in North America (the Society for Historical Archaeology, for example, was founded in 1968) and the advent of historic preservation laws in the United States, such as the 1966 National Historic Preservation Act, that required assessment of historical archaeological resources. Since then, the archaeology of Chinese railroad workers has largely been conducted as part of the growing field of overseas Chinese archaeology (Schuyler 1980; Greenwood 1993; Wegars 1993; Maniery 2004; Voss 2005; Voss and Allen 2008; Staski 2009; Ross 2013), also referred to as Chinese American archaeology and Asian American archaeology.

Most archaeological studies of Chinese railroad worker sites have been conducted to comply with historic preservation laws. In research for this overview, a thorough effort was made to locate site records and cultural resource management (CRM) reports related to Chinese railroad workers, but undoubtedly many more remain. Besides CRM studies, student theses have generated important bodies of research, most notably through anthropology programs at the University of Nevada at Reno, University of Idaho, University of Montana, Western Wyoming Community College, and University of Texas at Austin.

This overview of the history of archaeological research on Chinese railroad workers in North America is organized by railroad line, beginning with the western divisions of three United States transcontinental railways: the Central Pacific, the Southern Pacific, and the Northern Pacific. In all three, Chinese immigrants were the majority of workers for the western divisions, while white (American-born and European immigrant) workers were recruited for the eastern divisions. (Chinese immigrants also constructed two other transcontinental lines: segments of the Atchison, Topeka & Santa Fe Railroad and the western division of the Canadian Pacific Railway. However, no archaeological studies of Chinese work camps on these railroads have been identified.) Discussion of regional, branch, and narrow-gauge railroads follows.

Central Pacific Railroad, 1865–1869

Connecting Council Bluffs, Iowa, with Sacramento, California, the eastern (Union Pacific) and western (Central Pacific) divisions

of the first U.S. transcontinental were joined on 10 May 1869, at Promontory Summit, Utah, in the famous Golden Spike ceremony. The first known professional presentation of archaeological research on a Chinese railroad worker site was delivered nearly 100 years later, at the 1969 annual meeting of the Society for Historical Archaeology. Chace and Evans (1969) reported the findings of a surface survey at Summit Camp at Donner Pass, California, where Chinese immigrants labored for four years to blast tunnels through the Sierra Nevada summit. The transcript of Chace and Evans's presentation is printed as the opening article in this thematic issue, making it publically available for the first time. Their research at Summit Camp supported important descriptive analyses of artifacts commonly found on Chinese immigrant and Chinese American sites (Chace 1976; Etter 1980; Evans 1980). Summit Camp, in Tahoe National Forest, was formally recorded in 1997 and was recommended for eligibility to the National Register of Historic Places in 2008. The California State Office of Historic Preservation concurred with this recommendation in 2009. As one of the largest and longest-occupied residential bases for Chinese railroad workers in North America, Summit Camp has continued to be a focus of archaeological research (Baxter and Allen, this issue; Molenda, this issue).

Railroad grade survey in the Tahoe National Forest has also yielded evidence of two other substantial Chinese worker camps: Windmill Tree and China Kitchen (Molenda, this issue). The Tahoe basin is also notable for extensive studies of Chinese immigrant woodcutters and colliers who provided lumber and fuel to the Central Pacific Railroad during its construction and operation (Chung 2003; Smith and Dixon 2005; Lee 2008).

Promontory Summit near Ogden, Utah, has also been the subject of long-term archaeological research programs. The symbolic and historical importance of the "meeting of the rails" led to this area being designated as Golden Spike National Historic Site (GSNHS) in 1957. As Polk (this issue) summarizes, the archaeological and historical resources of the GSNHS have been the subject of multiple historical and archaeological surveys since the 1960s, although little subsurface work has been conducted. The GSNHS contains at least 19 construction camps, many of which likely represent worker residences during the bitterly cold 1868–1869 winter. At least four camps are identified as Chinese (Polk and Simmons Johnson 2012; Polk, this issue). The work camp sites in the GSNHS are notable for the variety of architectural remains represented, including dugouts, pit structures, leveled platforms, and masonry foundations (Anderson 1983).

One of the most unusual documented archaeological sites associated with Chinese workers on the first transcontinental is a deposit of Chinese cultural material, including a Chinese brown-glazed stoneware liquor jar, on a small knoll near Monument Rock on the Central Pacific Railroad grade near Promontory Summit. Unlike the large-group work camps at Summit Camp and Promontory Summit described above, the presence of this jar "indicates an individual act of agency, possibly seeking a place of quiet refuge from the daily toils of laboring" (Merritt 2013).

Prior archaeological work on the first transcontinental shows a tendency toward study of large base camps used for specialized operations. As Molenda (2013:5) notes: "larger and more permanent camps tend to be located near walls, culverts, and tunnels, with stone structural remains visible on the surface. ... In contrast, the Overseas Chinese seem to have occupied much more ephemeral 'tent camps' in areas where construction proceeded quickly." For example, archaeologists studying the Fenelon, Nevada, railroad grade identified sparsely distributed Chinese ceramic fragments that were interpreted as possible evidence of 1860s Chinese railroad construction crews (Turner 1982:19). Molenda's ongoing survey in the Tahoe National Forest identified several diffuse artifact scatters adjacent to the railroad grade that may also represent these ephemeral tent camps.

After the construction of the first transcontinental was completed, many Chinese workers were hired as section hands to repair and maintain the lines. Notably, the Union Pacific, which did not hire Chinese workers during construction, quickly engaged Chinese veterans of the Central Pacific to support railroad operations in the eastern division of the first transcontinental. Raymond and Fike (1981) conducted surface studies and historical research

on 25 Utah branch stations, 6 of which showed evidence of substantial Chinese habitation from the 1870s to the 1910s. Gardner (2004, 2005) and colleagues (Gardner et al. 2002; MacNaughton 2012) have studied Chinese workers at the Aspen and Hampton Union Pacific station camps on the first transcontinental railroad in Wyoming.

Southern Pacific Railroad, 1873–1883

Formally incorporated in 1865, the Southern Pacific Railroad was acquired by the Central Pacific Railroad in 1868, with the formal merger completed in 1870. Construction of this southern transcontinental railway began in 1873. The route connected Sacramento, California, to New Orleans, Louisiana, via Los Angeles, California. Strobridge, the former construction supervisor for the Central Pacific Railroad, came out of retirement to complete the job. The Southern Pacific relied heavily on the labor of veteran Chinese workers from the first transcontinental. By completion, the Southern Pacific employed an estimated 6,000 workers, 5,000 of whom were Chinese (Briggs 1974:31). The Golden Spike joining the western and eastern divisions was driven on a bridge crossing the Pecos River in Texas on 12 January 1883.

Fedick and Stone (Fedick and Stone 1988; Stone and Fedick 1990) conducted an archaeological survey near Phoenix, Arizona, on a 100 ft. wide corridor along 22 mi. of the historic Southern Pacific Railroad. They identified seven sites associated with railroad construction and maintenance. One of these, Site 12, was investigated through surface collection, test excavation, and data recovery. "An abundance of Chinese ceramics, and opium cans, and food remains associated with a traditional Chinese diet" (Stone and Fedick 1990:146) indicate the site was inhabited primarily by Chinese workers. Chronologically sensitive artifacts indicate that the site was more likely related to maintenance and repair of the railroad, pointing to the important role of Chinese employees in the operation of the Southern Pacific Railroad, as well as in its construction (Stone and Fedick 1990:144–145).

Briggs (1974) investigated two railroad construction worker encampments, the Langtry

Camp and the Upper Rio Grande Tunnel No. 1 Camp, at the Pecos River crossing in Val Verde County, Texas. The Langtry Camp, which housed Chinese workers, consisted of stone-lined tent platforms associated with double-hearth features. Briggs (1974:53) estimated the camp likely housed between 500 and 665 Chinese residents. Artifacts were primarily residential and include a much higher percentage of European- and American-produced goods than seen at Chinese construction camps on the first transcontinental. The remote location of the camp, distant from both the Pecos River and the railroad alignment, may have been selected to minimize confrontations with white and Mexican workers on the eastern division. This locale placed stress on Chinese workers by increasing distance to water sources and increasing Chinese dependence on company suppliers (Briggs 1974:197–204).

The Chinatown in El Paso, Texas, was established by Southern Pacific construction veterans, many of whom continued to work for the southern transcontinental railroad after its completion. Archaeological research has shown that in contrast to coastal Chinatowns where residents had ready access to imported goods from China, El Paso's Chinese community relied heavily on locally available material culture and foods. For example, American-manufactured bottles were often relabeled for secondary purposes, including laundry bluing, Chinese wines, and traditional Chinese medicines (Staski 1993).

Northern Pacific Railroad, 1870–1883

The Northern Pacific, linking Chicago to Seattle, employed an estimated 3,000 to 5,000 Chinese construction workers, most of whom were also veterans of the first transcontinental. The railway was completed on 8 September 1883, with the driving of a golden spike near Gold Creek, Montana.

Avocational archaeologist Gary Weisz (2003) and colleagues (Merritt 2010; Merritt et al. 2012; Akin et al., this issue) have identified and recorded nine line camps on the Northern Pacific Railroad (NPRR) alignment through the rugged valley of the Clark Fork River in western Montana. A 10th, the NPRR front town known as Cabinet Landing, was studied by

Landreth and colleagues (Landreth et al. 1985). Comparative analysis of the 10 sites shows several general similarities: they are oblong, linear camps along river valleys, and they all have tools representing the labor of railroad construction, along with horseshoes and other hardware from draft-animal tack (Merritt et al. 2012:677). Beyond this, the distribution of material culture bifurcates along ethnic lines. Spatial analysis shows clear segregation, with distinct separate areas for Chinese workers, often with natural topography creating a spatial buffer between Chinese and white workers. Chinese encampments were invariably located in uneven, mosquito-infested areas, indicating that camp geography reinforced ethnic hierarchies among workers. The material remains on Chinese camps "emphasize foodways, folk beliefs, and leisure—all of which represent means to help balance a life of hard work" (Merritt et al. 2012:686). The loss of life among Chinese railroad workers on the NPRR was severe, and the Thompson River, Heron, and Noxon camps include rare extant examples of graves and grave markers (Merritt et al. 2012:680–681). Additional work to document Chinese work camps along the NPRR is currently under way in Bonner County, Idaho, through the University of Idaho (Stokeld and Petrich-Guy 2014). Research by Urbaniak and Dixon (this issue) also documents the eventual replacement of Chinese workers on the NPRR with a multiethnic workforce including Japanese, Norwegian, and English immigrants.

Other Railroads

Along with the transcontinentals, railroad companies soon built "thousands of rail lines—large and small gauge—leaving extensive dendritic networks of railroad grades, trestles, and tunnels throughout the West" (Dixon 2014:193). From the 1860s to the 1890s, Chinese workers were central to the construction and operation of many of these railroads.

In Nevada, the Virginia & Truckee Railroad (V&TRR), linking the Comstock Lode in Nevada with silver ore processing and supply centers in Reno, Carson City, Silver City, and Virginia City, was constructed primarily by 1,200 Chinese workers recruited after the completion of the first transcontinental. Chinese workers on the V&TRR were especially targeted by the anti-Chinese movement, which marched on railroad work camps in American Flats near Virginia City and drove Chinese workers off the grade into the surrounding hills. Railroad executives brokered a deal that reserved some railroad segments for white workers. Wrobleski (1996) conducted a pedestrian survey of a 6 mi. section of the V&TRR grade and analyzed three Chinese construction worker sites. One site was badly eroded; the second was a residential site with 13 tent platforms, as well as numerous hearth features; and the third included a single flat area with a dense distribution of artifacts related to food, alcohol, and opium consumption. Wrobleski concluded that this third site likely represented a separate recreation area, possibly the headquarters of a sutler who sold goods to railroad workers. Wrobleski (1996:66–68) interprets this separation of recreational activities from sleeping and resting areas as a common aspect of working-class life, in which the shared consumption of foods and social drugs facilitated camaraderie in the midst of a harsh, centralized, and regimented work life.

A fourth V&TRR work camp, the Lakeview Camp, was recorded and excavated in the late 1990s (Rogers 1997; Furnis and Maniery, this issue). The site housed an estimated 40 to 70 Chinese men during grading and tunneling. In their contribution to this issue about the Lakeview Camp, Furnis and Maniery show how systematic excavation and recording methods can reveal patterns of activity areas even in shallow and ephemeral work camp sites. Echoing Wrobleski's findings, Furnis and Maniery found distinct public spaces for cooking, eating, and socializing separate from sleeping areas.

Like the V&TRR, the Eureka & Palisades Railroad was built to link silver mines in the Eureka, Nevada, region with the first transcontinental in Palisades, Nevada. Zier (1985) investigated a Chinese railroad workers' site representing a temporary camp possibly occupied for only a few days. The site included three artifact clusters, interpreted by Zier as each representing one group of 12–20 workers.

Other railroads in Nevada, such as the narrow-gauge Bodie & Benton Railroad, served local interests. Operated by the same

consortium as the V&T, the Bodie & Benton linked lumber mills with mining sites. Currently studied by Sunseri (this issue), the Mono Mills site associated with the Bodie & Benton was a locale in which Chinese workers lived alongside Native American Paiutes. Sunseri's investigations reveal evidence of transcultural interactions and cooperation between these two subjugated worker populations.

In Utah, archaeologists recorded a small itinerant Chinese railroad encampment associated with the Utah & Pleasant Valley Railway, completed in 1879, and identified rock structures likely representing Chinese work camps on the Denver & Rio Grande Western Railroad, completed in 1883 (Merritt 2013). In Mesa County, Colorado, Conner and Darnell (2012) conducted an archaeological assessment of the Excelsior Train Station site on the Denver & Rio Grande Railway. Their research identified a distinct concentration of Chinese artifacts, including porcelain tablewares, Chinese brown-glazed stoneware, and opium paraphernalia. They conclude that, although historical records for the railroad do not list any Chinese employees, the site represents a Chinese labor camp associated with the railroad's construction or operation (Conner and Darnell 2012:36)

In Roundup, Montana, Urbaniak and Dixon (this issue) identified rock inscriptions likely carved by Chinese workers employed to mine coal for the Milwaukee Road. In San Diego County, California, Hallaran et al. (1989) studied a late-1910s construction camp on the San Diego & Arizona Eastern Railway. Research revealed a diverse multiethnic workforce including Mexicans, European Americans, Native Americans, Indians, Pakistanis, Greeks, Swedes, and Chinese.

Existing Themes and New Directions

Prior archaeological research reveals tantalizing glimpses of the historical experience of Chinese railroad workers in the American West, and it also exposes large gaps in archaeological knowledge. Only a few short segments of historical railroad alignments have been systematically surveyed. Most archaeological investigations have centered on a few large, long-term work camps associated with intensive grading, tunneling, and bridgework.

These represent only one aspect of railroad construction: most railroad construction workers typically lived in small groups in isolated short-term camps. While archaeologists have developed models predicting the locations and attributes of railroad worker camps based on slope, water access, and relationship to railroad features (Briggs 1974; Buckles 1983; Wrobleski 1996:24), more field research is needed.

Methodologically, surface survey and collection predominate, although important case studies show the value of excavation at both short-term (Furnis and Maniery, this issue) and long-term work camps (Briggs 1974; Wrobleski 1996; Baxter and Allen, this issue; Sunseri, this issue).

Many of the reports are primarily descriptive, providing an account of the work camp's location, visible archaeological features, and observed artifacts. This provides a rich corpus of primary observations for comparative analysis, and since the 1970s archaeologists have successfully drawn on these descriptive reports to develop taxonomic studies of the material culture of Chinese immigrants in North America, including guides for ceramics (Chace 1976; Evans 1980), opium paraphernalia (Etter 1980; Wylie and Fike 1993), and gaming-related artifacts (Jolly 2012). Additionally, the study of Chinese railroad worker sites affords opportunities for fine-grained chronological comparison. Sando and Felton (1993) noted that Double Happiness–pattern rice bowls prevailed in camps in the 1860s, being replaced by Bamboo-pattern rice bowls after about 1870. Similarly, Akin, Bard, and Weisz (this issue) note that the temporal control afforded by railroad worker camps enables refined models of the import of Asian coins to North America.

Researchers have also used evidence from Chinese railroad worker camps as a point of comparison with daily life in historic Chinatowns, which had greater diversity in age, gender, and class. Felton and colleagues (Felton et al. 1984; Sando and Felton 1993) note that, while ceramic assemblages at Chinese railroad worker sites are dominated by inexpensive Double Happiness– and Bamboo-pattern rice bowls, urban Chinatowns tended to include the more expensive porcelains decorated with Winter Green and Four Seasons patterns. Wylie and Fike (1993:292) compared the relative frequency of opium-pipe bowls on nonurban work camps, including railroad sites, with that on urban Chinatown sites. They concluded that there was a pattern of heavier opium use in work camps, perhaps to buffer work-related discomforts. This finding was recently corroborated by research on Northern Pacific Railroad camps in Montana, where the ubiquity of opium paraphernalia was interpreted as a source of "relief from the physical and psychological pain of manual labor ... the most effective pain remedy on the market until the introduction of aspirin in the 1890s" (Merritt et al. 2012:689). Gust's (1993) foundational comparative study of faunal remains at Chinese immigrant sites included several historical communities formed largely through railroad construction and operation; drawing on more recent studies, Kennedy (this issue) expands on this analysis to highlight patterns and local variations in railroad workers' diet.

While artifact-focused studies of railroad worker sites have tended to emphasize material culture unique to Chinese immigrants, several recent projects have emphasized the importance of Chinese railroad camps to working-class history and the formation of the capitalist world system. In a programmatic archaeological research design for work camps, the California Department of Transportation (2013:8) notes that, from 1848 to 1941, most new migrants and immigrants to the American West participated in work camps at some point in their lives, yet for "most of the 19th century, neither the government nor private companies made any concerted effort to document the state's transient labor force or its work camps." Such camps, including those used by railroad workers, were "integral parts of profit-driven enterprises and often were the direct result of large expenditures of capital. ... The economy of work camps involved the flow not only of capital and commodities but also of the workers themselves" (California Department of Transportation 2013:10). In this context, Chinese railroad camps share characteristics with work camps associated with other industries in the American West: a narrow economic focus; relative geographic isolation; impermanence; and interconnections with and dependence on regional, national, and global economies (Van Bueren 2002; Dixon 2014). Engaging with this world-system approach, Gardner (2004, 2005) has argued that regional core–periphery relationships developed within Chinese immigrant communities in the American West: Chinatowns near large permanent operations, such as mines, functioned as core settlements, whereas peripheral Chinese settlements, such as those associated with railroad section camps, faced isolation, which is materially reflected in decreased dietary diversity and greater reliance on non-Chinese material culture.

Concern with race, ethnicity, and nationality circulates throughout prior research on the archaeology of Chinese railroad workers. But the question of how race, ethnicity, and nationality came to matter in these archaeological studies merits closer discussion. From the beginning, archaeologists have studied the distinctive assemblages left by Chinese railroad laborers to define and describe the material culture of overseas Chinese communities. Archaeological research aiming to investigate assimilation, acculturation, or traditionalism through the study of Chinese railroad worker assemblages is common, but archaeologists have rarely considered how the commodity chains created by railroad labor contractors and suppliers may have constrained workers' consumption practices. It is unclear, for example, whether the ubiquity of certain Asian ceramic types at railroad work camps reflects the preferences of the workers themselves or the profit-driven decisions made by the labor contractors, railroad suppliers, and their import/export partners.

Emergent capitalist enterprises throughout the 19th-century American West recruited their workforces from diverse local, regional, national, and international populations (Dixon 2014; Sunseri, this issue; Urbaniak and Dixon, this issue). Workers were often organized into ethnically distinct work groups—at times, as the opening vignette of this article indicates, in order to deliberately divide workers from each other and suppress labor organizing. The Central Pacific Railroad's approach to staffing the construction of the first transcontinental was particularly significant in forging and codifying this ethnic contract-labor system during the early stages of industrial development in the American West. Briggs (1974) and MacNaughton (2012) note that this practice provides an

opportunity for comparative archaeological research on ethnicity and consumption, for the archaeological record of railroad labor contains spatially discrete sites occupied by working-class men of different ethnic and racial groups. Yet, as Merritt et al. (2012) noted, the separation of workers' camps by ethnicity was itself a process of racialization that produced, not simply reflected, social categories. As Molenda (this issue) and Sunseri (this issue) demonstrate, Chinese railroad workers were not passive recipients of the racist ideologies that fostered a segregated workforce.

The articles presented in this issue also begin to contribute to the "inside-out" perspective on the historical experience of Chinese railroad workers that CRWNAP scholars requested. Chace and Evans's (this issue) study of Summit Camp introduces the suite of material culture that most Chinese railroad workers used in day-to-day life, while Molenda (this issue) questions whether such material culture can be studied to address common themes in the archaeology of labor, such as overt and covert resistance to capitalist ideals. Baxter and Allen's (this issue) article, also discussing Summit Camp, emphasizes the power of place in evoking the hardships and accomplishments of Chinese laborers in the High Sierras, while Polk's (this issue) synthesis of archaeological research at the Golden Spike National Historic Site calls attention to a landscape fractured by corporate greed and ethnic and religious divisions. Furnis and Maniery's (this issue) work presents a methodology for differentiating activity areas within ephemeral work camps. Sunseri's (this issue) study of Chinese laborers at Mono Mills documents the interconnections forged between Chinese immigrants and Native American Paiutes, while Urbaniak and Dixon's (this issue) report on rock inscriptions documents the presence of Chinese, Japanese, and European immigrant workers in railroad-associated labor contexts.

Other contributions move beyond site-specific research, bringing together evidence from multiple work camps and, in some cases, multiple railroads. Akin, Bard, and Weisz (this issue) analyzed Asian coins from railroad worker sites on the NPRR, noting the uses of such coins to promote health, bring good luck, and for gambling. Kennedy (this issue) traces dietary practices through comparative analysis of animal-bone studies, challenging stereotyped historical accounts with evidence of local variation. Heffner (this issue) examines health-related artifacts, affording an entry point into ways that railroad workers managed the physical stress of their work, as well as their vulnerabilities to exposure and disease. Harrod and Crandall (this issue) presents the findings of bioarchaeological research, revealing not only the physical toll caused by hard labor, but also the impact of interethnic violence on individual life histories. This thematic issue closes with two commentaries. Praetzellis and Praetzellis (this issue) and Chung (this issue) note the value, and the current limitations, of the rich, place-based, descriptive evidence generated by archaeology. Both commentaries encourage archaeologists to reach beyond the discipline to work closely with descendant communities in North America and in China as sources of new, interesting questions for future research.

The Other Materialities of Chinese Railroad Workers

The research presented in this thematic issue is a strong beginning for an ongoing collaboration that will open new research directions in the years to come. Along with conventional archaeological survey, excavation, artifact studies, and data analysis, plans are underway for geographic information systems, digital humanities archives, and three-dimensional visualizations that can integrate archaeological, archival, pictorial, geographic, oral-history, and cultural-studies sources. Transnational research partnerships promise to forge unprecedented collaboration between historical archaeologists in the United States and scholars in related fields in Asia.

As archaeologists and others develop new methods and new questions for analyzing the archaeological landscapes, features, architectural traces, dietary remains, and fragmented material traces of Chinese railroad workers, it is equally important to consider other materialities of railroad labor that are rarely represented in the archaeological record of laborers' camps.

The first is the bodies of the workers themselves. Although widely heralded as a vanguard of the industrial age, 19th-century railroads in the American West were built with manual labor. Brush clearing, grubbing, grading, tunneling, bridging, track laying—all of these relied primarily on human muscle. Most of the construction work was painstakingly completed with hand tools under time pressures driven by profit motives and government incentives. The pride of work that many laborers rightfully felt at their accomplishments was shadowed by a tremendous loss of life caused by work accidents, environmental exposure, illness, and interethnic violence. To fulfill their obligations, labor contractors and work-gang headmen on the first transcontinental often maintained a pool of able-bodied camp followers who could replace injured and dead workers at a moment's notice (Hoffmann 1879:221–225; Barth 1964; Saxton 1971:60–66). The Central Pacific and most other railroads did not keep records of Chinese construction casualties (Ambrose 2000:156; N. Lee 2002; I. Chang 2003:59). Many historical texts estimate that as many as 1,000 to 1,500 Chinese workers lost their lives in construction of the first transcontinental alone, which, if correct, would indicate a death rate of around 1 in 10 workers (Kraus 1969a; Saxton 1971; Yen 1976; Tsai 1986). For years following the completion of the first transcontinental, veteran railroad workers journeyed back to the Sierra to search for the human remains of their lost colleagues in a practice called *jup seen you* (retrieving deceased friends) (I. Chang 2003:63–64). In light of the precariousness of workers' bodies, seemingly mundane results of archaeological research—traces of shelter, nourishment, medicine, and pain-numbing opium—take on heightened significance as efforts to care for one's own and one's fellows in a dangerous environment.

The government incentives that rewarded speed of railroad construction without regard to worker safety no doubt contributed to the callous disregard for life shown by railroad magnates and construction bosses. The profits from railroad construction—and the financing schemes that developed around it—were considerable indeed (Riegel 1926; Saxton 1971; Mayer and Vose 1975; White 2011). It is no coincidence that the Chinese Railroad Workers in North America Project began at Stanford

University, which was founded by Leland and Jane Stanford with the wealth that they had amassed through the construction of the Central Pacific Railroad and their related economic and political enterprises. Leland Stanford had a particularly contradictory relationship with Chinese immigration: early in his political career, he supported legislation to restrict Chinese immigration, referring to Chinese immigrants as "an inferior race" (Stanford 1862). Yet as one of the "Big Four" owners of the Central Pacific Railroad, he reversed his anti-immigrant stance only two years later, at one point suggesting that it would be good if a half-million more Chinese immigrated to the United States (Williams 1988:97). The self-interested opportunism of this reversal is revealed by Stanford's later support of the 1892 Geary Act, which extended and strengthened exclusion of Chinese immigrants (Tsai 1986). Throughout these political machinations, the Stanfords continued to employ hundreds of Chinese workers at their ranches and vineyards, as well as in the construction and operation of Stanford University

(Figure 4). The lavish landscape and monumental architecture of the campus are one of many Gilded Age materialities that should be credited to Chinese workers.

Few Chinese railroad workers became wealthy themselves. Paid less than most white workers and responsible for their own room and board, they had few financial resources and often owed considerable debts to immigration recruiters and labor contractors (Griswold 1962:118–119; Chiu 1967:46–47; Kraus 1969b:217; Saxton 1971:60–66; Daniels 1988:19; Williams 1988:97–98; White 2011:294–297). For some, however, railroad construction led to steady careers in railroad operations (Southern Pacific Company Bureau of News 1917; Chiu 1967); for others, savings from their wages enabled them to pay off loans, support their kin in North America and China, and start small businesses that afforded greater stability and self-determination (Kraus 1969a; Cassel 2002). This opportunity to earn and invest wages, however small, is another significant materiality of Chinese railroad

FIGURE 4. The other materialities of Chinese railroad workers: entrance to the main quadrangle at Stanford University. (Photo by author, 2012.)

laborers' historical experience. In the American West, the business districts of towns and cities were transformed by expanding Chinatowns, fueled by businesses supplying workers and supplies to the railroad construction projects, as well as new businesses started by former railroad workers (Chiu 1967; Tsai 1986; Chan 1991:30). In China, remittances from railroad workers and other migrants transformed the landscape of 19th-century Guangdong Province, sponsoring public works, such as schools, orphanages, hospitals, assembly halls, roads, bridges, and even railroads (Dehua 1999).

The workers who built the railroads constructed far more than a new means of commercial transportation. The identities and communities they formed reshaped the fabric of social life in the Americas and China, and the wealth generated by their labor continues to influence commerce, education, and philanthropy today. Through the study of the material objects, residues, and places that the railroad workers left behind, archaeology provides a tangible point of entry into these dense webs of political machinations, economic relations, cultural meanings, and historical experiences.

Acknowledgments

My first thanks are to Gordon H. Chang and Shelley Fisher Fishkin, codirectors of the Chinese Railroad Workers in North America Project, for so warmly welcoming me and fellow archaeologists into this exciting collaborative project. CRWNAP Associate Director Hilton Obenzinger and Director of Research Denise Khor have been especially helpful in working through the details of archaeological participation. Lynn Meskell graciously offered the Stanford Archaeology Center as host institution for the October 2013 workshop of the Archaeology Network of the CRWNAP. Megan Kane served as workshop local-arrangements chair, Chris Lowman as information officer, and Christina MacDonald as note taker. Stanford University staff Ellen Christensen, Lancy Eng, Julie Hitchcock, Jen Kidwell, Monica Moore, Laura Rossi, and Beth Stutsman contributed invaluable assistance in workshop planning and organization, and several Stanford student volunteers assisted with registration and workshop logistics. Phil Choy and Connie Young Yu, both discussants at the workshop, contributed key perspectives that shaped the direction of this thematic issue. Funding for the workshop was provided by several Stanford University programs, including the Office of the President, the Department of Anthropology, the Stanford Archaeology Center, the Department of History, the American Studies Program, International and Comparative Area Studies, the Center for East Asian Studies, and Ming's Chinese Cuisine and Bar.

The review of prior archaeological research presented in this introduction relied heavily on unpublished reports and hard-to-find documents that members of the Archaeology Network shared with the CRWNAP. At *Historical Archaeology*, Rebecca Allen (past editor), Joe W. Joseph (past editor), Christopher Matthews (current editor), and Richard Schaefer (copy editor) provided support and guidance throughout the publication process. I am especially grateful to Keren He, who translated the titles and abstracts into Chinese, to Hsinya Huang and her colleagues at National Sun Yat-sen University in Taiwan for proofreading the Chinese titles and abstracts, and to Corey Johnson and Laura Daly, who assisted with various stages of manuscript preparation. My final thanks are to the contributing authors. I am truly fortunate to have such wonderful colleagues.

References

AMBROSE, STEPHEN E.
    2000 *Nothing Like It in the World: The Men Who Built the Transcontinental Railroad 1863–1869.* Simon & Schuster, New York, NY.

ANDERSON, ADRIENNE B.
    1983 Ancillary Construction on Promontory Summit Utah: Those Domestic Structures Built by Railroad Workers. In *Forgotten Places and Things: Archaeological Perspectives on American History*, A. E. Ward, editor, pp. 225–238. Center for Anthropological Studies, Albuquerque, NM.

BAIN, DAVID H.
    1999 *Empire Express: Building the First Transcontinental Railroad.* Penguin, New York, NY.

BARTH, GUNTHER
    1964 *Bitter Strength: A History of the Chinese in the United States, 1850–1870.* Harvard University Press, Cambridge, MA.

BRIGGS, ALTON KING
1974 The Archaeology of 1882 Labor Camps on the Southern Pacific Railroad, Val Verde County, Texas. Master's thesis, Department of Anthropology, University of Texas, Austin.

BUCKLES, WILLIAM G.
1983 Models for Railroad Construction-Related Sites in the West. In *Forgotten Places and Things: Archaeological Perspectives on American History*, A. E. Ward, editor, pp. 213–223. Center for Anthropological Studies, Albuquerque, NM.

CALIFORNIA DEPARTMENT OF TRANSPORTATION
2013 *Work Camps: Historic Context and Archaeological Research Design*. Prepared by HARD Work Camps Team and California Department of Transportation Staff, Sacramento, for California Department of Transportation, Sacramento.

CASSEL, SUSIE LAN
2002 To Inscribe the Self Daily: The Discovery of the Ah Quin Diary. In *The Chinese in America: A History from Gold Mountain to the New Millennium*, S. L. Cassel, editor, pp. 54–74. AltaMira Press, Walnut Creek, CA.

CHACE, PAUL G.
1976 Overseas Chinese Ceramics. In *The Changing Faces of Main Street: San Buenaventura Mission Plaza Project Archaeological Report, 1975*, R. S. Greenwood, editor, pp. 510–530. City of San Buenaventura Redevelopment Agency, Ventura, CA.

CHACE, PAUL G., AND WILLIAM S. EVANS, JR.
1969 Celestial Sojourners in the High Sierras: The Ethno-Archaeology of Chinese Railroad Workers (1865–1868). Paper presented at the Second Annual Conference on Historical and Underwater Archaeology, Tucson, AZ.

CHAN, SUCHENG
1991 *Asian Americans: An Interpretive History.* Twayne, New York, NY.

CHANG, GORDON H.
2001 *Asian Americans and Politics: An Exploration.* Stanford University Press, Stanford, CA.
2008 *Asian American Art: A History, 1850–1970.* Stanford University Press, Stanford CA.

CHANG, IRIS
2003 *The Chinese in America: A Narrative History.* Penguin, New York, NY.

CHEW, WILLIAM F.
2004 *Nameless Builders of the Transcontinental.* Trafford, Victoria, BC.

CHINESE RAILROAD WORKERS IN NORTH AMERICA PROJECT
2012 About Our Project. Chinese Railroad Workers in North America Project, Stanford University <http://web.stanford.edu/group/chineserailroad/cgi-bin/wordpress/about-our-project/>. Accessed 10 October 2013.

CHINN, THOMAS W., HIM MARK LAI, AND PHILIP P. CHOY (EDITORS)
1969 *A History of the Chinese in California: A Syllabus.* Chinese Historical Society of America, San Francisco, CA.

CHIU, PING
1967 *Chinese Labor in California, 1850–1880.* State Historical Society of Wisconsin/Department of History, University of Wisconsin, Madison.

CHUNG, SUE FAWN
2003 The Chinese and Green Gold: Lumbering in the Sierras. Report to Humboldt-Toiyabe National Forest, Carson Ranger District, Passport in Time, Carson City, NV, from University of Nevada, Las Vegas.

CLARK, GEORGE T.
1931 *Leland Stanford: War Governor of California, Railroad Builder and Founder of Stanford University.* Stanford University Press, Stanford, CA.

CONNER, CARL E., AND NICOLE DARNELL
2012 Archaeological Investigation of Site 5ME7351.1, Excelsior Train Station, Mesa County, Colorado. Report to Colorado Historical Society State Historical Fund and the Bureau of Land Management, Grand Junction, from Dominguez Archaeological Research Group, Grand Junction, CO. Manuscript, Colorado Historical Society, Office of Archaeology and Historic Preservation, Denver.

DANIELS, ROGER
1988 *Asian America: Chinese and Japanese in the United States since 1850.* University of Washington Press, Seattle.

DEHUA, ZHENG
1999 Taishan. In *The Encyclopedia of the Chinese Overseas*, L. Pan, editor, pp. 36–37. Harvard University Press, Cambridge, MA.

DEVERELL, WILLIAM
1994 *Railroad Crossing: Californians and the Railroad, 1850–1910.* University of California Press, Berkeley.

DIXON, KELLY J.
2014 Historical Archaeologies of the American West. *Journal of Archaeological Research* 22(3):177–228.

ETTER, PATRICIA A.
1980 The West Coast Chinese and Opium Smoking. In *Archaeological Perspectives on Ethnicity in America: Afro-American and Asian American Culture History*, R. L. Schuyler, editor, pp. 97–101. Baywood, Farmingdale, NY.

EVANS, WILLIAM S.
1980 Food and Fantasy: Material Culture of the Chinese in California and the West, circa 1850–1900. In *Archaeological Perspectives on Ethnicity in America: Afro-American and Asian American Culture History*, R. L. Schuyler, editor, pp. 89–96. Baywood, Farmingdale, NY.

FEDICK, SCOTT L., AND LYLE M. STONE
    1988   Working on the Railroad: Social and Organizational
            Aspects of an Historic Work Camp of the Southern
            Pacific Railroad near Maricopa, Arizona. Paper
            presented at the 21st Annual Conference on Historical
            and Underwater Archaeology, Reno, Nevada.

FELTON, DAVID L., FRANK LORTIE, AND PETER D. SCHULZ
    1984   The Chinese Laundry on Second Street: Archaeological
            Investigations at the Woodland Opera House Site.
            California Department of Parks and Recreation,
            California Archaeological Reports, No. 24.
            Sacramento.

FISHKIN, SHELLEY FISHER
    2005   Crossroads of Cultures: The Transnational Turn in
            American Studies. American Quarterly 57(1):17–57.

GARDNER, A. DUDLEY
    2004   The Chinese in Wyoming: Life in the Core and
            Peripheral Communities. In Ethnic Oasis: The
            Chinese in the Black Hills: South Dakota History, L.
            Zhu and R. Estep, editors, pp. 86–96. South Dakota
            Historical Society Press, Pierre.
    2005   Cores and Peripheries: Chinese Communities in
            Southwestern Wyoming, 1869–1922. Wyoming
            Archaeologist 49(1):19–39.

GARDNER, A. DUDLEY, BARBARA CLARKE,
AND LYNN HARRELL
    2002   Final Report for the Aspen Section Camp 48UT660
            and the Associated Union Pacific Railroad Grade
            48UT668. Report to Wyoming Bureau of Land
            Management, Cheyenne, from Western Wyoming
            Community College, Rock Springs.

GREENWOOD, ROBERTA S.
    1993   Old Approaches and New Directions: Implications
            for Future Research. In Hidden Heritage: Historical
            Archaeology of the Overseas Chinese, P. Wegars,
            editor, pp. 375–403. Baywood, Amityville, NY.

GRISWOLD, WESLEY S.
    1962   A Work of Giants: Building the First Transcontinental
            Railroad. McGraw-Hill, New York, NY.

GUST, SHERRI M.
    1993   Animal Bones from Historic Urban Chinese Sites:
            A Comparison of Sacramento, Woodland, Tucson,
            Ventura, and Lovelock. In Hidden Heritage:
            Historical Archaeology of the Overseas Chinese, P.
            Wegars, editor, pp. 177–212. Baywood, Amityville,
            NY.

HALLARAN, KEVIN B., KAREN K. SWOPE,
AND PHILIP J. WILKE
    1989   Historical and Archaeological Documentation of a
            Construction Camp ("China Camp") on the San Diego
            & Arizona Railway, Anza-Borrego Desert State Park,
            San Diego County, California. Report to California
            Department of Parks and Recreation, Sacramento,
            from Archaeological Research Unit, University of
            California, Riverside.

HEATH, EARLE
    1927   From Trail to Rail: The Story of the Beginning
            of the Southern Pacific. Southern Pacific Bulletin
            15(5):9–12.

HOFFMANN, HEMMANN
    1879   Californien, Nevada und Mexico: Wanderungen eines
            Polytechnikers (California, Nevada and Mexico: A
            polytechnic's wanderings). Hugo Richter, Basel,
            Germany.

HOWARD, ROBERT W.
    1962   The Great Iron Trail: The Story of the First Trans-
            Continental Railroad. Bonanza, New York, NY.

HUANG, ANNIAN
    2006   The Silent Spikes: Chinese Laborers and the
            Construction of North American Railroads. China
            Intercontinental Press, Beijing, China.

JOLLY, ELYSE
    2012   Chinese Gaming in the Nineteenth-Century American
            West: An Ethnic and Cultural Reassessment. Master's
            thesis, Department of Anthropology, University of
            Nevada, Reno.

KRAUS, GEORGE
    1969a   Chinese Laborers and the Construction of the Central
            Pacific. Utah Historical Quarterly 37(1):41–57.
    1969b   High Road to Promontory: Building the Central
            Pacific (Now the Southern Pacific) across the High
            Sierra. American West, Palo Alto, CA.

LANDRETH, KEITH, KEO BORESON,
AND MARY CONDON (EDITORS)
    1985   Archaeological Investigations at the Cabinet Landing
            Site (10BR413). Eastern Washington University
            Reports in Archaeology and History, Report Number
            100-45. Cheney.

LEE, JANE M.
    2008   "Fidelity and Industry": The Archaeology of a Late-
            Nineteenth Century Chinese Woodcutter Camp in
            Dog Valley, California. Master's thesis, Department
            of Anthropology, University of Nevada, Reno.

LEE, NANCY S.
    2002   Telling Their Own Stories: Chinese Canadian
            Biography as a Historical Genre. In The Chinese
            in America: A History from Gold Mountain to the
            New Millennium, S. L. Cassel, editor, pp. 106–121.
            AltaMira Press, Walnut Creek, CA.

MACNAUGHTON, JAMES W.
    2012   A Historical Investigation of Changing Ethnicity and
            Consumption Patterns at the Union Pacific Railroad
            Section Camp of Peru (48SW3795): How Changing
            Ethnicity Can Be Interpreted in a Nineteenth Century
            Railroad Landscape. Master's thesis, Department of
            Anthropology and Sociology, Illinois State University,
            Normal.

MANIERY, MARY L.
2004   The Archaeology of Asian Immigrants: Thirty-Five Years in the Making. *SAA Archaeological Record* 4(5):10–13.

MAYER, LYNN R., AND KENNETH VOSE
1975   *Makin' Tracks: The Story of the Transcontinental Railroad in the Pictures and Words of the Men Who Were There.* Praeger, New York, NY.

MERRITT, CHRISTOPHER W.
2010   *"The Coming Man from Canton": Chinese Experience in Montana (1862–1943).* Doctoral dissertation, Department of Anthropology, University of Montana, Missoula. University Microfilms International, Ann Arbor, MI.
2013   The Continental Backwaters of Chinese Railroad Worker History and Archaeology: Perspectives from Montana and Utah. Paper presented at the Archaeology Network Workshop of the Chinese Railroad Workers in North America Project, Stanford University, Stanford, CA.

MERRITT, CHRISTOPHER W., GARY WEISZ, AND KELLY J. DIXON
2012   "Verily the Road was Built with Chinaman's Bones": An Archaeology of Chinese Line Camps in Montana. *International Journal of Historical Archaeology* 16(4):666–695.

MOLENDA, JOHN
2013   Aesthetically-Oriented Archaeology. Paper presented at the Archaeology Network Workshop of the Chinese Railroad Workers in North America Project, Stanford University, Stanford, CA.

NORDHOFF, CHARLES
1874   *California: For Health, Pleasure, and Residence. A Book for Travellers and Settlers.* Harper & Brothers, New York, NY.

POLK, MIKE R., AND WENDY SIMMONS JOHNSON
2012   From Lampo Junction to Rozel: The Archaeological History of the Transcontinental Railroad across the Promontory Mountains, Utah. GOSP Synthesis Report. Manuscript, Golden Spike National Historic Site, National Park Service, Promontory, UT.

RAYMOND, ANAN S., AND RICHARD E. FIKE
1981   *Rails East to Promontory: The Utah Stations.* Utah State Office Bureau of Land Management, Cultural Resource Series No. 8. Salt Lake City. Reprinted 1997 by Pioneer Enterprises, Livingston, TX.

RIEGEL, ROBERT E.
1926   *The Story of the Western Railroads from 1852 through the Reign of the Giants.* University of Nebraska Press, Lincoln.

ROGERS, C. LYNN
1997   Making Camp Chinese Style: The Archaeology of a V&T Railroad Graders' Camp, Carson City, Nevada, ARS Project No. 865. Report to Silver Oak Development Company, Carson City, NV, from Archaeological Research Services, Virginia City, NV.

ROSS, DOUGLAS E.
2013   Overseas Chinese Archaeology. In *Encyclopedia of Global Archaeology*, Claire Smith, editor, pp. 5675–5686. Springer, New York, NY.

SANDO, RUTH ANN, AND DAVID L. FELTON
1993   Inventory Records of Ceramics and Opium from a Nineteenth Century Chinese Store in California. In *Hidden Heritage: Historical Archaeology of the Overseas Chinese*, P. Wegars, editor, pp. 151–176. Baywood, Amityville, NY.

SAXTON, ALEXANDER
1971   *Indispensable Enemy: Labor and the Anti-Chinese Movement.* University of California Press, Berkeley.

SCHUYLER, ROBERT L. (EDITOR)
1980   *Archaeological Perspectives on Ethnicity in America: Afro-American and Asian American Culture History.* Baywood, Farmingdale, NY.

SCOTT, ELIZABETH M. (EDITOR)
1994   *Those of Little Note: Gender, Race, and Class in Historical Archaeology.* University of Arizona Press, Tucson.

SMITH, CARRIE E., AND KELLY J. DIXON
2005   Determination of Eligibility for Inclusion in the National Register of Historic Places of 19 Historic Sites within the Heavenly Ski Resort, Douglas County, Nevada, Report No. R2004-0519-00048. Manuscript, U.S. Forest Service, Lake Tahoe Basin Management Unit, South Lake Tahoe, CA, and Heavenly Ski Resort, South Lake Tahoe, CA.

SOUTHERN PACIFIC COMPANY BUREAU OF NEWS
1917   Japanese and Chinese Section Hands Aid in Liberty Loan. *Bulletin* 5(21):2.

STANFORD, LELAND
1862   Inaugural Address, Delivered: January 10, 1862. Governors' Gallery, California State Library <http://governors.library.ca.gov/addresses/08-Stanford.html>. Accessed 5 July 2014.

STASKI, EDWARD
1993   The Overseas Chinese in El Paso: Changing Goals, Changing Realities. In *Hidden Heritage: Historical Archaeology of the Overseas Chinese*, P. Wegars, editor, pp. 125–149. Baywood, Amityville, NY.
2009   Asian American Studies in Historical Archaeology. In *International Handbook of Historical Archaeology*, T. Majewski and D. Gaimster, editors, pp. 347–359. Springer, New York, NY.

STOKELD, RACHEL, AND MARY PETRICH-GUY
2014   Documenting Chinese Railroad Laborer Camps in Northern Idaho: A Professional/Amateur Collaboration. Paper presented at the 67th Annual Northwest Anthropological Conference, Bellingham, WA.

STONE, LYLE M., AND SCOTT L. FEDICK

1990 The Archaeology of Two Historic Homestead and Railroad-Related Sites on the Southern Pacific Main Line near Mobile, Maricopa County, AZ. Report to Dibble and Associates, Phoenix, AZ, from Archaeological Resources Services, Inc., Tempe, AZ.

TSAI, SHIH-SHAN HENRY

1986 The Chinese Experience in America. Indiana University Press, Bloomington.

TURNER, ARNIE L.

1982 The History and Archaeology of Fenelon, a Historic Railroad Camp. Bureau of Land Management, Archaeological Studies in the Cortez Mining District, Technical Report No. 8. Reno, NV.

U. S. CONGRESS

1877 Report of the Joint Special Committee to Investigate Chinese Immigration. 44th Congress, 2nd session, Senate Report No. 689. Washington, DC.

UNITED STATES PACIFIC RAILWAY COMMISSION

1887 Testimony Taken by the United States Pacific Railway Commission, 9 vol. 50th Congress, 1st session, Senate. Washington, DC.

VAN BUEREN, THAD M.

2002 The Changing Face of Work in the West: Some Introductory Comments. Historical Archaeology 36(3):1–7.

VOSS, BARBARA L.

2005 The Archaeology of Overseas Chinese Communities. World Archaeology 37(3):424–439.

VOSS, BARBARA L., AND REBECCA ALLEN

2008 Overseas Chinese Archaeology: Historical Foundations, Current Reflections, and New Directions. Historical Archaeology 42(3):5–28.

WEGARS, PRISCILLA (EDITOR)

1993 Hidden Heritage: Historical Archaeology of the Overseas Chinese. Baywood, Amityville, NY.

WEISZ, GARY

2003 Stepping Light: Revisiting the Construction Camps on the Lake Pend d'Oreille and Clark Fork Division of the Northern Pacific Railroad, 1879–1883, 3 vols. Manuscript, Idaho State Preservation Office, Boise.

WHITE, RICHARD

2011 Railroaded: The Transcontinentals and the Making of Modern America. W. W. Norton, New York, NY.

WILLIAMS, JOHN HOYT

1988 A Great and Shining Road: The Epic Story of the Transcontinental Railroad. University of Nebraska Press, Lincoln.

WROBLESKI, DAVID E.

1996 The Archaeology of Chinese Work Camps on the Virginia and Truckee Railroad. Master's thesis, Department of Anthropology, University of Nevada, Reno.

WYLIE, JERRY, AND RICHARD E. FIKE

1993 Chinese Opium Smoking Techniques and Paraphernalia. In Hidden Heritage: Historical Archaeology of the Overseas Chinese, P. Wegars, editor, pp. 255–303. Baywood, Amityville, NY.

YEN, TZU KUEI

1976 Chinese Workers and the First Transcontinental Railroad of the United States of America. Doctoral dissertation, Department of Asian Studies, St. John's University, Jamaica, NY. University Microfilms International, Ann Arbor, MI.

ZIER, CHARLES D.

1985 Archaeological Data Recovery Associated with the Mt. Hope Project, Eureka County, Nevada. Bureau of Land Management, Cultural Resource Series, No. 8. Reno, NV.

BARBARA L. VOSS
DEPARTMENT OF ANTHROPOLOGY
STANFORD UNIVERSITY
450 SERRA MALL, MAIN QUAD, BUILDING 50
STANFORD, CA 94305-2034

Paul G. Chace

Introductory Note to Chace and Evans's 1969 Presentation

In 1966 and 1967, Williams Evans, Jr. and I conducted research at Summit Camp, a cluster of Chinese railroad worker camps near Donner Pass in California; see also Baxter and Allen (this issue). As a private personal and self-funded exploration, the project was conducted well before the rigorous regulations of cultural resource management (CRM) archaeology emerged, and even before the techniques and theories of prehistoric archaeology were commonly applied to historical era sites. Even the California Archaeological Survey Office (now the California Historical Resources Information System) did not record historical era site locations back then.

The paper Evans and I wrote, with 30 slide illustrations, was originally presented in January 1969 at the second annual meeting of the Society for Historical Archaeology (SHA), held in Tucson, Arizona. We also distributed a printed table that listed 18 U.S. states and 16 other countries to which Chinese initially immigrated during this historical period. I believe that our paper is the earliest known professional presentation of research archaeology on a Chinese railroad worker locale—and perhaps of a Chinese immigrant site—in North America.

Presentation of this paper led to the formation of the SHA's Overseas Chinese Research Group. Now it is useful to measure paradigmatic shifts in the field. This 1969 presentation (1) summarized the then-known ethnographic descriptions of Chinese railroad workers, (2) described the archaeological materials found at their work camps at Donner Pass nearly 50 years ago, and (3) proposed that these cultural materials represented an archaeological "horizon style," one indicative of the immigration of Chinese laborers worldwide, with their initial arrivals in many countries dating between 1850 and 1870.

The transcript of this 1969 presentation is published in full here, making it available to other archaeologists and to the public for the first time. (The presentation abstract was printed in the 1969 SHA meeting program and in the Society for California Archaeology newsletter [Chace and Evans 1969]). This presentation launched the archaeology of Chinese immigrants and Chinese Americans. Throughout the 1970s, I edited a quarterly column, "Overseas Chinese Archaeology," for the Society for Historical Archaeology newsletter. In 1976, I published "Overseas Chinese Ceramics" (Chace 1976), a descriptive catalog of artifacts from Ventura, California, that built on the analysis conducted at Summit Camp. Artifacts from Summit Camp were discussed in chapters contributed by Evans (1980) and Etter (1980) in *Archaeological Perspectives on Ethnicity in America* (Schuyler 1980). At the Second National Conference on Chinese American Studies in 1980, I summarized the emergent new field in a presentation: "Archaeological Perspectives on the Overseas Chinese in America" (Chace 1984).

Both Evans and I were trained as anthropologists—William Evans at the University of California, Berkeley, and myself at the California State University, Long Beach. We framed our study as an "ethnoarchaeology" because we interpreted the archaeological remains through the lens of historical sources that documented Chinese immigrants involved in railroad construction. Although the term "ethnoarchaeology" has since come to have a very different meaning—e.g., Gould and Watson (1982) and Binford (1983)—I believe our approach resonates with current methodologies in ethnohistory and historical anthropology. We also predicted that Chinese immigrant material culture would represent an *archaeological horizon*, a term that denotes a widely disseminated set of artifacts that uniquely represent a particular culture and time period (Taylor 1948; Willey and Phillips 1958).

The presentation transcript is printed here exactly as it was originally delivered. The

Historical Archaeology, 2015, 49(1):24–26.
Permission to reprint required.

transcript contains no bibliographic citations and is written in a conversational style, in keeping with the style of an oral presentation. Some terms used here, such as "celestial" and "sojourner," are common in primary and secondary historical sources, but are rarely used by scholars today. Researchers have refuted the often-repeated myth that Chinese workers came to the United States only to earn money and return to China; in fact, the rate of return for 19th-century Chinese immigrants was about the same as that for European and Latin American immigrants (Takaki 1998). Likewise, I stopped using the term "Overseas Chinese" around 1980 upon realizing that this term was offensive to some modern Chinese Americans because it often implied People's Republic of China citizenship. Archaeological terminology has also changed. The archaeological locale at Donner Pass has been formally recorded as Summit Camp. Asian coins found at Summit Camp are today referred to by national currency names (e.g., *wen, dong,* etc.) (Akins et al., this issue). Despite these changes, the 1969 presentation speaks directly to research issues that are central to the archaeology of Chinese railroad workers today. Additionally, it provides a snapshot of Summit Camp as it was before the landscape was changed by modern utility development, tourism, and recreation.

Acknowledgments

William S. Evans, Jr. (1922–2009) (Figure 1) was a co-principal in the "Celestial Sojourners in the High Sierras" Project reported to the SHA in 1969. He held bachelor's and master's degrees from the University of California, Berkeley, where he focused on anthropology, archaeology, and geography, and later did postgraduate studies at the University of California, Los Angeles. He was the first curator at the Rancho Los Cerritos Museum in Long Beach, California, where he initiated historical archaeology studies. Evans taught anthropology at Santa Monica College for two decades before retiring in 1985.

FIGURE 1. William "Bill" S. Evans (1922–2009) standing next to the rough stone walls of an 8 × 12 ft. room at a work-camp locale below the summit, 21 August 1967. (Photo by author.)

References

BINFORD, LEWIS
    1983   *In Pursuit of the Past.* Thames & Hudson, London, UK.

CHACE, PAUL G.
    1976   Overseas Chinese Ceramics. In *The Changing Faces of Main Street: San Buenaventura Mission Plaza Project Archaeological Report, 1975,* R. S. Greenwood, editor, pp. 510–530. City of San Buenaventura Redevelopment Agency, Ventura, CA.
    1984   Archaeological Perspectives on the Overseas Chinese in America. In *The Chinese American Experience: Papers from the Second National Conference on Chinese American Studies (1980),* G. Lim, editor, p. 311. Chinese Historical Society of America and Chinese Culture Foundation, San Francisco, CA.

CHACE, PAUL G., AND WILLIAM S. EVANS, JR.
   1969   Abstract of "Celestial Sojourners in the High Sierras:
          The Ethno-Archaeology of the Chinese Railroad
          Workers (1865–1868)." *Newsletter of the Society
          for California Archaeology* 2(6):13–14.

ETTER, PATRICIA A.
   1980   The West Coast Chinese and Opium Smoking. In
          *Archaeological Perspectives on Ethnicity in America:
          Afro-American and Asian American Culture History*,
          R. L. Schuyler, editor, pp. 97–101. Baywood,
          Farmingdale, NY.

EVANS, WILLIAM S., JR.
   1980   Food and Fantasy: Material Culture of the Chinese
          in California and the West, circa 1850–1900.
          In *Archaeological Perspectives on Ethnicity in
          America: Afro-American and Asian American Culture
          History*, R. L. Schuyler, editor, pp. 89–96. Baywood,
          Farmingdale, NY.

GOULD, RICHARD A., AND PATTY JO WATSON
   1982   A Dialogue on the Meaning and Use of Analogy in
          Archaeological Reasoning. *Journal of Anthropological
          Archaeology* 1(4):355–381.

SCHUYLER, ROBERT L. (EDITOR)
   1980   *Archaeological Perspectives on Ethnicity in America:
          Afro-American and Asian American Culture History*.
          Baywood, Farmingdale, NY.

TAKAKI, RONALD
   1998   *Strangers from a Different Shore: A History of Asian
          Americans*, updated and revised edition. Back Bay/
          Little, Brown, New York, NY.

TAYLOR, WALTER WILLARD, JR.
   1948   *A Study of Archeology*. American Anthropological
          Association, Memoir 69. Washington, DC.

WILLEY, GORDON R., AND PHILIP PHILLIPS
   1958   *Method and Theory in American Archaeology*.
          University of Chicago Press, Chicago, IL.

PAUL G. CHACE
PAUL G. CHACE & ASSOCIATES
2665 KUANA LOA DRIVE
ESCONDIDO, CA 92029

Paul G. Chace (保罗·切斯)
William S. Evans, Jr. (小威廉·艾文斯)

Celestial Sojourners in the High Sierras: The Ethno-Archaeology of Chinese Railroad Workers (1865–1868)

西墅山[1]的天国来客：对中国铁路工人的民族考古学 (1865-1868)

ABSTRACT

This exact paper with 30 slide illustrations was presented originally at the 1969 meeting of the Society for Historical Archaeology (SHA) and led to the formation of the SHA's Overseas Chinese Research Group. It is useful for measuring paradigmatic shifts in the field. The presentation summarized the then-known ethnographic descriptions of Chinese rail-road workers, described the archaeological materials found at their work camps at Donner Pass nearly 50 years ago, and proposed that these cultural materials represented an archaeological "horizon style," one indicative of the immigration of Chinese laborers worldwide, with their initial arrivals in many countries dating between 1850 and 1870.

本论文最初连同30张幻灯片发表于1969年历史考古学学会的会议，并在该学会内促成了海外华人研究群的诞生。缘此，我们将衡量这个领域所发生的典范转换。本报告内容如下：概括当时已知的关于中国铁路工人的民族志学描述；描述50年后在多纳关中国劳工营考古发掘的材料；论证这些文化材料展现了一种"横向"的考古模式：此一模式表明了中国劳工始于1850至1870年之间，在世界范围内向多个国家移民的状况。

Presentation Transcript

Introduction

In the third quarter of the nineteenth century two events of international impact occurred. One was the construction of the transcontinental railroad, and the second was the mass immigration of Chinese to the countries of the Western Hemisphere. These two events are the context of this paper, "Celestial Sojourners in the High Sierras." It was the Chinese sojourners who built the Central Pacific Railroad over the difficult Sierra Nevada in California. They labored three years to carve a mile of tunnels at the Donner Pass summit.

In this paper we have three purposes: first, to summarize the ethnographic descriptions of these Chinese railroad workers; second, to describe the materials found in their work camps; and third, to propose this description as an "horizon style" useful in assessing materials of this temporal horizon from countries throughout the Western Hemisphere.

Our attention was brought to this material in 1962 by Joe Hickox who brought us a carton of broken Chinese rice bowls from a Donner Pass site. I spent three days surveying the region in 1966 and Evans joined me for three more days in 1967.

Donner Pass is 7,000 feet high in the Sierra Nevada, on the route between San Francisco and Reno, Nevada. The terrain is solid granite, and soil of any kind is rare. There are few spots that are flat or habitable. In winter snow accumulates to depths of forty feet. Here the Chinese camped while they whittled the railroad tunnels through the granite dome beneath them, from October 1865, through winters and summers to June of 1868.

Historical Archaeology, 2015, 49(1):27–33.
Permission to reprint required.

Ethnography

These Chinese were young men of little means who had emigrated from south China as indentured sojourners to earn their fortunes. Ultimately, after several years of labor, they hoped to return with money to their south China villages and their families. Thus, acculturation to American ways was not their purpose. They maintained Chinese culture in all spheres not requiring accommodation of local circumstances.

The sojourners wrote no histories of themselves. Descriptions by contemporary American travelers and journalists are meager. Worse, they are fraught with problems for the "celestial citizens" were new and totally unfamiliar to most European and American writers, who understood little, if anything, of the Chinese culture. Only a patch-work ethno-history is possible.

The first Chinese arrived in California in 1848 and thousands came with the gold rush. Gangs of Chinese were first employed on the railroad construction in 1865, and 14,000 sojourners were on the payrolls three years later. Organized in crews of 10 to 40 men, each with a Chinese foreman and a cook, they had a European supervisor. The Chinese foreman directed the men and maintained order, and received and distributed the monthly pay in gold coin for the gang and their cook. The Chinese gangs camped apart from other workers. They had cramped wooden huts or small tents, depending on the location and season. They worked six days each week, using American made tools. After work, they rushed to camp to bathe and change into fresh clothes. Clothing included the long, full Chinese blouse and wide straw hat but American boots and maybe trousers. Each gang messed together on Chinese fare, primarily rice and tea, but with a variety of meats and vegetables. Gambling was a common evening pastime in the camps as apparently was the consumption of quantities of whiskey of the cheapest and rawest varieties. Holiday trips to larger Chinese communities, particularly San Francisco's Chinatown, provided the men with fuller participation in the Canton culture established in these settlements.

Archaeology

The location illustrated is the largest of the twelve camp locations we surveyed at Donner Pass (Figure 1). The power pole has fallen between two huts sites. The earth floor is held in place by a rough stone foundation. The floor was twelve by twenty-five feet. The presence of nails indicated a wooden superstructure. The adjacent hut was twelve by thirty feet. Both had extra stone outside one end which probably was the remains of a fire hearth. We discovered a third hut at another site. This one, which employed a huge granite monolith as a rear wall, was fifteen foot square with the extra stone again in the center of one end. The other camps were simple, open sites in the places the terrain was flat and treeless. These areas invariably had a surface litter of camp debris. All of the materials were on the surface. We undertook no excavations.

The materials in each of the camps was essentially the same. Identical forms and patterns were found in each location.

Bottle glass was found in most camps. Large bottles with hand formed collars, they are primarily whiskey and wine bottle forms. One bottle panel is even marked "Bitters." Buttons were not uncommon, and we found some metal buckles such as are used today on work overalls. These metal buttons indicate the adoption of some American clothing as the traditional Chinese button is cloth. We also recovered in several of the camps rusted fragments of marked American made shovels, but other tools were lacking. A number of coins, Chinese "cash," were picked up (Figure 2). The characters in relief, the square hole, and the large sizes

FIGURE 1. Donner Pass, 21 August 1967. Photograph shows house floors of Site 2, looking northeast. Note the telephone pole fallen between floors. (Photo by Paul G. Chace.)

make them easy to identify. We know that wagering was important, and apparently the "cash" was so traditional that imitation pieces were cut from copper and iron. Illustrated are three of these locally fashioned gaming tokens. We also picked up an 1853 dime and a Sacramento druggist's trade token. There were also brass opium boxes with Chinese characters embossed in the center.

Of the ceramics, the crude, heavy porcelain rice bowl illustrated was by far the most common form and pattern (Figure 3). We have several score vessels of this same, repetitious, underglaze blue pattern. The motif is repeated three times around each bowl. There is a tree on the left and on the right is the character for "Double Happiness." This simple, mass-produced, provincial Canton ware was packaged and sold in lots of ten in Canton markets, according to one informant. Certainly, many times ten were used at Donner Pass. Some of the bases are marked with other words wishing fortune and prosperity. There were other underglaze patterns on rice bowls forms: this dotted floral, and this stylized leaf combined with this tailed figure. The three circles motif also appears with the tailed figure.

Besides the peasant wares, we did recover a few rare pieces of finer porcelain. This small celadon cup and bowl are very fine, thin porcelain. This "green bean blue," as it is termed in Cantonese, is used traditionally by rural doctors. Some of this celadon is distinctively marked. A Canton born informant told us the glaze comes from "Quan-see." We found some overglaze enamel painted porcelain. The tree-in-the swamp motif appeared at several sites. These hand-painted blue, underglaze designs were unique.

This tiny redware item with a matt finish is the bowl of an opium pipe (Figure 4). We found this redware at several sites but only in tiny fragments. Similar matt

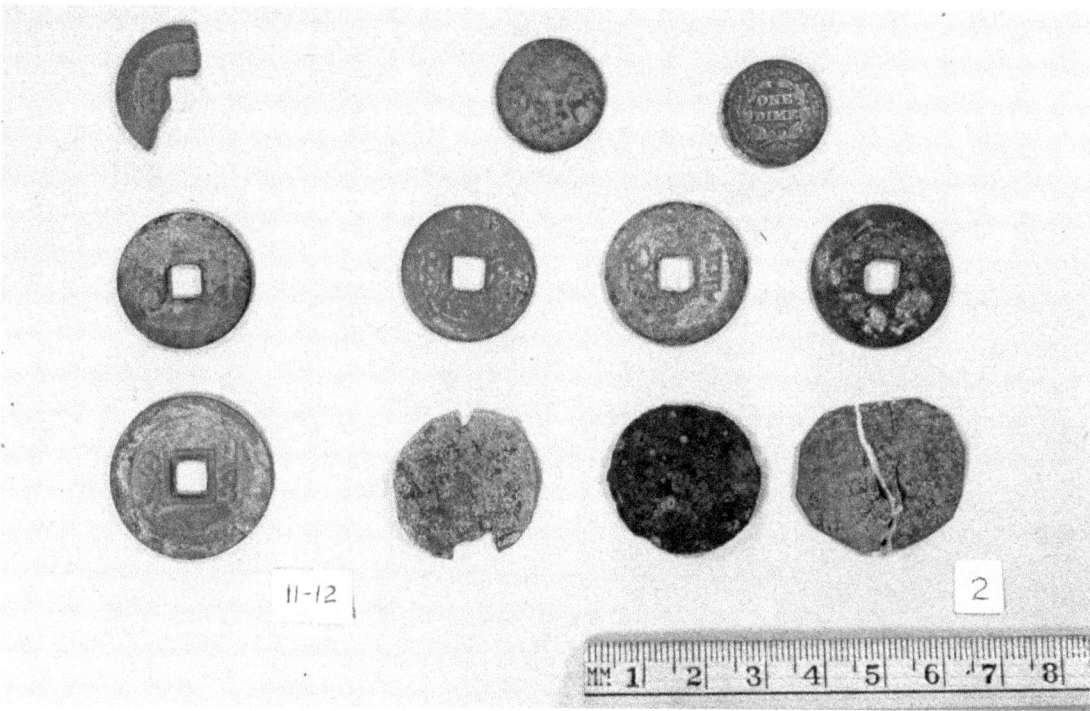

FIGURE 2. Coins and tokens found at Donner Pass. Most are Chinese "cash," easily identified by the square center hole. *Top row, center*: trade token from a Sacramento druggist. *Top row, right*: 1853 dime. *Bottom row, right*: three locally fashioned gaming tokens. (Photo by Paul G. Chace.)

FIGURE 3. Porcelain rice bowl, "Double Happiness" pattern. (Photo by Paul G. Chace.)

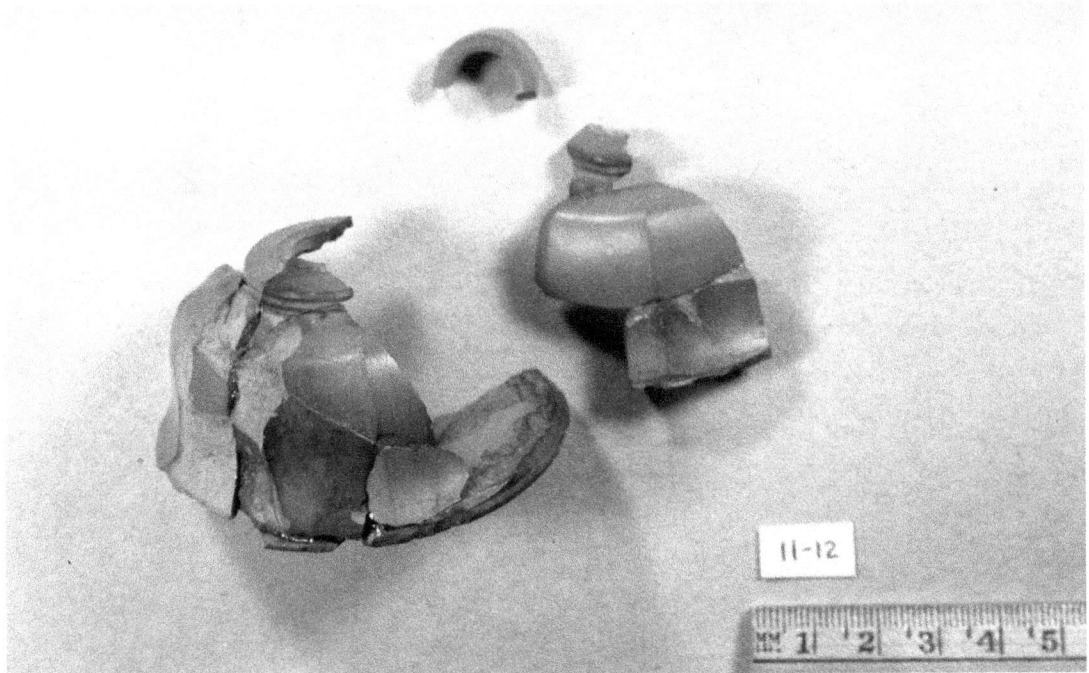

FIGURE 4. Red-earthenware opium-pipe bowl. (Photo by Paul G. Chace.)

finished black ware opium pipes bowls were also present at two of the camps, but no complete forms could be reconstructed.

A group of buff earthenware had an exterior white slip. The form was a globular, wide mouthed, jar or tea pot.

This huge, barrel shaped vessel is a brown stoneware with a rich black-brown glaze (Figure 5). The rim, wiped clean of glaze, has a medium color between the unglazed body and the dark, glazed surface. This huge crock is nineteen inches tall. Presumably this transported some food stuff from China across the Pacific to San Francisco and then to Donner Pass. We found a number of these. There were also more globular jar forms with tie lugs near the small mouth. An identical, complete specimen from a San Francisco collector measured fifteen inches in height. Our Canton born informant identified this as the stoneware made near Canton at Shek-wan. This Shek-wan Brown Ware is not unknown in the literature. These small, crudely fashioned, saucer shaped items just may be lids for the globular pot, although waxed paper covers tied with string are known to be used.

Fragments of very large, flat pans, like an American milk pan, are the same Shek-wan Ware only they are unglazed. They may be cooking pans. We found similar pans in Chinatown, said to be for cooking herbs. Other sherds represent smaller vessels of the Shek-wan Brown Ware. These are wide and narrow mouth jars without curving rims, some with spouts. These are containers for Chinese spirits, soy sauce, and salted foods. The glaze color varies from black to a rich chocolate brown. The glaze is unusually glossy and rarely dull. The vessels forms are flat based, and the shoulder are high and rounded. Soy sauce and liquor packaged in this or nearly identical ware can still be purchased today in San Francisco's Chinatown.

FIGURE 5. Barrel-shaped jar, Chinese brown-glazed stoneware. (Photo by Paul G. Chace.)

An Horizon Style

The material just described, particularly the ceramics, we would propose are an horizon style. This particular style of cultural materials is indicative of an archaeological horizon. Fortunately, that horizon can be well defined historically as the wide dispersal of Chinese laborers during the third quarter of the nineteenth century. The concept of horizon denotes a style of materials found over a very broad space and which were spread there during a very short period of time. Broad space and short time are the particular features of an horizon, and this Chinese immigration fits the concept perfectly. The presence of provincial Canton style ceramics, particularly peasant wares, is an horizon marker.

These wares should be found everywhere the sojourners labored. That area includes the South Pacific and most countries in the Western Hemisphere. We have a table to hand out which indicates the countries the sojourners immigrated to and the dates of their arrivals. The Chinese were in Canada, the U.S., Mexico, Peru, Cuba, many of the West Indies, and elsewhere. Notably, and most useful for historical archaeologists, the dates for their arrival in these various countries are all very close, most are between 1850 and 1870.

The horizon style defined from the 1865–1868 Donner Pass sites in California should be particularly useful in assessing archaeological materials throughout the Americas and elsewhere. We are looking forward to learning of materials from this horizon from other areas for comparative study. Several collections have already come to our attention. We are anxious to see more. We invite your communication.

PAUL G. CHACE
PAUL G. CHACE & ASSOCIATES
2665 KUANA LOA DRIVE
ESCONDIDO CA 92029

WILLIAM S. EVANS, JR.
(1922–2009)

Endnote

[1]西 垔 山（the High Sierras, or the Sierras-Nevada），在中国通常译为内华达山脉。但因为此山主体仍在加利福尼亚州，为避免歧义，此处按音译作西垔山。

R. Scott Baxter (R · 巴克斯特)

Rebecca Allen (瑞贝卡 · 阿伦)

The View from Summit Camp
从"山巅营地"望去

ABSTRACT

Chinese laborers occupied Summit Camp in California from 1865 to 1869 while they excavated the tunnels, built the grade, and laid the track over the most daunting obstacle facing the construction of the transcontinental railroad. Several archaeologically driven and tourist-related artifact collecting activities have occurred at Summit Camp, but it still contains important archaeological information. Study of this camp expands the typical historical view of Chinese laborers as subsidiary players in railroad construction. During their stay here, they made Summit Camp their own, building a small town that included many aspects of traditional Chinese culture. The laborers transformed the land that they built and lived in. Patterns of camp organization and layout reflect issues of labor relations and highlight their adaptive skills. The site of Summit Camp retains a remarkable *power of place.* Its location and landscape convey a sense of the history, resiliency, and labor contribution of Chinese railroad workers.

一批中国劳工在1865至1869年间居住在加利福尼亚州的山巅营地。他们在此开凿隧道，建筑坡道，并为横贯大陆铁路上最险峻的路段铺设轨道。山巅营地已举办过多次带有考古学背景，且与旅游相关的文物搜集活动，但它仍含有很多重要的考古学信息。关于这个营地的研究已经扩展了将中国劳工作为铁路建设中的辅助工作者的传统历史观点。中国劳工在其居留期间，已将山巅营地发展为自己的领地，建立了一个具有多重中国传统文化特色的小镇。他们转变了这块由他们建筑和居住的土地。该营地的组织和布局模式反映了劳工关系中的若干议题，并突出了工人们适应环境的技能。山巅营地保有显著的所谓"场所的权力"。其位置与景观传递出一种历史感，也体现了中国铁路工人的坚毅不拔以及其劳动的贡献。

Introduction

The Pacific Railroad people are making wonderful progress on the Summit Tunnel. Some persons—even engineers—calculated that this great work would require three or four years for its completion, and so it would in other countries, or if it were under the control of laggards, but here, and in the hands of go-ahead Californians, tunnel-time is annihilated. The tunnel is 1,660 feet long. It was begun in September last—at four points—on the east and on the west ends, and two other faces were created by a shaft in the centre. Thus, there are four faces, with three sets of hands to each, or twelve sets in all. Each set works eight hours, and the work goes on night and day! And now, on the 1st of the present month, of all these 1,660 feet, there were but 681 remaining to be cut! The progress last week was sixty feet, and at this rate the tunnel will be completed by the middle of August next. By measurement, on the 1st instant, there were but 346 feet in the east heading and 335 in the west heading, making, as before stated, 681 feet in all to be cut. And so in the space of eleven months from the period of its commencement will this tunnel be finished! (*Daily Alta California* 1867)

Donner Pass is 7,000 feet high in the Sierra Nevada, on the route between San Francisco and Reno, Nevada. The terrain is solid granite, and soil of any kind is rare. There are few spots that are flat or habitable. In winter snow accumulates to depths of forty feet. Here the Chinese camped while they whittled the railroad tunnels through the granite dome beneath them. (Chace and Evans 1969)

Summit Camp is in Placer County, California, near Donner Summit and Interstate 80. Site occupation is related to the main Chinese transcontinental railroad work camp, used during the construction of the Donner Summit tunnels. These tunnels were constructed between 1865 and 1869, and the camp was occupied during that same period. The camp is one of the largest and earliest examples of a Chinese labor camp in the United States. It is inherently important to the transcontinental railroad and Chinese American history as a symbol of the efforts expended in the construction of the railroad and the establishment of a permanent Chinese American population.

In 2006 the Tahoe National Forest asked for a damage assessment and National Register evaluation of Summit Camp. The site had been impacted by repeated leaks from a petroleum pipeline that runs through the site and subsequent cleanup efforts. The U.S. Forest Service wanted to make an informed decision about whether further protection or mitigation measures were needed to address this resource that was being

Historical Archaeology, 2015, 49(1):34–45.

Permission to reprint required.

repeatedly challenged by pipeline construction (and destruction), as well as by archaeologists and tourists (Allen and Baxter 2006).

Chinese Laborers at Summit Camp

To build what became known as the trans-continental railroad, the Central Pacific Railroad constructed rails from Sacramento eastward, and the Union Pacific Railroad constructed the railroad westward. Leland Stanford, E. B. Crocker, Charles Crocker, Mark Hopkins, Collis P. Huntington, and Theodore Judah were controlling partners of the Central Pacific line. Stanford, Hopkins, Huntington, and Charles Crocker, known as the "Big Four," came to dominate most of the politics and commerce of California for the next three decades.

Several acts of Congress, collectively known as the Pacific Railroad Acts, stipulated that both the Union Pacific and the Central Pacific be allotted bonds in proportion to the miles of track they laid. The acts also provided the companies timber and quarrying rights, along with 20 sections of land for each mile of rail laid. Each company was granted a 200 ft. wide strip of land on both sides of the right-of-way and 640 ac. (1 sq. mi.) for each mile of railroad completed, awarded in a checkerboard pattern on alternating sides of the track. The companies could then sell this land to raise more money. Apparently the land and subsidies were the most attractive part of the deal (Kibbey 1996:18). The Big Four's coffers from land sales alone paid for construction of the railroad, although keeping labor and material costs at a minimum was always an important consideration.

The first spike of the transcontinental railroad was driven in January 1863 at the foot of K Street on the Sacramento waterfront (Steinheimer and Dorn 1989:10; McClain 1995:8; Kibbey 1996:22). Construction proceeded as planned through the Central Valley. As the railhead advanced into the Sierra foothills, it was the practice to run excursion trains from Sacramento so that interested citizens could view the latest construction efforts. After leaving the valley and adjoining foothills, progress slowed, as heavy snow and tunneling through granite rock near Donner Pass presented major obstacles. By the summer of 1867, the railroad was still not completed between Cisco and Truckee. To speed

progress, a second phase of construction, east of the summit, was worked simultaneously with that at the summit; locomotives, rails, cars, and parts were hauled over the Dutch Flat Donner Lake Wagon Road to Coburn's Station (Truckee). Although the railroad was completed between Truckee and Reno by May 1868, the final gap between Cisco and Truckee was not officially closed until June of that year (Myrick 1962:18).

The story behind how and why Chinese laborers came to work on the railroad has become part of the lore of the American West. Originally thought to be too small of stature to handle the rigors of the job, they quickly built a reputation for themselves as hard workers capable of accomplishing dangerous tasks away from which others shied. It was this reputation that landed them at Summit Camp. At Donner Summit, the railroad was faced with the unen-viable chore of excavating a series of seven tunnels within 2 mi. of the summit (Figure 1). The longest tunnel, designated No. 6, was 1,659 ft. long, excavated 124 ft. below the surface of solid granite (Griswold 1962:117), with a 30 ft. change in elevation. Laborers dug holes into the granite face to place black-powder charges to blast the rock free, with another crew work-ing afterward to remove the loosened rock after each explosion. Between the tunnels, extensive rockwork was needed to build up the grade. Accomplishing this took four long years of hard labor, often with more than 40 ft. of snow on the ground (Figure 2). As a result, what would have been a temporary labor camp developed into what was essentially a small town, known as Summit Camp.

Work was grueling and dangerous, blasting away rock and mucking out the debris by hand. The Chinese laborers worked sunrise to sunset six days a week, earning $35 a month from which their living expenses were taken, leav-ing them about $20 in take-home pay at the end of the month. In comparison, non-Asian workers were paid about the same, but had their board included as part of their compensa-tion. Work carried on year-round, even through the dead of winter. In the winter of 1866, an avalanche swept away and killed five Chinese graders. Their fellow workers could not recover their bodies until the following summer when the snow finally melted away, exposing their remains (Gillis 1870:157).

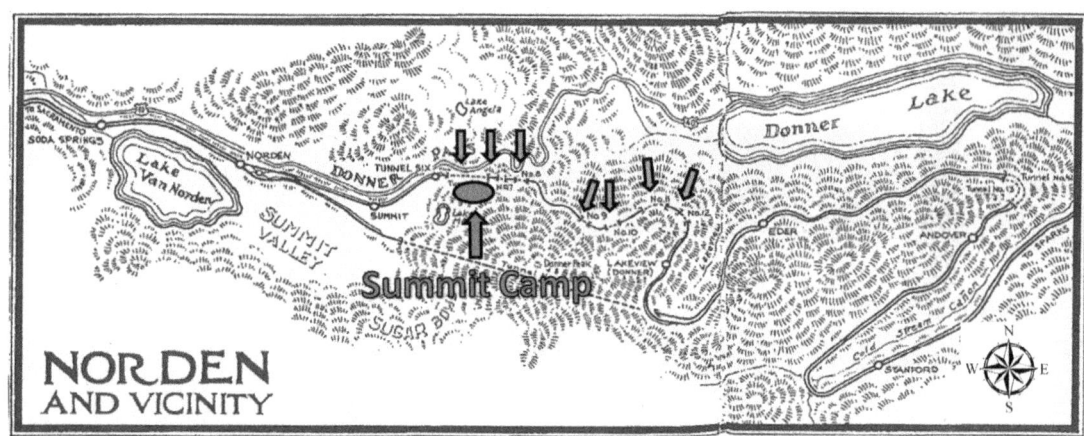

FIGURE 1. Seven tunnels (noted by arrows) were excavated by Chinese railroad workers, all within two miles of Summit Camp. (Map adapted from Signor [1985:114–115] by R. S. Baxter, 2008.)

FIGURE 2. Chinese railroad workers, working in the midst of snow. (Photo <http://scalar.usc.edu/anvc/the-knotted-line/media/railroad-in-winter.jpg>, late 19th century.)

Typical construction camps along the railroad were a simple conglomeration of tents and temporary structures that could be easily taken down and moved as the railroad progressed eastward. In some instances, rolling bunkhouses were used and moved along the track as it was laid. Because Summit Camp was occupied for a relatively long period of time, the Chinese railroad workers erected more permanent structures. The desire for protection against the severe winter environment at the summit was another incentive encouraging construction of more substantial structures. Figure 3 shows an historic photograph by Alfred Hart that illustrates a portion of Summit Camp at the east portal of Tunnel No. 6, also known as Summit Tunnel.

Archaeological Discoveries at Summit Camp

The authors were able to correlate one of the cabins shown in Figure 3 with the archaeological record (Baxter and Allen 2008) and designated this feature as Locus 10. Here the archaeological crew found a stone foundation in the exact location of the photograph and identified the layout of the cabin, including a hearth (Figure 4) that may have been used for heating the cabin and/or cooking. Outside the cabin foundation was what appeared to be a second collapsed hearth and a small hearth typically referred to as a wok oven or stove. Historical drawings of Chinese campsites often illustrate temporary hearths. Archaeologists excavated several shovel-test pits around the cabin and recovered artifacts, including nails, window glass, gaming pieces, coins, Chinese and European American tablewares, and opium-pipe bowl fragments (Baxter and Allen 2008).

FIGURE 3. A portion of Summit Camp at the east portal of Tunnel No. 6. Note the presence of small wooden cabins. (Photo by Alfred A. Hart, <http://www.donnersummithistoricalsociety.org/PDFs/newsletters/news12/july12.pdf>, ca. 1865–1869.)

FIGURE 4. Hearth feature at Summit Camp. (Photo by R. S. Baxter, 2007.)

Archaeologists also identified another roughly cylindrical hearth built up against a hillside, similar in appearance to large roasting features found at other overseas Chinese sites (Medin 2002). Chinese cooks frequently used these cooking features for large communal cooking efforts, including smoking or roasting meats. Some roasting hearths were large enough to cook whole animals, such as pigs. While clearing away surface debris, archaeologists also noted more ephemeral remains of another cabin foundation, at either end of which were a pair of wok stoves. Shovel-test pits in this area recovered nails, window glass, wok fragments, Chinese brown-glazed stoneware, Chinese and European American tablewares, opium-pipe bowl fragments, and opium or spice cans (Baxter and Allen 2008). A limited number of gaming pieces and liquor bottles hint at recreational activities. The presence of tins and bowl fragments suggests regular opium consumption, perhaps for medicinal, recreational, or social purposes, or,

more likely, a combination of all three motives.

Soil samples taken from in and around the hearths and submitted for microfloral, macrofloral, and lipids tests indicated the consumption of indigenous foodstuffs, including elderberry and bearberry, as well as imported foodstuffs, including rice, barley, and legumes (Puseman and Cummings 2008). Historical records indicate that the diet of the Chinese workers included dried oysters and abalone, dried bamboo, seaweed, mushrooms, dried fruits, rice, crackers, vermicelli, salted cabbage, Chinese sugar, peanut oil, Chinese bacon, pork, and poultry. There is also a lake near Summit Camp with a thriving population of catfish, which the Chinese railroad workers reportedly planted there to provide a ready supply of fresh fish.

Results of the field efforts were rather mixed, in that the number of artifacts present at the site were relatively few in number and offered only limited information. This was unexpected, as Chinese laborers occupied the site for nearly four continuous years. The authors were aware of previous archaeological studies at the summit, further detailed below, but in the absence of finding a variety and quantity of materials, the authors instead focused field efforts on mapping the features visible on the surface of the site. Through this documentation, the authors were able to associate several of the stone foundations and cooking features with the cabin locations seen in historical photographs, allowing for a better understanding of the layout of the camp and the size of the cabins and their method of construction. Archaeologists also identified a number of cooking features, providing evidence for use of traditional cooking methods and suggesting that communal cooking occurred on the site. Historical records indicate that men were grouped in teams of 12 to 20,

with one designated as the headman, responsible for organizing the men during the workday and providing them with food and shelter. A second man was designated as the cook, who, aside from cooking meals, was responsible for making sure that a steady supply of tea was provided to the workers during the day, and that hot water was available for bathing in the evenings (Lindström et al. 1999). Figure 5 shows one of the men delivering tea at the east portal of Tunnel No. 8 at Donner Summit.

Why So Few Artifacts at the Site?

As noted above, the quantity of artifacts recovered from the site was unexpectedly low for a place that had been occupied for at least four years. Artifacts were highly fragmented,

FIGURE 5. East portal of Tunnel No. 8; the man in photograph is delivering tea to the workers. (Photo by Alfred A. Hart, <http://content.cdlib.org/ark:/13030/tf058005hz/>, ca. 1865–1869.)

with few items larger than a quarter dollar. This is the result of several factors. First, there is very little soil deposition in this granitic environment, so most of the artifacts remained on the ground surface. This contributed a second factor in the paucity of artifacts: most of the material was on the surface in an area of sparse vegetation, making it easily visible. Old Highway 40 is near the site, as is the Pacific Crest Trail, a petroleum pipeline, and a railroad grade going through the site that is now used by hikers, bikers, and off-road vehicles. A popular ski resort is also within walking distance. All of this access contributes to a fairly steady stream of pedestrian traffic through the site. According to Forest Service sources, at one point a park ranger was leading walking tours of the site and had encouraged people to pick up artifacts as souvenirs of their trip.

Installation of the Santa Fe Pacific Pipeline (for natural gas) occurred in 1956. The pipeline crossed through the center of the site, creating a disturbance corridor about 45 ft. wide. A fiber-optic cable, installed around 1987, crosses through the center of the site. At least two generations of utility lines run overhead, and foundation holes for utility poles have been excavated in many places across the site.

Previous Archaeological Collection

Previous archaeologically driven activities resulted in a series of collections from the 1960s through the 1980s that removed much of the archaeological record from the site's surface. Documentation of these collections also helps explain why so few artifacts were found at the Summit Camp site in 2006. Most of the large artifacts were picked up more than 30 years prior to the authors' own field efforts. While the Forest Service did not authorize these collections, they are documented in the archaeological literature.

In 1962 Paul Chace received a box of rice bowls collected from the Summit Camp site by a non-archaeologist. Chace later surveyed and collected from the area in 1966 and again with William Evans in 1967. Chace and Evans (1969) presented a paper on the Donner Summit site and the Chinese railroad workers who labored there at the annual meeting of the Society for Historical Archaeology. That paper is reproduced

in this volume in its original conference-paper format. Chace and Evans said that the purpose of their paper was to highlight the history of the railroad workers, describe the artifacts found at the site, and establish a "style" of artifacts that characterized Chinese archaeological sites of the period. They noted the remnants of the wooden structures and described a plethora of artifacts, all of which were found on the surface. Ceramics received the most attention. Their paper was one of the first historical archaeological descriptions of ceramic patterns/styles known as Double Happiness, Celadon ware, Bamboo ware (also known as Three Circles and a Dragonfly in early literature), and what came to be known as Chinese brown-glazed stoneware (CBGS). The authors also noted other Chinese artifacts, such as coins and opium bowls, and described European American bottles and buttons as "American" influence.

Chace and Evans's paper established two important precedents. First, the authors acknowledged that Chinese-inhabited sites contain immediately identifiable artifacts that have become the hallmark of archaeological studies of Chinese American sites: "They maintained Chinese culture in all spheres not requiring accommodation of local circumstances." Second, Chace and Evans established the importance of using cultural consultants to help interpret the material culture. In this case, they consulted a "Canton-born informant," who offered information on the origins of Celadon wares and the forms of the Chinese brown-glazed stoneware.

In part, based on his experience from the Summit Camp site, Evans (1980) wrote an article that further defined the material culture of Chinese-occupied sites. He also included comparative material from Bear Valley, Columbia, Harmony Borax Works, Riverside, and Ventura, California, as well as Virginia City, Nevada. Some of this information was from other archaeological sites; other details were from historical accounts. Evans (1980:90) particularly paid attention to food, "the paraphernalia of subsistence," and relaxation (evidence of opium and gambling). His article focused on ceramic utilitarian ware, tableware, opium pipes, tins, lamp covers, gaming pieces, coins, and medicine bottles. He concluded that the assemblage associated with Chinese workers in the American West was notable for its lack of diversity and association with a male-dominant society. Only in Virginia City, where women and families were present, did the material culture present much variation.

This material is now housed at the Chinese Historical Society of Southern California. The historical society has been kind enough to lend Scott Baxter the collection so that it can be fully cataloged and analyzed, a process that is ongoing. This collection includes everything from tools and food-storage vessels to personal items, such as buttons; opium paraphernalia, including cans and pipe bowls; and tableware.

In 1984 another archaeologist collected additional materials from the Summit site. John Molenda is now studying this collection (Molenda, this issue). Susan Lindström and colleagues recorded the site after a pipeline accident and its subsequent repair damaged the site (Lindström et al. 1999). Although archaeologists did not collect artifacts, they noted impacts to the site, and Lindström (2005) later revisited for the same reason. William Self Associates recently completed an evaluation of several other sites, slightly north of the area described in this article, that may be extensions of or related to the occupation at Summit Camp (Arrigoni et al. 2013). Scott Baxter's current goal is to address nearly five decades of archaeological research at Summit Camp and highlight and expand the material and archaeological findings and importance of this site.

A Sense of Place and Heritage

What is apparent about this site is that, despite its checkered archaeological and surface-collected history, it retains the ability to convey a better understanding of the lives of the thousands of virtually anonymous Chinese workers who toiled on the construction of the transcontinental railroad. Although only limited excavations were carried out at the site in 2006, archaeologists found domestic-related material and more information about camp layout. These materials, coupled with information found in the previous collections from the site, have the potential to address research themes, such as architecture, land use, diet, culture change, and labor relations.

Summit Camp represents one of the oldest and largest settlements of Chinese workers in California that has been archaeologically documented. The building of the transcontinental railroad probably ranks below only statehood and the Gold Rush in the shaping of California's economy, politics, and social systems. Summit Camp was a vital link in the development of the transcontinental railroad, one of the greatest engineering feats in American history. Without the Chinese workers who occupied this and other camps, the completion of the tunnels through Donner Summit would have been delayed by months or possibly longer, effectively hamstringing the Central Pacific Railroad. Summit Camp was one of the largest and longest-lived camps, due to the difficult nature of the work in which the residents were engaged, which took several years to complete. Construction of the railroad was also the driving force in bringing waves of Chinese immigrants to California, planting the seeds of the state's still-thriving Chinese American community. The residents of Summit Camp were not the transient, transnational "sojourners" that Chace and Evans (1969) named them, a label that has since fallen out of anthropological favor, as the historical and archaeological literature (including essays in this issue) demonstrates how interconnected the Chinese workers were with the communities around them before, during, and well after the construction of the railroad.

Despite site impacts, including archaeology; artifact collection; and pipeline construction, repair, and destruction, Summit Camp retains much of its physical integrity. The authors' recent test excavations demonstrate that the shallow soils still hold quantities of artifacts, albeit in limited numbers, although study of previous collections adds to the understanding of the archaeological record. Intact hearths and cabin foundations remain, providing insight into camp layout and activity areas. Visually impressive, the site retains excellent integrity of setting. Most of the 20th-century development that has sprung up around the site remains out of sight and offsite. Even the original railroad grade, although now abandoned, is still present. The viewshed from this site retains its ability to affect the visitor. Standing at the site, with its view of Donner Lake, the railroad grade, and tunnel, it is easy to imagine the hardship, fortitude, and contribution of the Chinese railroad workers. Summit Camp retains its purpose and power of place. Remarkably, the view from Summit Camp today is very much the same as it was in 1865 (Figure 6). In 2009, the California State Historic Preservation Officer concurred with the Forest Service and authors' recommendation that the site is eligible for listing on the National Register of Historic Places.

Motivations for Documenting the Past

Neville R. Ritchie (2003:6) noted that "Chinese heritage sites" have different meanings for different groups, and that regional social and political climates account for many of those opinions. Although Ritchie was discussing sites in New Zealand and Australia, the sentiment can be applied to the American West. Celebration of the 150th anniversary of the transcontinental railroad is certainly tied to the social and political climate of 21st-century California and other western states. Creation of the Chinese Railroad Workers in North America Project (2014) at Stanford University recognizes the contribution of Chinese laborers who "helped to shape the physical and social landscape of the American West," and attempts to reverse the "unjust" exclusion of these workers from the majority of western histories.

While the railroad workers at Summit Camp were internally organized and inclusive of the camp inhabitants, the amount of external marginalization that they faced is only now coming to the forefront of history told. The National Park Service (2013) launched an initiative to highlight its role as America's "storyteller" agency; the initiative is intended to "increase the number of historic and cultural resources associated with the nation's diverse cultural groups that are identified, documented, preserved, and interpreted." This is a self-reflecting effort that, as the demography of the United States changes, so too does the need to revisit the past, reflect upon historical populations, and make the conscious effort to make the past more relevant to the present, as well as to the future. Recent historical archaeological literature (Voss and Allen 2008; Dixon 2014) emphasizes the importance of working within a transnational paradigm for the study of migrant communities, with local and regional heritage groups, and engaging

historical and historians' perspectives, as well as those of other colleagues and disciplines. It is this integration of approaches and understanding that best represents the study of marginalized populations, such as the railroad workers, especially those who have no documentation of their own history.

Revisiting Summit Camp has added a nuance of significance to the study of the laborers' contribution—capturing the landscape and sense of place that grounds this contribution. Standing at Summit Camp, most people can only begin to imagine the hardships and determination of the laborers, but they can appreciate the workers' place of belonging in the story of the creation of the American West.

Acknowledgments

We would like to thank Carrie Smith for giving us the opportunity to work at the Summit Camp site. Brad Deveraux, Alex Armstrong, and Maher Tleimat helped us in the field to document the site. Susan Lindström and Connie Young Yu helped us to document the site's history. The visit to the site by Connie and her husband John helped to open our eyes to the power of the place and its deep meaning in Chinese American history. Eugene Moy and the Chinese Historical Society of Southern California lent Scott the collection to study. Thanks also to Barbara L. Voss, Gordon Chang, Shelly Fisher Fishkin, and others for their efforts in pulling together the Chinese Railroad Workers in North America Project and asking us to participate. Our fellow archaeologists provided critical peer review that definitely improved this paper and its contents. Thank you all.

FIGURE 6. The view from Donner Summit has remained remarkably unchanged since construction of the transcontinental railroad: (a) Traveler Charles Nordhoff (1874) drew his view from Summit Camp to illustrate his travel book; (b) a diorama at the California State Railroad Museum envisions the same view with workers present (Photo by R. Allen, 2009); and (c) the modern view from Summit Camp with Tunnels 6, 7, and 8 visible on the *right* of the photo. (Photo by R. Allen, 2007.)

References

ALLEN, REBECCA, AND R. SCOTT BAXTER
2006 Historical Archaeological Damage Assessment, Evaluation Proposal, and Research Design for FS Site 05-17-57-633. Report to Tahoe National Forest, Truckee, CA, from Past Forward, Inc., Garden Valley, CA.

ARRIGONI, AIMEE, PAUL FARNSWORTH, AND NAHIZ FINO
2013 Final Cultural Resources Assessment Report for the Three Historic Sites near Line Section 12, Nevada County, California. Report to Tahoe National Forest, Truckee, CA, from William Self Associates, Inc., Orinda, CA.

BAXTER, R. SCOTT, AND REBECCA ALLEN
2008 National Register of Historic Places Evaluation and Damage Assessment for CA-PLA-2002/H (Summit Camp). Report to Tahoe National Forest, Truckee, CA, from Past Forward, Inc., Plymouth, CA.

CHACE, PAUL G., AND WILLIAM S. EVANS, JR.
1969 Celestial Sojourners in the High Sierras: The Ethno-Archaeology of Chinese Railroad Workers (1865–1868). Paper presented at the Second Annual Conference on Historical and Underwater Archaeology, Tucson, AZ.

CHINESE RAILROAD WORKERS IN NORTH AMERICA PROJECT
2014 Chinese Railroad Workers in North America Project. Stanford University <https://www.stanford.edu/group/ chineserailroad/cgi-bin/wordpress/>. Accessed 4 January 2014.

DAILY ALTA CALIFORNIA
1867 State Items—The Summit Tunnel. *Daily Alta California* 10 May, 19(6265):1. San Francisco.

DIXON, KELLY J.
2014 Historical Archaeologies of the American West. *Journal of Archaeological Research* 22(4):177–228.

EVANS, WILLIAM S., JR.
1980 Food and Fantasy: Material Culture of the Chinese in California and the West, circa 1850–1900. In *Archaeological Perspectives on Ethnicity in America: Afro-American and Asian American Culture History*, Robert L. Schuyler, editor, pp. 89–96. Baywood, Farmingdale, NY.

GILLIS, JOHN R.
1870 Tunnels of the Pacific Railroad. *American Society of Civil Engineers Transactions* 1(13):153–169.

GRISWOLD, WESLEY S.
1962 *A Work of Giants: Building the First Transcontinental Railroad.* McGraw-Hill, New York, NY.

KIBBEY, MEAD B.
1996 *The Railroad Photographs of Alfred A. Hart, Artist.* California State Library Foundation, Sacramento.

LINDSTRÖM, SUSAN
2005 Letter Report to Greg Taylor and Levine Fircke, Re: Kinder Morgan Donner Summit Incident Release Site: Restoration Phase Preliminary Archaeological Metal Detection Survey, 1 September. Manuscript, Tahoe National Forest, Truckee Ranger District, Truckee, CA.

LINDSTRÖM, SUSAN, JOHN BETTS, LEON SCHEGG, AND DON WIGGINS
1999 Santa Fe Pacific Pipeline Partners, L.P., Donner Pass Incident, Heritage Resources Inventory, Vol. 1: Report, Tahoe National Forest, Truckee Ranger District (Report 05-17-1223), Nevada and Placer Counties, California [Draft]. Manuscript, Santa Fe Pacific Pipeline Partners, L.P., Orange, CA.

McCLAIN, JIM
1995 Drilling through Granite: Construction of the Summit Tunnel. *Sierra Heritage* 13(6):8–11.

MEDIN, ANMARIE
2002 Chapter 7. Cooking Features. In Excavation of the Woolen Mills Chinatown CA-SCL-807H, San Jose, Vol. 1, Rebecca Allen, R. Scott Baxter, Anmarie Medin, Julia Costello, and Connie Young Yu, authors, pp. 105–120. Report to California Department of Transportation, District 4, Oakland, from Past Forward, Inc., Richmond, CA, California Department of Transportation, Sacramento, Foothill Resources, Ltd., Mokelumne Hill, CA, and EDAW, Inc., San Diego, CA.

MYRICK, DAVID F.
1962 *Railroads of Nevada and Eastern California, Vol. 1: The Northern Roads.* University of Nevada Press, Reno.

NATIONAL PARK SERVICE
2013 Program Description. National Park Service, Cultural Resources Diversity Program, U.S. Department of the Interior <http://www.cr.nps.gov/crdi/description/ prgm.htm>. Accessed 4 January 2014.

NORDHOFF, CHARLES
1874 *California: For Health, Pleasure, and Residence. A Book for Travelers and Settlers.* Harper & Brothers, New York, NY.

PUSEMAN, KATHRYN, AND LINDA SCOTT CUMMINGS
2008 Macrofloral and Organic Residue (FTIR) Analysis of Sediment from Summit Camp (FS Site 05-17-57-633), California. Report to Past Forward, Inc., Garden Valley, CA, from Paleo Research Institute, Golden, CO.

RITCHIE, NEVILLE R.
2003 Taking Stock: 20 Years of Australasian "Overseas Chinese Archaeology." *Australian Archaeology* 21:4–10.

SIGNOR, JOHN R.
1985 *Donner Pass: Southern Pacific's Sierra Crossing.* Golden West, San Marino, CA.

STEINHEIMER, RICHARD, AND DICK DORN
    1989 *Diesels over Donner*. Interurban Press, Glendale, CA.

VOSS, BARBARA L., AND REBECCA ALLEN
    2008 Overseas Chinese Archaeology: Historical Foundations, Current Reflections and New Directions. *Historical Archaeology* 42(3):5–28.

R. SCOTT BAXTER
ENVIRONMENTAL SCIENCE ASSOCIATES
2600 CAPITOL AVENUE, SUITE 200
SACRAMENTO, CA 95816

REBECCA ALLEN
ENVIRONMENTAL SCIENCE ASSOCIATES
2600 CAPITOL AVENUE, SUITE 200
SACRAMENTO, CA 95816

John Molenda (约翰·莫兰达)

Moral Discourse and Personhood in Overseas Chinese Contexts
海外华人语境中的道德话语与人格

ABSTRACT

Resistance and agency have been important themes in archaeological sites of labor. But how should archaeologists address archaeological contexts where resistance seems attenuated? This article takes the construction of the transcontinental railroad (1865–1869) as a case study to explore this question, focusing on the High Sierras section of the railroad around Tahoe National Forest. Chinese laborers in the mid-19th century were oriented toward and empowered by a moral discourse quite different from that of their Western capitalist employers, and these moral differences were intimately connected with divergent understandings of personhood. While Western capitalists understood labor relations through the dominant discourse of possessive individualism and the spirit of capitalism, Chinese workers were invested in a discourse of relational personhood and filiality. Understanding these differences can transform archaeological interpretation of Chinese work camps in regard to the presence of agency and the significance of labor.

在对劳工的考古学研究中，抵抗与能动性一直是重要的议题。但是对于那些抵抗显薄弱的考古学场景，我们又应该如何看待？本文将横贯大陆铁路的建设（1865–1869）作为探索这一问题的个案研究，将重点放在围绕太浩国家公园、在西垩山上的一段铁路建设。我认为，十九世纪的中国劳工曾受到一种与他们的西方资本家雇主截然不同的道德话语的调节和激励。而他们之间的道德差异又与其对于人格的不同理解密切相关。西方资本家基于一种占有性个人主义的主流话语和资本主义精神来理解劳动关系，而中国工人则笃信关系性的人格与孝道话语。理解这种不同，将转变我们对于中国劳工营中能动性的存在以及劳动的意义所作出的考古学诠释。

Resistance

Work camps and other sites of labor have been regarded by many historical archaeologists as having pronounced potential to address issues of class and class conflict. According to Hardesty (2002:94), "the often stark faces of labor and capital at work camps make such social formations ideal cases for the application of conflict theories." McGuire and Reckner (2002:47) stated: "[T]he archaeological record of the historic West is largely the result of day-to-day lived experiences, and these experiences *must* have included class struggle [emphasis added]." Over the past several decades, historical archaeologists have demonstrated the active role workers have played in resisting capitalist dominance. Such "collective resistance by workers in an industrial setting can take many forms, including malingering, sabotage of machinery, and destruction of products" (Saitta 2007:40). Examples range from the explicit violence of the Ludlow Massacre (Ludlow Collective 2001) to more subtle expressions of resistance, including drinking on the job and destruction of property (Nassaney and Abel 1993; Mrowzowski et al. 1996; Shackel 2000).

In these studies, the archaeological material suggests that laborers understood the conflicting interests of capitalists and laborers, and took an active role in defending their class interests. But such an understanding of resistance causes a problem: how can archaeologists interpret sites of labor where "resistance" seems relatively attenuated? The work camps occupied by Chinese laborers on the transcontinental railroad in the 1860s present just such a case. If documentary or archaeological evidence for resistance cannot be found, does this mean that Chinese laborers were "more docile" and had "less will of their own against their bosses" (U.S. Congress 1877)? If researchers take the documentary evidence (written by European Americans) at face value, this is exactly the impression received. Take, for instance, the congressional testimony of Charles Crocker, the supervisor of the construction of the transcontinental railroad:

> So far as the controlling of large bodies of laborers on works of the magnitude of the Central Pacific, we had one strike with the Chinese. ... The Chinese circulated a document among themselves, all through the camp, and on the next Monday morning they refused to come out. ... If there had been that number of white laborers on that work in a strike there would have been murder and drunkenness and disorder of

all kinds; it would have been impossible to have controlled them; but this strike of the Chinese was just like Sunday all along the work. These men staid in their camps; that is, they would come out and walk around, but not a word was said, nothing was done; no violence was perpetrated along the whole line. (U.S. Congress 1877)

Crocker is commenting on the single instance of labor agitation among Chinese laborers on the transcontinental railroad for which there is documentary evidence, occurring in late June 1867 (*Daily Alta California* 1867). The strike was not limited to a specific camp, but took place "along the whole line" (U.S. Congress 1877) in the High Sierras. Thus, all the work camps mentioned in this article can be considered associated with this event.

Crocker responded to this lone strike with "coercive measures," such as stopping the supply of provisions. Within the week "they returned peaceably to work" (U.S. Congress 1877). This implies that while Chinese laborers had some degree of class consciousness, or at least a sense of shared interests with other workers, relative to other workers they were far less likely to engage in overt resistance,

and the one occasion they actually did so was relatively benign. To explain this by saying Chinese laborers were somehow less agentive or more docile is merely to reproduce orientalist stereotypes (Said 1978), yet a narrative of class struggle does not readily fit with the archaeological data.

Archaeology

During the summer of 2013, I conducted pedestrian survey and surface mapping of sites associated with the construction of the transcontinental railroad in and around Tahoe National Forest in the High Sierras of California (Figure 1). This project aims both to find previously unrecorded work camps associated with the railroad (via pedestrian survey of relatively flat areas within 500 m of the railroad, supplemented with metal detection) and also perform a more detailed mapping and analysis of previously identified work camps within the project area. Previously recorded sites were identified through a records search of the North Central Information Center at California State University, Sacramento; archival research at the

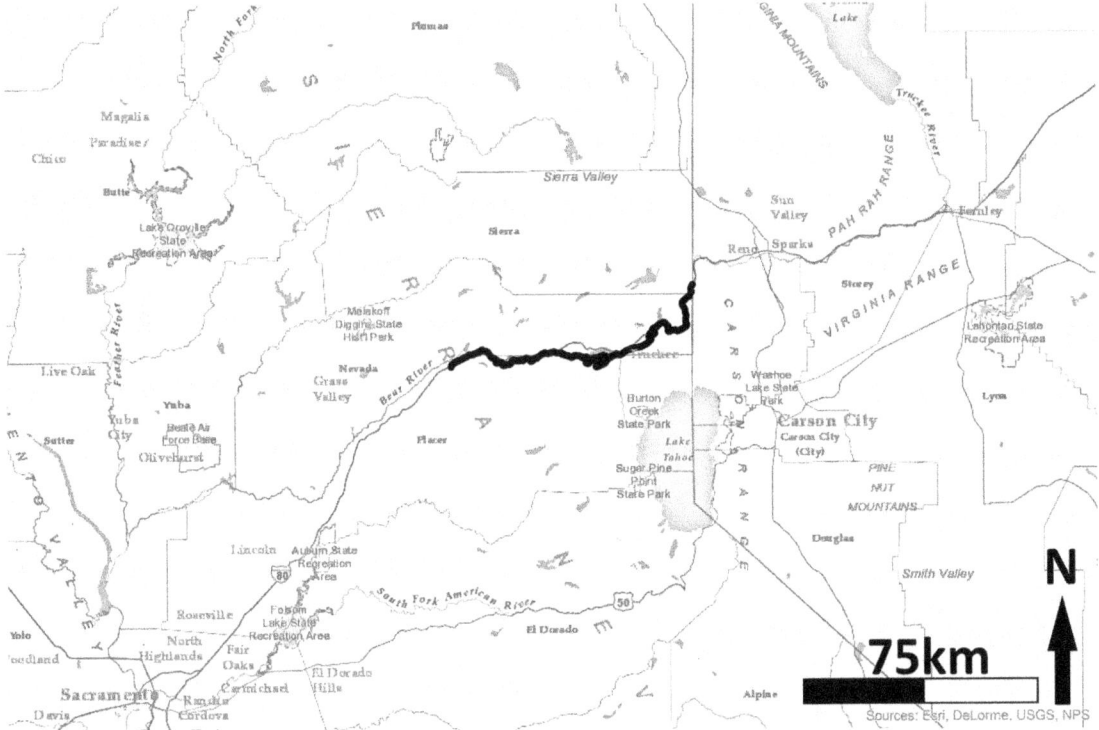

FIGURE 1. Regional map showing the project area, Placer and Nevada counties, California. (Map by author, 2014.)

California State Railroad Museum Library in Sacramento; the Bancroft Library in Berkeley; the Nevada Historical Society in Reno; and the Truckee Historical Society in Truckee; as well as consultation with archaeologists Susan Lindström (private consultant), R. Scott Baxter (Environmental Science Associates), and Carrie Smith (Heritage Resource Manager at the Tahoe National Forest).

While the survey is not yet complete, at least one previously unrecorded work camp, Windmill Tree or Camp 5 (Figure 2), included multiple visible structural remains and nearly 200 recorded surface artifacts. This site and two previously recorded railroad work camps, Summit Camp (Baxter and Allen 2008) and China Kitchen (Gralia and Gralia 2004), are the most intact reported Chinese work camps associated with the construction of the transcontinental railroad in the High Sierras (Figure 3).

Summit Camp has been studied by archaeologists since the 1960s (Baxter and Allen, this issue; Chace and Evans, this issue). One important assemblage of artifacts from Summit Camp was collected by archaeologist Julia Costello. Costello conducted pedestrian surface collection of Summit Camp in 1984, grouping collected artifacts by loci. At the time of the analysis presented here, the field records for the Costello Summit Camp Collection were not available, and the assemblage was studied as a group for the purposes of intersite comparison. Recently, Costello located a sketch map of the survey loci that may allow future studies to incorporate intrasite comparative analysis.

In this article, I compare the results of my reanalysis of the Costello Summit Camp Collection with the findings of my preliminary field research at the Windmill Tree site. In summer 2013, Lindsay Montgomery and I conducted mapping and pedestrian surface survey of the Windmill Tree site using 5 m transects. Like Summit Camp, the Windmill Tree site has minimal vegetation, affording excellent surface visibility. All artifacts were marked with a pin flag, mapped with compass and tape in relation to the site data, photographed, and measured.

Preliminary comparisons between the Costello Summit Camp Collection and surface survey data from the Windmill Tree site offer an opportunity to explore expectations for archaeological evidence of overt or covert resistance among Chinese laborers.

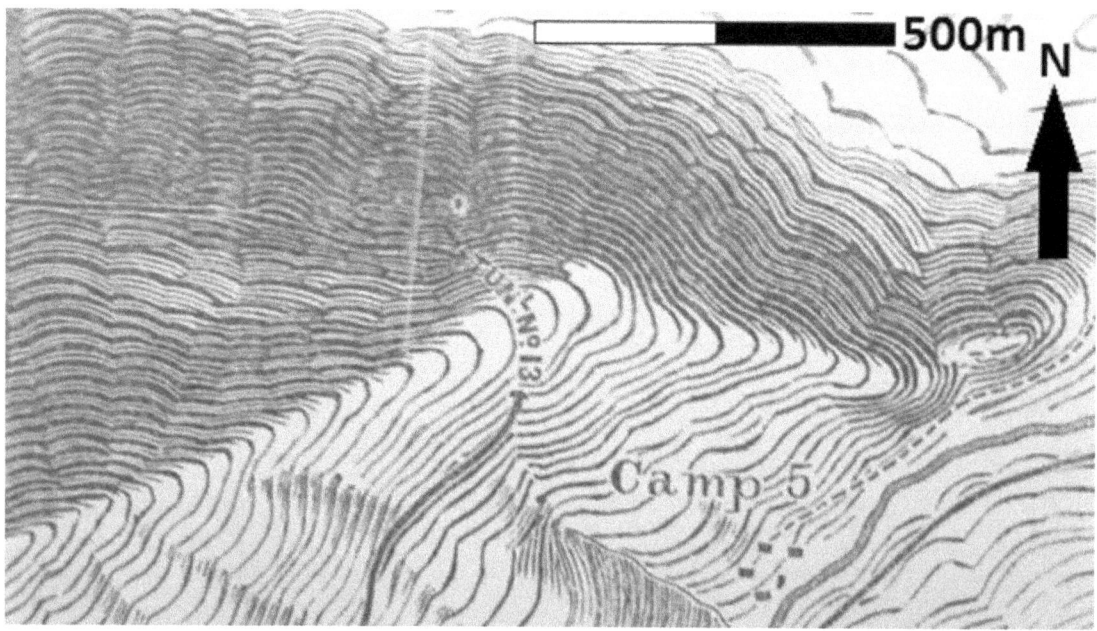

FIGURE 2. Detail of the *Map of the Central Pacific Railroad from Summit Valley to the Truckee River* (Vose 1882) showing the location of Camp 5, also known as Windmill Tree.

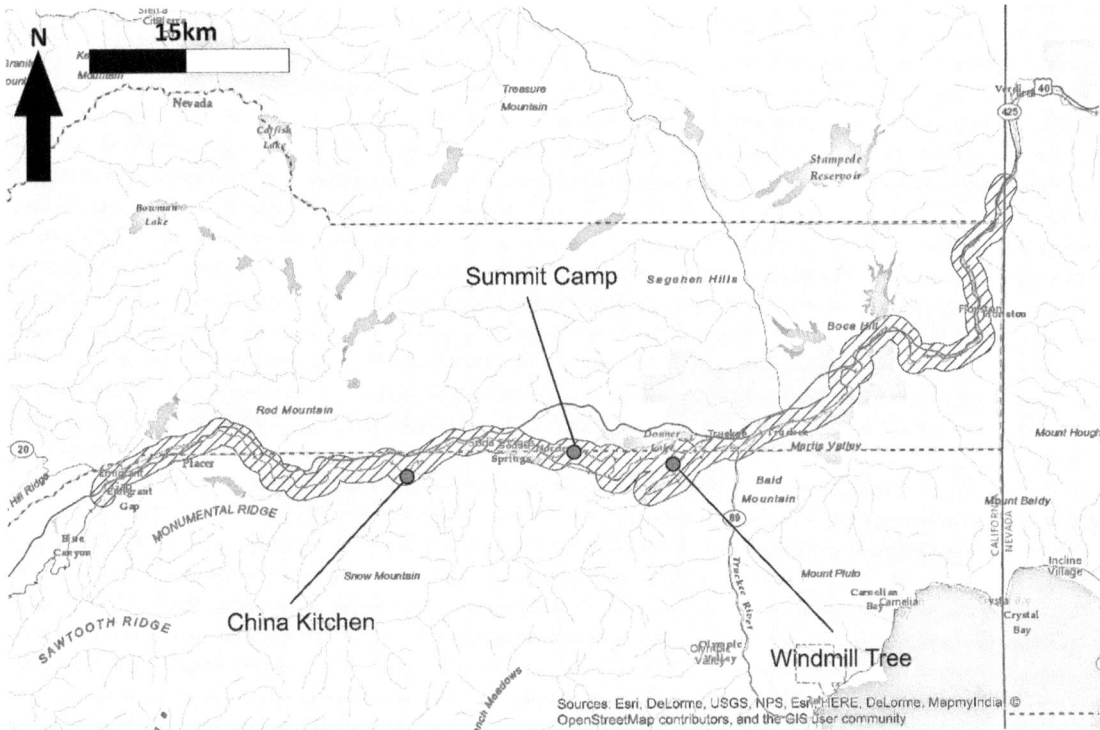

FIGURE 3. Project area showing three known work camps in Placer and Nevada counties, California, associated with the transcontinental railroad and mentioned in the text. (Map by author, 2014.)

The Costello Summit Camp Collection provides a general expectation of the types and proportions of artifacts found in Chinese work camps in the High Sierras. The ceramic assemblage consists mostly of Double Happiness porcelain rice-bowl sherds (Figure 4) and Chinese brown-glazed stoneware (CBGS) (Figure 5) (Table 1). There are also fragments of ceramic opium-pipe bowls. Diagnostic metal artifacts include wok fragments, Chinese coins, and opium boxes. Of these, opium-box fragments were the most abundant metal artifact in both specimen count (Number of Individual Specimens [NISP]=183, 73.8%) and weight (282.4 g, 28.3%). Other than occasional medicine vials and gaming pieces, the glass assemblage consists primarily of bottle-glass shards. Beside a few wine-bottle bases, most of the identifiable glass-bottle shards represent European American medicine bottles and glass vials used in traditional Chinese medicine (Heffner, this issue).

Because both the Summit Camp and Windmill Tree sites were long-term camps where Chinese railroad workers lived for extended periods, a comparison of these two sites provides a preliminary measure of consistency or variety in material practices among different groups of Chinese railroad workers. Overall, it is the similarity in the material culture assemblage that is striking. So far, not only are the types of artifacts found at each site very consistent, but so also their relative abundance. For example, Table 1 shows that the relative frequency of Double Happiness rice-bowl sherds and CBGS sherds at both sites is very similar. While further research at the Windmill Tree site and other work camps on the transcontinental railroad may reveal more nuanced findings, at present the evidence suggests that both artifact types and their relative proportions may be relatively homogeneous among Chinese work camps. This in turn supports a picture of collective purchasing and organized distribution of everyday goods (Stanford 1865; U.S. Congress 1877).

The artifacts from the Summit Camp and Windmill Tree sites have indexical relationships

FIGURE 4. Double Happiness porcelain rice-bowl sherds in situ, Windmill Tree site. (Photo by author, 2013.)

with some of the daily activities of Chinese railroad laborers. Beside the artifacts associated with food storage (CBGS vessels), production (woks), and consumption (porcelain rice bowls and other tablewares), the presence of coins and gaming pieces suggests active recreation and socialization among Chinese workers. The presence of glass fragments of opioid tonics, along with opium-pipe bowls and opium boxes, suggests that opium was used for medicinal as well as pleasurable purposes, and perhaps even that the distinction between enhancing pleasure and anesthetizing pain is not altogether clear. The consistent presence of Double Happiness porcelain rice bowls, one of the least expensive ceramic patterns available during this period (Sando and Felton 1993), suggests that individualized choice of ceramic styles was not a concern, if it was even possible. Rather, such a distribution system seems motivated by frugality.

The activities indicated by these archaeological remains—food preparation, gaming, opium

use, and so on—can be marshaled to support many different interpretations and moral stories, but I would argue they cannot be used as evidence of resistance traditionally conceived without extreme artificiality and theoretical mediation. While the supervisors of the building of the railroad repeatedly lament the effect of alcohol on white workers, Charles Crocker testified to Congress that he had "no recollection of ever having seen a drunken Chinaman" (U.S. Congress 1877). While alcohol is almost invariably condemned when discussed, when Crocker mentioned opium use among the Chinese it was seemingly without opprobrium, merely stating: "It stupefies them. They lie in a state of stupor and dream pleasant dreams, as I understand it" (U.S. Congress 1877). When asked whether he found Chinese laborers reliable and honest, Superintendent of Construction James Harvey Strobridge testified: "Yes, as much so as other people; much more reliable; they would not get drunk and go away as white men" (U.S. Congress 1877). There is thus no

FIGURE 5. Brown-glazed stoneware in situ, Windmill Tree site. (Photo by author, 2013.)

textual warrant to interpret opium use among the Chinese as a form of resistance parallel to the use of alcohol.

A narrative of class struggle does not readily fit with the archaeological data left behind by Chinese railroad workers. What interpretive alternatives are there for conceptualizing agency and the meaning of labor?

Absent Evidence

I suggest that, in order to think more fruitfully about resistance, agency, and labor in Chinese contexts, archaeologists and other researchers need to make an interpretive shift in understanding personhood and its relation to variant moral discourses. But linking the archaeological data

TABLE 1
CERAMICS FROM COSTELLO SUMMIT CAMP COLLECTION AND WINDMILL TREE

Ceramic Type/Pattern	Windmill Tree Number of Sherds (Percentage)	Costello Collection Number of Sherds (Percentage)	Costello Collection Weight in Grams (Percentage)
Double Happiness	3 (7.3)	108 (9.6)	185 (4.5)
Brown-glazed stoneware	36 (87.8)	906 (80.7)	3,796.1 (91.8)
Celadon	0 (0)	17 (1.5)	9.2 (0.2)
Opium-pipe bowls	2 (4.8)	42 (3.7)	36.2 (0.9)
Other	0 (0)	50 (4.5)	109.1 (2.6)

with such a theoretical discussion begins with examination of an archaeologically invisible practice of profound importance for interpreting the material remains on Chinese work camps and indeed overseas Chinese contexts generally: the pervasive practice of remittances (Lawton 1987; Hsu 2000; Costello et al. 2004; Cohen 2005; Voss and Allen 2008). A remittance is the sending of income from a transnational worker to his or her family back home. While remittances clearly leave an archaeological signature at the location in which they are received (Hsu 2000), their impact on the archaeological remains left behind by their senders is more subtle.

It is difficult if not impossible to measure the percentage of income Chinese laborers sent home to their families, but there is no doubt it was significant. Madeline Hsu (2000) demonstrates how transformative the reception of these remittances was for the Four Counties area of Guangdong Province, where most of the Chinese laborers on the railroad originated. European Americans also noted the amount of money returning, though they were less than sanguine in their assessment of the practice (*Nevada State Journal* 1876). Any interpretation of the archaeological remains of Chinese work camps should give great weight to the fact that all the artifacts recovered were purchased with only a fraction of the workers' income. The artifacts used and their distribution mechanisms were likely chosen because they enabled Chinese workers to survive while performing their primary task: the sending of funds back to their families in Guangdong.

Remittances constitute an absent presence in the archaeological assemblages of Chinese work camps, and archaeological interpretations must take them into account when discussing the motivations and agency of Chinese laborers. Although archaeologically invisible, they constitute a real-world material flow linking visible archaeological remains with interpretation.

Moral Discourse and Personhood

In his analysis of the historical sources of the modern Western understanding of the self, Charles Taylor (1989:28) suggests a "link between identity and a kind of orientation. To know who you are is to be oriented in moral space, a space in which questions arise about what is good or bad, what is worth doing and what not, what has meaning and importance for you and what is trivial and secondary." Taylor (1989:33) suggests that, within this moral space, "we cannot do without some orientation to the good." By "the good," Taylor (1989:19) means making "qualitative distinctions" and acting with "the sense that some action, or mode of life, or mode of feeling is incomparably higher than the others."

Anthropologists have long been aware of the particularistic variation that exists among human societies in regard to these qualitative distinctions. That is to say, notions of "the good" and, thus, of identities, are intimately entangled with the cultural frameworks that make distinctions about what is worth doing, and these frameworks vary wildly within time and space.

Given this understanding, the encounter of European American capitalists and Chinese American laborers in the mid-19th century is particularly interesting. Chinese emigration from Guangdong Province to the United States increased dramatically in the mid-19th century, and this cultural interpenetration involved not only the flows of people and material goods, but also the meeting of genealogically distinct moral discourses.

Williams (2008) productively discusses the gendered aspect of these discourses in his contrast between Western and Chinese understandings of masculinity. On the one hand, there is a colonial and orientalist understanding of Chinese masculinity dominant among Americans of European descent (Said 1978). Chinoiserie, the use of "dainty" drinking vessels, and the display of the queue, the braided hairstyle similar to a ponytail, were all used to code Chinese males as effeminate and simultaneously reinforce the machismo of European American males. On the other hand, there is an indigenous Chinese understanding of the proper ways to be men, as expressed through the correlative contrast of *wen* and *wu* (to gloss: intellectual masculinity and tough-guy masculinity).

There is much worth emulating in Williams's study, but what is most remarkable is the mode of argumentation applied. Numerous students of Chinese culture, both Chinese and non-Chinese, have noted the pervasiveness of correlative contrasts in the Chinese intellectual tradition. From this stance, "every phenomenon is viewed from a perspective that enables the perceiver to summarize and label it with a pair of terms" (Yang 2006:330). Correlative contrasts are "two possible states or statuses of events or situations that are developing along a time dimension. They do not mean anything when they are presented alone, but when they are put together they represent a relationship of 'one can be transformed to become the other'" (Yang 2006:331). Hall and Ames refer to this as a "polar" sensibility, in which "terms are clustered in such a way as to be essentially incomplete unless paired with opposing or complementary alter-terms," in contrast to a "dualistic" sensibility in which "strictly delimitable" terms have a "univocal sense." They suggest this may make the Chinese intellectual tradition "uncongenial to the development of univocal propositions" (Hall and Ames 1998:127). To explain briefly, the term *left* has no univocal sense, no internal and delimitable content that would make it intelligible as a singular term. It is essentially incomplete until it is paired with the "alter-term" *right*. In the Chinese intellectual tradition, all terms get their sense from being paired in this fashion. The distinctions drawn between first orientalist and indigenous discourses, and then between *wen* and *wu* masculinities, along with a refusal to understand these terms in a dualistic or essentialist fashion, are thus especially felicitous modes in which to understand Chinese discourse from a more emic point of view.

I employ a similar strategy in order to contrast dominant Western and Chinese discourses on what it is to be a person (Fowler 2004). I will first contrast possessive individualism with relational personhood, then discuss two poles of moral possibility available to Chinese workers in their self-fashioning: the *junzi* (gentleman) and the *xiaoren* (small person). Finally, I will discuss how understanding these differences can influence archaeological interpretation and the meaning of labor, agency, and resistance.

It should be noted that both possessive individualism and relational personhood are forms of "conceptual selves" (Neisser 1988).

Whether they are best understood as accurate representations or ideology is less important here than their role in empowering and moving people to act as though they were certain sorts of selves. Nor do I want to present these poles in a normative fashion, as if to claim in an unproblematic way that Westerners are possessive individuals, whereas Chinese are relational persons. Rather, I regard relational personhood as "the model that modern Chinese people deal with and depart from" (Yang 2006:328) in the same sense that the possessive individual is the model Western people deal with and depart from.

Charles Crocker and Becoming a Possessive Individual

The term *possessive individualism* was coined by C. B. Macpherson (1962:3), who explained that individualism's "possessive quality is found in its conception of the individual as essentially the proprietor of his own person or capacities, owing nothing to society for them. The individual was seen neither as a moral whole, nor as part of a larger social whole, but as an owner of himself." This is the human as always already in the marketplace, where relations are seen as voluntary and based on self-interest, the characteristic form being the contract (Macpherson 1962:263–277). Leone (2005:34) claims individualism is "the single most motivating concept in the American quest for freedom." Matthews (2010:10) states that "when persons begin to regard their self-interest as distinct from the interests of their family and community, they are behaving as individuals," and describes possessive individuals as existing "within and against the interests of their communities."

The possessive individual is the idealized subject of capitalism in the sense that, as a person becomes more and more a possessive individual, he or she embodies the prerogatives of capitalist accumulation itself. Weber (1930) perhaps did more than anyone else in advancing understanding of the moral underpinnings of this form of personhood. Taking Benjamin Franklin as his exemplar, Weber states:

> The peculiarity of this philosophy of avarice appears to be the ideal of the honest man of recognized

credit, and above all the idea of a duty of the individual toward the increase of his capital, which is assumed as an end in itself. Truly what is here preached is not simply a means of making one's way in the world, but a peculiar ethic. (Weber 1930:17)

Weber (1930:33) goes on to describe "the ideal type of capitalistic entrepreneur," who

avoids ostentation and unnecessary expenditure, as well as conscious enjoyment of his power, and is embarrassed by the outward signs of the social recognition which he receives. His manner of life is ... distinguished by a certain ascetic tendency. ... He gets nothing out of his wealth for himself, except the irrational sense of having done his job well.

The crucial point is that, in this state of affairs, the circuit of capital is endless and has no human purpose. Money becomes an end unto itself, and woe to any human activity, sentiment, institution, or idea that stands in the way of its increase.

The papers of Charles Crocker provide illuminating examples of how possessive individualism and the asceticism of the spirit of capitalism are expressed in the behavior of their exemplars:

I used to quarrel with Strowbridge [sic] when I first went in. Said I, "Don't talk so to the men; they are human creatures—don't talk so roughly to them." Said he, "You have got to do it, and you will come to it; you cannot talk to them as though you were talking to gentlemen, because they are not gentlemen; they are about as near brutes as they can get." I found that it was true, there was no need of sympathy for those men, for they would build upon your sympathy and would pay no attention to your rights or your orders, and you [threw] away your kindness on them. The only way to do was to rule them with an iron hand. (Crocker [1866–1868]:51–52)

Crocker's initial stance toward the railroad workers was one of sympathy; they were "human creatures" and deserved to be treated with dignity. However, he quickly came to realize this fellow feeling was in contradiction with his structural role as capitalist and master of men and abandoned it. Crocker illustrates this transformation with an anecdote in which he preemptively intimidated workers into abandoning demands for higher wages:

One day I was paying off and noticed a little knot of men talking together. Said I, "Strowbridge [sic], there is something breeding there." He replied, "They are getting up a strike or something of the kind." "Let me handle them," said I. ... As soon as they got close up, I turned around and said, "Strowbridge, I think you had better reduce wages on this cut, we are paying a little more than we ought to; there is no reason why we should pay more on this cut and on that tunnel than on the other work; you better reduce them about 25[¢] a day." The men heard this, and they stopped, and chatted together awhile.

Finally one of them stepped forward, and said, "We thought, Sir, that we ought to have our wages raised a little on this tunnel. ... I think you better not reduce it; we thought we ought to get an advance, but you ought not to reduce it certainly." "Well, Strowbridge," said I, "what do you think? Can we afford to pay them that wage?" "Oh," said he, "I wouldn't make a fuss over it; we had better let them go on at the same figure." "All-right," said I and they went on satisfied with what we had been paying them. (Crocker [1866–1868]:52)

This is a dramatic transformation from Crocker's initial attitude of sympathy. He had begun his path toward embodying capital, toward becoming a possessive individual. To see as ethical the setting aside of human sympathy in favor of treating humans in an instrumental fashion is dependent on a certain understanding of the nature of humans (as uniformly rational, self-interested, etc.). It is also dependent on what Taylor (1989:20) calls a "'strong evaluation': the fact that these ends or goods stand independent of our own desires, inclinations, or choices, that they represent standards by which these desires and choices are judged." In effect, Crocker was empowered to dismiss his feelings of sympathy because of a commitment to external standards considered equally binding on all involved. Capitalists and laborers are construed as being motivated by the same factors, flattening any qualitative distinctions between them and essentially recoding their structural distinction quantitatively: both are self-interested, but the capitalist is more successful. Personal feeling must be set aside in order to fulfill one's duties to an externalized standard of behavior. Thus, maximizing one's advantage at the expense of others is what anyone would do were they he. Take, for instance, these 1876 exchanges between Crocker and William Piper, then the Democratic congressional representative from San Francisco:

Piper: Did you make any money out of that contract?
Crocker: Yes, sir; I made all I could; just as you would, and just as other men would do.
[later]
Piper: How much did you get?
Crocker: That is my business. I got all I could, I assure you. (U.S. Congress 1877)

When those in a position of power argue that others would do as they do if only they were in their position, it can have the effect of justifying their dominance and whatever means they use to maintain it. It is a claim to the right of mastery because one is quantitatively closer to the "ideal capitalist entrepreneur" as described by Weber (1930). Indeed, Crocker's memoirs contain claims of self-denial and ascetic devotion to work typical of the self-mythologizing possessive individual, such as when he describes his habits:

> My habits were: Total abstention from liquor of all kinds; total abstention from tobacco; and my habit was to work night and day. I used to get up at four o'clock in the morning and go to work and work till I went to bed. In the evening, after dark, I made hickory brooms and ax-handles and such articles; spent my evenings working by firelight. (Crocker [1866–1868]:16–17)

Charles Crocker was obviously a more complicated person than the one I have presented here. In his memoirs, he recalls the shame he felt when he realized the transformation he was undergoing, as in this exchange with his wife:

> I became so that my wife used to be afraid of me. ... "Well," said she, "your manner is overbearing and gruff, that is the way you talk with me and with everybody." I got so that I was really ashamed of myself; that sort of bearing was entirely foreign to me. (Crocker [1866–1868]:51)

My purpose in highlighting how possessive individualism transformed Charles Crocker through the building of the railroad is not to reduce the whole of his life to a few paragraphs (he was also, for example, an abolitionist), but to show just how powerful its pull and demands were, even in the face of doubts and internal contradictions, even among those who were not cynical hypocrites, but apparently acted with good conscience. Possessive individualism was not an homogeneous and accepted standard, even among those who

took on the role of capitalist. Rather, it was something that had to be cultivated—through personal discipline, through flattening structural and motivational differences between capitalists and laborers, through the setting aside of human sympathy, and through the externalization of the standards of behavior involved.

Relational Personhood and Becoming Human

Archaeologists have become increasingly aware that the possessive individual is but one of a variety of different ways of construing the self (Fowler 2004; Thomas 2004). The self-interpretation of the possessive individual is sharply at odds with the dominant Chinese understanding of personhood.

In the dominant Chinese tradition, "the self is not construed as a solid thing, or even a concept, but a term paired with other collective terms to represent many whole/part relations" (Yang 2006:342). Returning to correlative contrasts, a person or self cannot be understood in isolation, but must be paired with another term in order to have significance. Construed in this way, an atomistic individual (possessive or not) is absurd. Rather, "it is in the way one tries to become an all-around moral person that one sees the significance of the self" (Yang 2006:343). This is distinguished qualitatively in terms of another correlative contrast, this one between the "properly human" and "merely human" (Davies 2011), between the *junzi* (gentleman) and *xiaoren* (small person).

While the framework of possessive individualism flattens qualitative differences between people and their motivations,

> the person is conceived of in Confucian ideology as capable of cultivating himself or herself, as long as he or she chooses to do so, of becoming a moral being, and of having the virtue of *ren* (benevolence/humanity). The *junzi* and *xiaoren* form a spectrum of moral possibilities from which a person can choose. (Yang 2006:339)

One of the most important distinctions between the *junzi* and *xiaoren* is the "orientation toward the good" (Taylor 1989:33) that empowers and moves them. While the *junzi* is moved by *yi* (righteousness/justice/meaning), the *xiaoren* is moved by *li* (gain/advantage/profit). To be moved by *yi* is to make oneself a person. One's status as fully human is dependent on one's capacity for *ren* (benevolence/humanity). This is in large part demonstrated by being *xiao* (filial). Filiality is the lifelong duty to honor, remember, and care for one's parents and ancestors, springing from the unpayable debt of one's being brought into existence and ideally motivated by a sense of gratitude.

To the degree this framework is operative, one cannot be a possessive individual in Macpherson's (1962) sense. Insofar as one embodies the possessive individual, one has severed non-contract-based social ties. Sentiment and human feeling (*renqing*) are seen as absolutely vital for the relational person and are in fact the basis for proper human relationships (Oxfeld 2010). In contrast, they have no place in the rationalized instrumental relationships of the possessive individual, as is seen in Crocker's memoirs.

Consequences

One interesting consequence of this is how deficient each moral framework appears if it is construed in terms of the other. For the possessive individual, relational persons appear chained to a set of moral debts, obligations, and duties not of their own choosing and are thus bereft of freedom and autonomy. For a relational person, the possessive individual appears as a degenerate, bereft of basic human capacities. Rather than understood as variant forms of personhood with distinct "strong evaluations" and orientations toward "the good," however construed, they tend toward being defined in terms of what they lack relative to the other. This dynamic, at least in part, animated the encounters and misunderstandings between Americans of European and Chinese descent in the mid-19th century.

This dynamic also affects archaeological interpretations regarding agency, resistance, and the meaning of labor in Chinese contexts. Archaeology, as a discipline with Western origins, has historically tended toward interpretations implicitly understanding human persons as individuals, and has seen agency in terms of the capacity to manipulate and control the surrounding human and natural environment. For the relational person, in contrast,

agency is not exhausted by struggles for or against domination. Rather, "the self is also seen as a process of action-taking by which the person improves relationships with [his or her] surroundings" (Yang 2006:343). In other words, archaeologists should not necessarily see the absence of archaeological evidence for overt or covert resistance as evidence of the absence of agency. Furthermore, researchers should not construe the sacrifices made and labor performed by Chinese railroad workers as evidence of selfless behavior, but rather as evidence of their active self-fashioning as fully human moral beings.

Acknowledgments

I would like to thank Zoe Crossland, Nan Rothschild, Barbara Voss, Bryn Williams, and several anonymous reviewers for reading and commenting on earlier versions of this article. I would also like to thank the members and organizers of the Chinese Railroad Workers in North America Project. Thanks to R. Scott Baxter, Susan Lindström, Adrian Praetzellis, and Carrie Smith for giving advice and sharing their knowledge of Chinese archaeology in the High Sierras. I am indebted to Julia Costello for making her Summit Camp collection available for analysis, and to Alison Damick and Lindsay Montgomery for helping with fieldwork. This research would not have been possible without financial support from the Columbia University Department of Anthropology and the Robert Stigler Fund for Archaeological Fieldwork. The author is solely responsible for the content of this article.

References

BAXTER, R. SCOTT, AND REBECCA ALLEN
2008   National Register of Historic Places Evaluation and Damage Assessment for CA-PLA-2002/H (Summit Camp). Report to Tahoe National Forest, Truckee, CA, from Past Forward, Inc., Plymouth, CA.

COHEN, MYRON L.
2005   *Kinship, Contract, Community, and State: Anthropological Perspectives on China*. Stanford University Press, Stanford, CA.

COSTELLO, JULIA G., KEVIN HALLARAN,
AND KEITH WARREN
2004 The Luck of Third Street: Historical Archaeology
Data Recovery Report for the Caltrans District 8
San Bernardino Headquarters Demolition Project.
Manuscript, Foothill Resources, Ltd., Mokelumne
Hill, CA.

CROCKER, CHARLES
[1866–1868] Facts Obtained from the Lips of Charles
Crocker, Regarding His Identification with the
Central Pacific Railroad, and Other Roads Growing
of It. Manuscript, Bancroft Library, University of
California, Berkeley.

DAILY ALTA CALIFORNIA
1867 Strike of the Chinese for Eight Hours' Work and
Twelve Hours' Pay on the Pacific Railroad. *Daily
Alta California* 30 June:1.

DAVIES, GLORIA
2011 Homo Dissensum Significans, or the Perils of Taking
a Stand in China. *Social Text* 109:29–56.

FOWLER, CHRIS
2004 *The Archaeology of Personhood: An Anthropological
Approach.* Routledge, London, UK.

GRALIA, ROSS, AND MAYA GRALIA
2004 Primary Record for Site #05-17-55-525 Tahoe NF.
Manuscript, State of California, Resources Agency,
Department of Parks and Recreation, Sacramento.

HALL, DAVID L., AND ROGER T. AMES
1998 *Thinking from the Han: Self, Truth, and Transcendence
in Chinese and Western Culture.* State University of
New York Press, Albany.

HARDESTY, DONALD L.
2002 Commentary: Interpreting Variability and Change
in Western Work Camps. *Historical Archaeology*
36(3):94–98.

HSU, MADELINE Y.
2000 *Dreaming of Gold, Dreaming of Home:
Transnationalism and Migration between the
United States and South China, 1882–1943.* Stanford
University Press, Stanford, CA.

LAWTON, HARRY W.
1987 A Chinese Merchant Returns to His Native Land.
In *Wong Ho Leun: An American Chinatown*, pp.
291–294. Great Basin Foundation, San Diego, CA.

LEONE, MARK P.
2005 *The Archaeology of Liberty in an American Capital:
Excavations in Annapolis.* University of California
Press, Berkeley.

LUDLOW COLLECTIVE
2001 Archaeology of the Colorado Coal Field War,
1913–1914. In *Archaeologies of the Contemporary
Past*, Victor Buchli and Gavin Lucas, editors, pp.
94–107. Routledge, London, UK.

MACPHERSON, C. B.
1962 *The Political Theory of Possessive Individualism:
Hobbes to Locke.* Clarendon Press, Oxford, UK.

MATTHEWS, CHRISTOPHER N.
2010 *The Archaeology of American Capitalism.* University
Press of Florida, Gainesville.

MCGUIRE, RANDALL H., AND PAUL RECKNER
2002 The Unromantic West: Labor, Capital, and Struggle.
Historical Archaeology 36(3):44–58.

MROWZOWSKI, STEPHEN A., GRACE H. ZIESING, AND MARY
C. BEAUDRY
1996 *Living on the Boott: Historical Archaeology at the
Boott Mills Boardinghouses, Lowell, Massachusetts.*
University of Massachusetts Press, Amherst.

NASSANEY, MICHAEL, AND MARJORIE ABEL
1993 The Political and Social Contexts of Cutlery
Production in the Connecticut Valley. *Dialectical
Anthropology* 18:247–289.

NEISSER, ULRIC
1988 Five Kinds of Self-Knowledge. *Philosophical
Psychology* 1(1):35–59.

NEVADA STATE JOURNAL
1876 Where the Money Goes. *Nevada State Journal* 27
June:3. Reno.

OXFELD, ELLEN
2010 *Drink Water, but Remember the Source: Moral
Discourse in a Chinese Village.* University of
California Press, Berkeley.

SAID, EDWARD W.
1978 *Orientalism.* Vintage, New York, NY.

SAITTA, DEAN J.
2007 *The Archaeology of Collective Action.* University
Press of Florida, Gainesville.

SANDO, RUTH A., AND DAVID L. FELTON
1993 Inventory Records of Ceramics and Opium from
a Nineteenth Century Chinese Store in California.
In *Hidden Heritage: Historical Archaeology of
the Overseas Chinese*, Priscilla Wegars, editor, pp.
151–176. Baywood, Amityville, NY.

SHACKEL, PAUL
2000 Craft to Wage Labor: Agency and Resistance in
American Historical Archaeology. In *Agency Theory
in Archaeology*, M.-A. Dobres and J. Robb, editors,
pp. 232–246. Routledge, London, UK.

STANFORD, LELAND
1865 *Statement Made to the President of the United States
and Secretary of the Interior of the Progress of the
Work, October 10th, 1865.* H. S. Crocker & Co.,
Sacramento, CA.

TAYLOR, CHARLES
  1989   *Sources of the Self: The Making of Modern Identity.* Harvard University Press, Cambridge, MA.

THOMAS, JULIAN
  2004   *Archaeology and Modernity.* Routledge, London, UK.

U. S. CONGRESS
  1877   *Report of the Joint Special Committee to Investigate Chinese Immigration.* 44th Congress, 2nd session, Senate Report No. 689. Washington, DC.

VOSE, GEORGE L.
  1882   *Manual for Railroad Engineers.* Lee & Shepard, Boston, MA.

VOSS, BARBARA L., AND REBECCA ALLEN
  2008   Overseas Chinese Archaeology: Historical Foundations, Current Reflections, New Directions. *Historical Archaeology* 42(3):5–28.

WEBER, MAX
  1930   *The Protestant Ethic and the Spirit of Capitalism.* Routledge, London, UK.

WILLIAMS, BRYN
  2008   Chinese Masculinities and Material Culture. *Historical Archaeology* 42(3):53–67.

YANG CHUNG-FANG
  2006   The Chinese Conception of Self: Towards a Person-Making (做人) Perspective. In *Indigenous and Cultural Psychology: Understanding People in Context*, Uichol Kim, Kui-Shu Yang, and Kwang-Kuo Hwang, editors, pp. 327–356. Springer, New York, NY.

JOHN MOLENDA
DEPARTMENT OF ANTHROPOLOGY
COLUMBIA UNIVERSITY
NEW YORK, NY 10027

Michael R. Polk (迈克·波克)

Interpreting Chinese Worker Camps on the Transcontinental Railroad at Promontory Summit, Utah

试论犹他突顶山上的中国劳工营

ABSTRACT

The first transcontinental railroad was completed at Promontory Summit, Utah, on 10 May 1869. Unique to this construction was the employment of thousands of ethnic Chinese railroad workers. The Promontory Mountains portion of the route had the largest concentration of railroad construction camps. Of 19 camps recorded during an inventory of the Golden Spike National Historic Site, four appear to be of Chinese ethnic origin. These camps were smaller than European American camps, with fewer features. Both Chinese and European American artifacts were found at Chinese worker camps, revealing the practicality of and need for locally produced and railroad-issued items, as well as the workers' desire to use ethnically familiar items. A comparison with Chinese construction camps in Nevada and California reveals important similarities, suggesting that up to 500 Chinese construction laborers may have lived at the four Utah sites. A multifaceted explanation is provided for the separation of Chinese camps from other workers' camps.

1869年五月10日，第一条横贯大陆铁路在犹他州的突顶山峻工。这一工程的独特之处，在于它雇佣了成千上万的中国工人。突顶山路段聚集了该铁路工程中最多的劳工营。在金色道钉国家历史纪念地的目录所记载的19个营地中，有四个属于中国工人。这些营地比欧美营地规模小，而遗迹较少。在中国劳工营，来自中国与欧美的文物均有出土。这既显示出当地产品和铁路周边物品的实用性以及他们对这些物品的需求，也显示出他们对故乡熟悉物件使用的渴望。内华达州与加州境内类似的中国劳工营相比较，显示了两者重要的相似之处。据估计，有多达500名中国劳工曾居住在这四个营地内。本文还将对中国劳工营与其它国家劳工营的分隔提供多面向的解释。

Introduction

Promontory Summit lies in a cold, windswept, high-desert environment in rural northern Utah. It is a place far removed from the urban population of the nearby Wasatch Front and lacks significant water resources. The area remains sparsely populated nearly a century and a half after the completion of the transcontinental railroad, one of the most significant events to occur in the United States. Such a construction feat had never before been undertaken anywhere. Not only was the achievement a technological marvel, but it had equally important social, political, and economic significance for the country and the world as a whole. This railroad stretched from Omaha, Nebraska, westward to the Pacific Ocean, ending at Oakland, California. It bridged the vast unknown spaces of the Great American Desert and accelerated the processes whereby the American frontier was eventually eliminated. It opened the great western lands to settlement, hastening the creation of western territories and states. It united East and West. Instead of taking six weeks to cross the nation by pony express, mail now took six days from coast to coast. The railroad led to the almost complete annihilation of the American bison, changing Native American lifeways. Historians count completion of the transcontinental railroad among the most significant and far-reaching events in the nation's history.

The area surrounding the Last Spike location was the site of the most intense construction activity undertaken during the period from 1868 to 1869. There construction culminated when the Union Pacific Railroad (UPRR) from Omaha and the Central Pacific Railroad (CPRR) from Sacramento, California, eventually met to join their railroads in a grand celebration on 10 May 1869. The area set aside in 1957 as a national historic site was designated the Golden Spike National Historic Site (GSNHS) to commemorate the completion of the first transcontinental railroad and to acknowledge the tremendous historical consequences that occurred as a result (Public Law 89-102). On 30 July 1965, it became part of the U.S. National Park System. The site was listed in the National Register of Historic Places in 1966, and its significance was documented for the register in 1986 (Hendricks 1986). In addition, the "Joining of the Rails/Transcontinental Railroad" was designated a National Civil Engineering Landmark in 1969 by the American Society of Civil Engineers.

Historical Archaeology, 2015, 49(1):59–70.
Permission to reprint required.

Within this historic site are a great many historical resources, including railroad grades and cuts along the eastern slopes of the Promontory Mountains, along with railroad workers' camps, all dating from late 1868 to May 1869 (Figure 1). It also includes remains of the former town site of Promontory, along with the former roundhouse and associated railroad structures. The GSNHS was the subject of a multiyear investigation to document and understand these resources (Polk 2013). In 2001 the U.S. National Park Service's Western Archaeological and Conservation Center (WACC) initiated a survey and inventory of resources, followed by similar efforts by Sagebrush Consultants, LLC (Sagebrush) from 2002 to 2008. This effort built upon previous studies and investigations, including Robert Utley's (1960) early documentation of the park's national historical significance; James Ayres's (1982) archaeological investigation of the town site of Promontory Station; Homstad et al.'s (2000) preparation of a cultural landscape report; and Sagebrush's overview of the archaeology and history of the

Promontory route (Polk 1998). The most recent work culminated in a series of interim reports covering each year of fieldwork, followed by a compilation of the information in a report entitled: "From Lampo Junction to Rozel: The Archeological History of the Transcontinental Railroad across the Promontory Mountains, Utah" (Polk and Simmons-Johnson 2012).

Of the many books and articles that have been published about the transcontinental effort, very few have focused on the archaeology, and even fewer on the construction workers themselves, those who were largely responsible for completion of the world's first transcontinental railway. The focus of this article is on the workers' efforts to complete the final section of the transcontinental railroad during late 1868 and early 1869. The politics and story of the actual construction leading up to the railroads' arrival at Promontory have been told many times, in works such as Klein (1987), Bain (1999), Francaviglia (2008), Ambrose (1990), Galloway (1950, 1989), Kraus (1969), and Utley (1969). Particularly valuable for an overview of Promontory Summit during this time

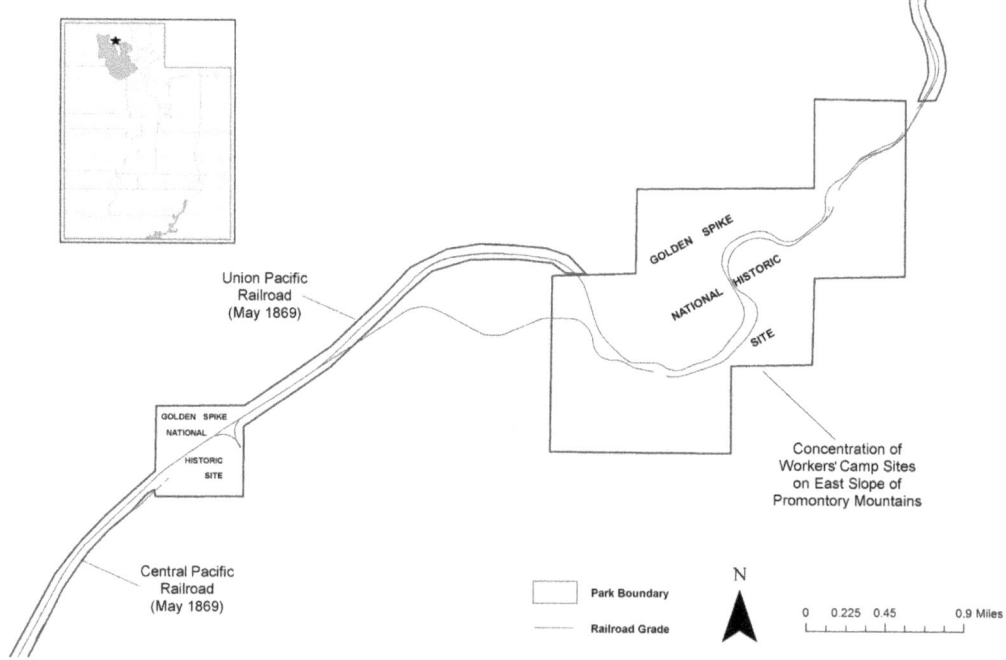

FIGURE 1. Map showing the Promontory Summit area in the Golden Spike National Historic Site where the Central Pacific Railroad and the Union Pacific Railroads united, May–November 1869. (Map developed from USGS 7.5' quadrangles: Sunset Pass [1968], Lampo Junction [1972], Golden Spike Monument [1967], and Thatcher Mountain SW, Utah [1966], by Jamie Morrison, Sagebrush Consultants, 2014.)

is Francaviglia's *Over the Range: A History of the Promontory Summit Route of the Pacific Railroad* (Francaviglia 2008). The broad history will not be repeated here, other than to provide context where it is critical to an understanding of the construction and workers at Promontory, Utah. However, a brief contextual history is necessary to understand better the local activities carried out by workers of the UPRR and CPRR, and the archaeology discussed later.

Promontory Summit

GSNHS, which straddles the area of Promontory Summit, contains the largest concentration of worker camp archaeological sites along the routes of both the UPRR and CPRR. Not only are these camp sites sources of information about railroad company activity, but also about the cultural and ethnic origins of the workers who lived in those camps and labored on the railroads (Figure 2).

It is estimated that during the final push to complete the line in 1868–1869 as many as 6,000 workers toiled across northern Utah (Francaviglia 2008:88–89). Goodwin (1991:181) indicates that during the final construction phase of CPRR work on the transcontinental, the railroad had 12,000 Chinese construction workers on its payroll. Where all these men were working is not clear, although it is likely that most would have been in the Promontory area, where both railroads concentrated most of their resources in May 1869. This was a multicultural effort that included, almost entirely, men who were Irish, Cornish, Chinese, German, African American, English, and Native American, as well as Mormons and former Civil War officers and soldiers. There were also some women who contributed. The

FIGURE 2. Big Trestle, photo by A. J. Russell, May 1869. This trestle, just east of Promontory Summit, Utah, lies on the east slope of the Promontory Mountains, where intensive construction took place in early 1869. Note the remaining worker camp tents on the ridge in the *upper right* of the photograph. (Courtesy Utah State Historical Society.)

magnitude, significance, and very nature of the effort has encouraged historians to focus on the powerful men who were behind the building of the railroad, and on its economics and politics. Few have spent much time picking out bits of information from histories, documents, diaries, and, especially, archaeology to examine and understand better the role of common workers in the effort. Legends about the Union Pacific's Irish track layers, construction contractor "General" John Casement's work gangs, and the Central Pacific's loyal Chinese workers have become part of historical lore and overshadow the many other individuals and groups who participated in the construction effort. For example, the fact that Brigham Young's Mormon work crews, as contractors to both the UPRR and the CPRR, built most of the grade across northern Utah has been generally obscured (Galloway 1950:103; Strobridge 2002:3). There is also a smattering of information suggesting Native American involvement was not only in construction, but also in maintenance operations along the

transcontinental railroad. Davis (1894:153) writes that at the 10 May 1869 ceremony "[c]urious Mexicans, Indians and half-breeds, with the Chinese, Negro, and Irish laborers, lent to the auspicious little gathering a suggestive air of cosmopolitanism." George Kraus, cited in Fike and Raymond (1981: 9), notes that "Indians, indigenous to the area, also worked alongside the Chinese" (Figure 3).

Despite the fact that there are many published anecdotal accounts about transcontinental railroad workers of a variety of ethnicities, it is known that a significant segment of the workforce was from a number of backgrounds other than European American. By far the largest single group was ethnic Chinese, the extraordinary contribution of whose members was largely in support of CPRR construction from California to Promontory Summit during the years 1865 to 1869. Most of the 19 construction camps recorded at GSNHS were dominated by European Americans and likely represented groups associated with the UPRR construction. Four or five camps contain

FIGURE 3. Site 42BO1134, Chinese workers' camp, on the edge of the Central Pacific Railroad grade near Promontory Summit. The image shows the location of a tent platform and rock clusters. The view is to the east southeast with Great Salt Lake in the background. (Photo by Heather Weymouth, Sagebrush Consultants, 2002.)

artifacts of ethnic Chinese, the predominant material culture present. The distinct artifact assemblage, the moderate size, and other evidence strongly indicate occupation by Chinese railroad workers during 1868 and 1869. Almost certainly these camps were occupied by the Chinese who worked for the CPRR. There is no indication that the UPRR hired Chinese crews for its work, and, according to Strobridge (2002:2): "No Chinese ever worked east of Promontory," a further indication that the UPRR did not hire Chinese railroad workers. The Chinese who worked on the railroad at Promontory were the most documented ethnic group there. The presence of these men in Utah was the result of a chain of events dating back to the late 1840s in China and California.

Railroad Construction Approaching Promontory Summit

The CPRR and UPRR could operate independently when their respective construction sites were hundreds or thousands of miles apart, but the federal government, the promoter and funder of a significant part of this effort, expected cooperation to fulfill the ultimate goal of the project. This came into play as construction entered the Territory of Utah. Initial examinations of possible routes for the proposed railroad line through the northern portion of Utah were carried out as early as 1863 and 1864 (Rigdan 1951:1480). Following these initial reconnaissance efforts, more detailed surveys were carried out by UPRR engineers in 1867. During 1868 final location surveys were made from the mouth of Weber Canyon to Humboldt Wells in Nevada. At the same time, the CPRR was making its own surveys for the transcontinental route through the area. In 1867 CPRR engineers explored the Wasatch Range, its valleys and basins, and as far as the Ham's Fork River in Wyoming. In 1868 the CPRR engineers filed their preliminary survey with the U.S. Department of the Interior (Rigdan 1951:1481).

While grading and laying track moved rapidly along for the UPRR, the CPRR also pushed its crews to move more quickly. Both railroads, using Mormon contract laborers, undertook grading along the Promontory route from Corinne (east of Promontory) to Rozel

(just west of Promontory). The UPRR did not begin construction west of Ogden until February 1869 (Utley 1960:46). By March 1869, construction activity by both railroads was moving at a frenzied pace. The UPRR tracks reached Ogden on 8 March 1869 (*Salt Lake Daily Telegraph* 1869). A letter to the *Deseret Evening News* dated 25 March 1869 provided a firsthand account of this activity in the area between Corinne and Junction City (now known as Lampo Junction):

> Work is being vigorously prosecuted ... both lines running near each other and occasionally crossing. Both companies have their pile drivers at work where the lines cross the [Bear] river [near Corinne]. From Corinne west thirty miles, the grading camps present the appearance of a mighty army. As far as the eye can reach are to be seen almost a continuous line of tents, wagons and men. (*Deseret Evening News* 1869)

The CPRR tracks did not reach Promontory from the west until 30 April 1969 (Dodge 1910:943). Track was not completed to the summit by the UPRR until 9 May (Ames 1969:336). On 10 April, Congress ratified the railroad agreement to join the rails at Promontory Summit. The rails were officially joined on 10 May 1869.

Railroad Construction Camps

Thousands of workers were involved in this construction. Closer inspection of the archaeology of construction camps from a relatively early time period for the intermountain West provides fascinating, though limited, insights into camp structure, ethnicity, group dynamics, and labor relations among large corporate entities, their subcontractors, and the workers. Reaching the "end of the line" for both railroads at Promontory, in the latter half of 1868 and early 1869, resulted in a number of unique circumstances, certainly something that had not been encountered anywhere else up to that time. At least three of these are significant:

> 1. The topographic challenges for the railroads were considerable. The east slope of the Promontory Mountains is very steep and rocky. Except for tunnels, this location posed the greatest challenge for construction anywhere along the 86 mi. stretch of the UPRR from Promontory Summit eastward to Echo, Utah (Morris 1876:6). This alone resulted in an enormous expense for both railroads, as well as in the use of an army of workers.

2. Congress had not yet established a meeting point for the railroads. Each company had been working to gain advantage by building past and far beyond the other. In early 1869, CPRR crews were grading as far east as Echo Summit, near the Wyoming border, while Union Pacific crews were working in the vicinity of Humboldt Wells, in eastern Nevada (Utley 1960:18), a distance of about 250 mi. More local to Promontory Summit, each railroad spent enormous sums of money building railroad grades and culverts, filling washes, and even building trestles more than 25 mi. past the other in order to gain the advantage mentioned above. It was not until 10 April 1869, when Congress chose Promontory Summit as the meeting place, that this frenzied work ceased, and both railroads worked toward a logical joining of their respective tracks. The competition prompted both railroads to expend far more resources and men than would have normally been the case.

3. The close proximity of each railroad's crews (at least 19 camps located within a few miles of one another), coupled with the difficult terrain, strategic maneuvering for position by each railroad, and the fact that all resources available were called upon with little concern for cost, created an unusual mix of elements. Every construction crew, including the Irish, Cornish, Native Americans, Chinese, African Americans, Germans, English, Mormons, and Civil War veterans, was represented and interacted at this place to some degree, (McCague 1964:117).

It was at Promontory that the track layers caught up with the graders, those responsible for blasting rock ledges, spanning the arroyos, filling the washes, and leveling the terrain upon which to lay the ties and track. Histories of the great effort to cross the continent often gloss over the details of how it was done and who was responsible for the backbreaking jobs of construction that were completed in an era with few machines to ease the process. Picks, shovels, pry bars, and horse- and mule-drawn carts and wheelbarrows, coupled with blasting powder, were the commonly used tools.

During the GSNHS archaeological inventory between 2002 and 2008, 19 railroad construction sites were recorded. It is certain that more camps exist outside the park boundary. Site locational data indicate that a construction camp was established every 3 to 5 mi. and even closer together on the eastern slopes of the Promontory Mountains. Identification of sites by company, subcontractor, or ethnicity will require more historical research and analysis than has been possible as part of this project, but some interesting details have emerged from the basic data recovered. At least two camps

can almost certainly be tied to a particular railroad. The largest two workers' camp sites lie adjacent to particular company track lines, providing evidence of the railroad with which they were affiliated. Site 42BO851, closest to the "Big Fill" structure built by the CPRR, is likely to have been a Central Pacific camp. Site 42BO852, located closest to the UPRR-constructed "Big Trestle," is probably a Union Pacific camp (Figure 4).

Features common to almost all of the camps in the area include dugouts, some with dry-laid rock walls and many larger ones with collapsed dry-laid chimneys. There are tent platforms at all of the camps as well. Artifacts found at all of the sites are consistent with occupation during the construction period, and, at many, evidence of much later occupation suggests that they may have been used as maintenance camps. A wide variety of bottle glass, much of it reflecting beer and wine consumption; clothing fasteners; a lot of unidentifiable metal; and some wood were found across the sites. Many cut nails were found around a dry-laid stone building foundation, but none were found around dugouts or tent platforms. There were four brass military buttons found, one U.S. Army cavalry button dating to before 1861, and three Civil War–era general-service buttons issued by the U.S. Army. While some artifacts that can be attributed to ethnic Chinese were present on several sites, four sites in particular contain the best evidence of being exclusively Chinese construction camps (Polk 2013).

The 19 railroad construction sites were recorded as part of the research project undertaken by the U.S. National Park Service and Sagebrush during the early 2000s (Giles and Frost 2001; Weymouth and Southworth 2002; Weymouth, Pagano, and Garrison 2006; Weymouth, Pagano, Williamson et al. 2006). Within these 19 sites 219 features were recorded, including 144 depressions, 26 room blocks, 18 tent platforms, 12 rock shelters, and 2 blacksmith platforms. Other features identified were hearths, collapsed-chimney rubble/rock piles, an earthen mound, check dams, and a diversion ditch.

Excavation was not a part of the investigation. The aridity of the region has limited the vegetation present on the surface, making it possible to gain considerable insight into the

Golden Spike National Historic Site
Site 42BO1134

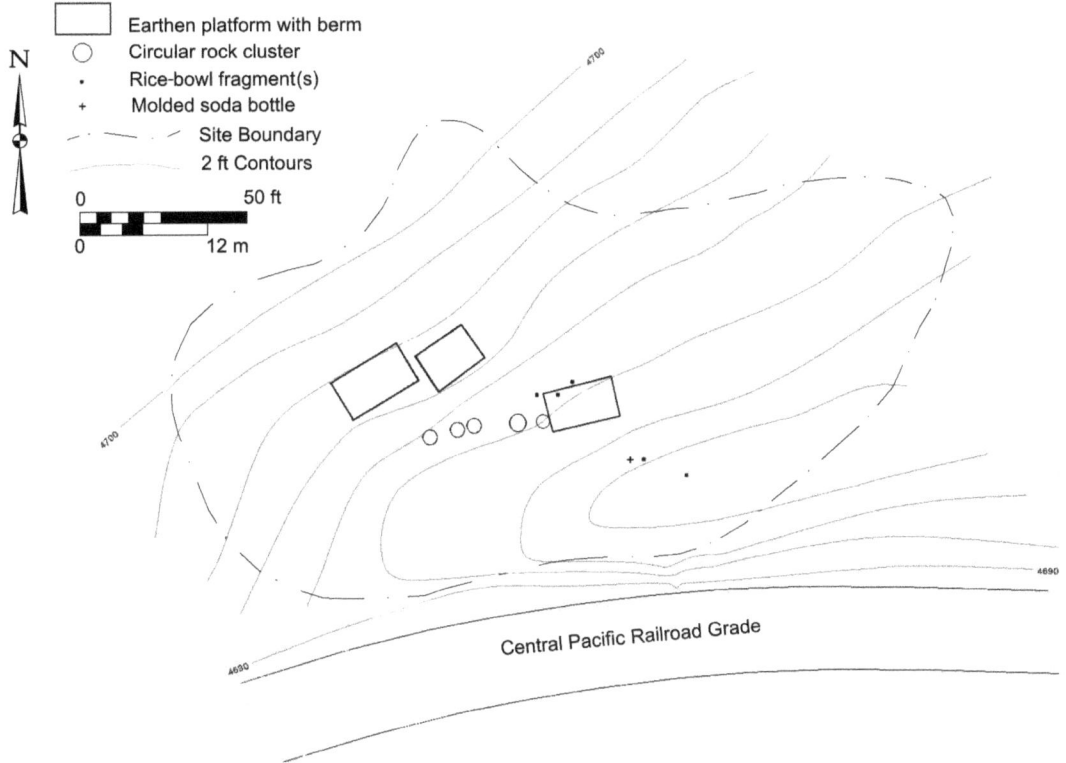

FIGURE 4. Sketch map of Site 42BO1134, Chinese worker camp, near Promontory Summit, Utah. (Map by Heather Weymouth, Sagebrush Consultants, 2002.)

nature and function of the archaeological sites. Fifteen of the camps have evidence strongly associating them with European American occupation. This includes stoneware jar fragments and earthenwares; nails; soda, liquor, and medicine bottles; cartridges; fasteners; utensils; buttons; blasting powder–can fragments; cast-iron pot fragments; and many other commonly discarded artifacts dating to the 1868–1869 period. These camp sites are distinct in other ways. Most contain habitation features. Habitation structures include small-to-large housing units; and large, rectangular structures likely representing barracks, communal mess halls, and Union Pacific or Central Pacific corporate structures. Other moderately sized structures may represent supply sheds, machinery sheds, and stores. Specific types of ground structures at Promontory have been described by Anderson (1983:227–236):

1. Pit structures, largely circular in shape with a pile of stone off to one area where a fireplace was built;
2. Square-to-rectangular masonry foundations or rooms consisting of foundations made of unshaped rocks, which were dry laid;
3. Dugout features, excavated into the sides of hills, with pits that were lined or reinforced with rock; and
4. Tent platforms, a very common feature, with the largest in area measuring 12 × 36 ft. The largest could represent mess tents, corporate headquarters, or areas to park wagons.

These features, along with others, such as check dams, mounds of indeterminate origin, and hearths, account for 138 formal features within 15 sites, averaging about 9 features per camp. The largest site, 42BO852, alone has 67 features.

One other significant physical characteristic of these camps is their size. The sites range from about 0.1 ac. to more than 24 ac. in area, averaging about 2.4 ac.

Chinese Worker Camps at Promontory

Four camp sites were identified as Chinese, largely through ethnically identifiable artifacts. The fact that only superficial evidence could be examined limited interpretation and comparison, but there are still useful metrics to describe and ponder. These sites tended to be much smaller in size and have fewer visible features than the European American sites in the area. Despite years of locals collecting artifacts along the railroad, a significant number of artifacts were still present, likely eroding out of the ground over time. Table 1 lists the site identification numbers, features, and size for each of the identified Chinese sites.

Selected artifacts were collected, and others were noted at the sites. These artifacts provide a broader understanding of occupation here. Many artifacts of European American manufacture appear to have been for domestic use and were likely purchased or supplied by the railroads for the workers. Also, at least a small portion of the artifact assemblage includes work-related artifacts associated with railroad construction (i.e., blasting-can fragments and nails). Most significantly, however, a high percentage of ethnic Chinese artifacts was found. A summary of those artifacts that were collected as part of this research follows.

White porcelain tableware fragments, most commonly rice bowls, were found at each of the sites. Most fragments could be identified as having painted blue (dominant) or polychrome patterns with a clear glaze finish. Specific designs could be identified on fewer fragments. The most common pattern identified was Bamboo, followed by the Double Happiness pattern. There were also a few examples of the Four Seasons pattern. More fragments of rice bowls and other tableware ceramics exist at Site 42BO1070 than any of the other sites (Figure 5). About the same number were found at Sites 42BO1068, 42BO1060, and 42BO1134. Other ceramic fragments found at the sites were stoneware rice wine– and soy sauce–bottle, or ginger-jar fragments, and many fragments of orange earthenware opium-pipe bowls.

At Site 42BO1060, opium-tin fragments were found, along with a cast-brass Chinese coin from the reign of Emperor Zhi He (A.D. 1054–1055) of the Song Dynasty, which lasted from 960 to 1279 (Kevin Aiken 2014, pers. comm.). While this is not a Chinese coin commonly found in western North America, apparently it is not unusual, even though it dates to a very early time period (Figure 6).

Comparisons with Other Railroad Construction Camps with Chinese Components

While not numerous, there have been studies carried out at a number of railroad construction camps in Nevada and California, from the same general time period, that included Chinese workers who almost certainly followed a living pattern similar to those workers at Promontory in 1868 and 1869. A few of those studies are discussed below.

Investigations and excavations with ethnic Chinese components have been undertaken at a transcontinental railroad site called Summit Camp in California (Baxter and Allen, this issue), a workers' camp site known as Lakeview Camp on the Virginia & Truckee Railroad (V&TRR) in western Nevada, dating to 1872 (Rogers 1997; Furnis and Maniery,

TABLE 1
FEATURES AND SIZES OF ETHNIC CHINESE WORKER CAMP SITES NEAR PROMONTORY
SUMMIT

Site Number	Features	Site Size
42BO1060	2 dugouts, 2 hearth remnants	60,500 sq. ft. (1.4 ac.)
42BO1068	Unknown (disturbed)	54,000 sq. ft. (1.2 ac.)
42BO1070	1 possible tent platform, 2 wooden posts	1,450 sq. ft. (0.03 ac.)
42BO1134	3 tent platforms, 5 limestone rock clusters	46,170 sq. ft. (1.1 ac.)

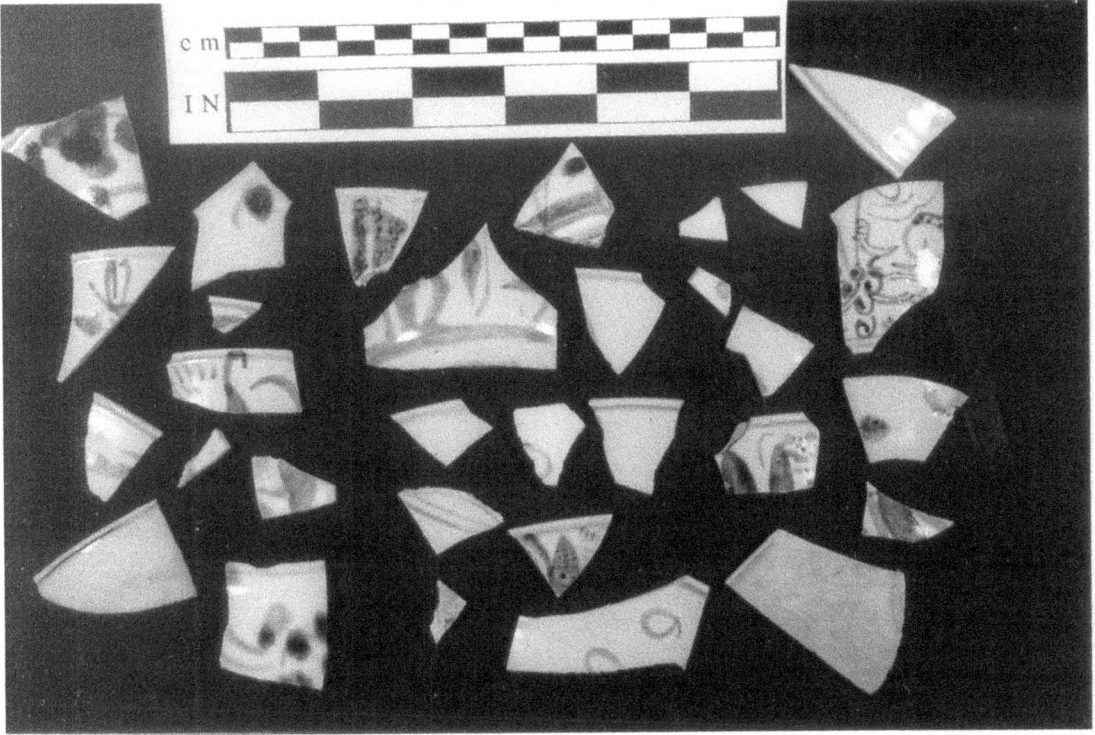

FIGURE 5. Porcelain utilitarian-ware bowl fragments from Chinese worker camps on the east slope of the Promontory Mountains, where the most intense construction activity on the transcontinental railroad took place. (Photo by Heather Weymouth, Sagebrush Consultants, 2002.)

FIGURE 6. Chinese coins recovered from a National Park Service excavation of an 1869 Central Pacific Railroad stone culvert headwall (Hutchinson 1988). This work was done in support of restoration efforts.

this issue), and a workers' camp associated with construction of the Eureka & Palisade Railroad in central Nevada in 1875 (Zier 1985). All of these investigations seem to suggest that similar occupation patterns and activities took place in each of these disparate areas over a fairly short period during or shortly after completion of the transcontinental railroad (1865–1875).

The Summit Camp site shows some similar traits, including the kinds of domestic and Chinese artifacts present at Promontory sites and a hearth feature, but the length of occupation and the fact that a cabin was once present on the site make meticulous comparisons difficult.

The Lakeview Camp was occupied for several weeks in 1872. Studies of the site reveal that the camp was certainly a temporary camp, probably occupied by a large group of Chinese individuals during the construction of the V&TRR (Rogers 1997; Furnis and Maniery, this issue). No evidence of permanent structures or of extensive ranch features was found at the site. The archaeological deposits are fairly shallow (approximately 50 cm below surface) and limited in their artifact quantities and functional types, suggesting short-term occupation of a domestic nature. The Lakeview Camp report (Rogers 1997) further elucidates that the overwhelming majority of artifacts found were manufactured in China. Also, it indicates that the site was organized into public and private, socializing and work areas.

The worker camp in central Nevada, 26EU790, on the Eureka & Palisade Railroad offers particularly useful comparisons to Promontory (Zier 1985). Occupied for what appears to have been only a few days in 1875, there were three artifact clusters found. Cluster A measured 90 × 100 ft. (9,000 sq. ft.), Cluster B measured 60 × 100 ft. (6,000 sq. ft.), and Cluster C measured 75 × 100 ft. (7,500 sq. ft.). These probably represent occupation by 12 to 20 workmen for one or two nights (Zier 1985:149). Artifact categories found at the site were similar to those at the Lakeview Camp. Also similar to Lakeview, relatively few artifacts were present on the site.

With the exception of Summit Camp (where remains of a permanent building were found), the sites discussed lacked evidence of permanent structures. Also, all the sites had few artifacts present, and most of those artifacts were

of Chinese origin. Cultural features present (except at the central Nevada site) consisted of hearths or stone concentrations. Of particular note here are the three measured areas of activity at site 26EU790. Using this as a guide and extrapolating from the Lakeview Camp, which likely represented multiple gangs congregating in a central place over time, a similar projection could be made for the Promontory Chinese sites. For instance, if Site 42BO1060, measuring 60,500 sq. ft., was divided into separate, adjacent camps of 12- to 20-man work gangs (Goodwin 1991:184), one could speculate that up to eight different worker groups congregated at this site; similarly, for 42BO1068, seven work gangs; for Site 42BO1070, perhaps only one; and for 42BO1134, six. Adding these together, one could project that as many as 250 to 500 Chinese, and possibly more, may have lived at these sites during railroad construction.

Further Thoughts about Construction Camps

Despite the limited survey and surface-collection information about the sites at Promontory, more comparative analyses between similar sites along other western railroads can provide valuable insights on and important understanding of these camps. Even various demographic and sociological analyses may offer more insights. For instance, the fact that Chinese workers are known to have built distinct camps, separate from other railroad workers, is an important subject to explore. In addition to environmental and technological variables influencing camp layout, social-structure variables created conventions for behavior in many construction camps (Buckles 1983). Buckles argues that native-born laborers would not tolerate the presence of the nonnative laborers employed, such as Chinese, Italians, Mexicans, and African Americans, and suggests that ethnic separation in camps was common and even enforced by management. This would also apply to Mormons, who made up a large percentage of the construction crews at Promontory. Their strict moral code and religious beliefs, not to mention attachment to separate construction companies (and railroads), would almost certainly have led them to set up camps physically separated from others working in the area. These ideas are supported and enhanced by Goodwin and colleagues, who describe in detail the reasons for separation of the Chinese, including those described above, as well as the fact that the Chinese bosses and workers themselves chose this pattern (Goodwin 1991:182–183). Labor contractors found it easier to maintain discipline this way, and naturally workers sought familiar company and the customs of their fellow countrymen.

These and other important aspects of railroad workers' camps will be difficult to tease out without further archaeological investigation. It is expected that more detailed analyses of the features and artifacts from the construction camps found on the Promontory Mountains slope will allow a better understanding of who occupied each camp. These analyses will also help identify camp affiliation with either UPRR or CPRR, the amount of ethnic diversity at each camp, and more information concerning the origin of camp occupants.

References

AMBROSE, STEPHEN E.
  1990 *Nothing Like It in the World: The Men Who Built the Transcontinental Railroad, 1863–1869.* Simon & Schuster, New York, NY.

AMES, CHARLES U.
  1969 *Pioneering the Union Pacific: A Reappraisal of the Builders of the Railroad.* Appleton-Century-Crofts, New York, NY.

ANDERSON, ADRIENNE
  1983 Ancillary Construction of Promontory Summit, Utah: Those Domestic Structures Built by Railroad Workers. In *Forgotten Places and Things: Archaeological Perspectives on American History*, Albert E. Ward, editor, pp. 225–238. Center for Anthropological Studies, Albuquerque, NM.

AYERS, JAMES E.
  1982 *Archaeological Survey of Golden Spike National Historic Site and Record Search for Promontory, Utah.* Arizona State Museum, Tucson.

BAIN, DAVID HAWARD
  1999 *Empire Express: Building the First Transcontinental Railroad.* Viking, New York, NY.

BUCKLES, WILLIAM G.
  1983 Models for Railroad Construction Related Sites in the West. In *Forgotten Places and Things: Archaeological Perspectives on American History*, Albert E. Ward, editor, pp. 213–223. Center for Anthropological Studies, Albuquerque, NM.

DAVIS, JOHN P.
  1894 *The Union Pacific Railway; A Study in Railway Politics, History, and Economics.* S. C. Griggs, Chicago, IL.

DESERET EVENING NEWS
  1869 No title. *Deseret Evening News* 7 April:5. Salt Lake City, UT.

DODGE, GRENVILLE M.
  1910 *How We Built the Union Pacific Railway: And Other Railway Papers and Addresses.* U.S. Congress (Senate), Washington, DC.

FIKE, RICHARD E., AND ANAN S. RAYMOND
  1981 *Rails East to Promontory: The Utah Stations.* Bureau of Land Management, Cultural Resource Series No. 8. Salt Lake City, UT.

FRANCAVIGLIA, RICHARD V.
  2008 *Over the Range: A History of the Promontory Summit Route of the Pacific Railroad.* Utah State University Press, Logan.

GALLOWAY, JOHN DEBO
  1950 *The First Transcontinental Railroad: Central Pacific and Union Pacific, 1863–1869.* Simmons-Boardman, New York, NY.
  1989 *The First Transcontinental Railroad.* Dorset Press, New York, NY.

GILES, RALPH B., AND DAWN A. FROST
  2001 Golden Spike National Historic Site: Systemwide Archeological Inventory Program Fiscal Year 2000 Interim Report. Manuscript, National Park Service, Western Archeological and Conservation Center, Tucson, AZ.

GOODWIN, VICTOR
  1991 Transportation. In *Nevada's Northeast Frontier*, Victor Goodwin, Edna B. Patterson, and Louise A Ulph, authors, pp. 133–206. University of Nevada Press, Reno.

HENDRICKS, RICKY
  1986 Golden Spike National Historic Site, UT. National Register of Historic Places Registration Form, Utah State Historic Preservation Office, Salt Lake City.

HOMSTAD, CARLA, JANENE CAYWOOD, AND PEGGY NELSON
  2000 *Cultural Landscape Report Golden Spike National Historic Site Box Elder County, Utah.* National Park Service, Intermountain Region, Cultural Resources Selections, No. 16. Denver, CO.

HUTCHINSON, SAYRE
  1988 List of Classified Structures, Stone Box Culvert, Record 11858. National Park Service, List of Classified Structures <http://hscl.cr.nps.gov/insidenps/report.asp?STATE=&PARK=&STRUCTURE=&SORT=1&RECORDNO=11858>. Accessed 9 August 2014.

KLEIN, MAURY
    1987 *Union Pacific: Birth of a Railroad, 1862–1893.* Doubleday, Garden City, NY.

KRAUS, GEORGE
    1969 *High Road to Promontory: Building the Central Pacific (Now the Southern Pacific) across the High Sierra.* Castle, New York, NY.

MCCAGUE, JAMES
    1964 *Moguls and Iron Men: The Story of the First Transcontinental Railroad.* Harper & Row, New York, NY.

MORRIS, ISAAC N.
    1876 *Condition of the Union Pacific Railroad.* 44th Congress (House), 1st sess., Executive Document 180. Washington, DC.

POLK, MICHAEL R.
    1998 Cultural Resources Overview and Preservation Recommendations, Promontory Route Corinne to Promontory, Utah, Report No. 1134. Manuscript, Sagebrush Consultants LLC, Ogden, UT.
    2013 The History and Influence of Chinese Railroad Workers on the Transcontinental Railroad: A View from the End of the Line at Promontory Summit. Paper presented at the Archaeology Network of the Chinese Railroad Workers in North America Workshop, Stanford University, Stanford, CA.

POLK, MICHAEL R., AND WENDY SIMMONS-JOHNSON
    2012 From Lampo Junction to Rozel: The Archeological History of the Transcontinental Railroad across the Promontory Mountains, Utah, GOSP Synthesis Report. Manuscript, Golden Spike National Historic Site, National Park Service, Promontory, UT.

RIGDAN, PAUL
    1951 Historical Catalogue: Union Pacific Historical Museum. Manuscript, Western Heritage Museum, Omaha, NE.

ROGERS, C. LYNN
    1997 Making Camp Chinese Style: The Archaeology of a V&T Railroad Graders' Camp, Carson City, Nevada. Manuscript, Archaeological Research Services, Virginia City, NV.

SALT LAKE DAILY TELEGRAPH
    1869 No title. *Salt Lake Daily Telegraph* 15 March:2. Salt Lake City, UT.

STROBRIDGE, EDWIN
    2002 Fiction or Fact? Did the Chinese and Irish RR Workers Really Try to Blow Each Other Up? Central Pacific Railroad Photographic History Museum <http://cprr .org/Game/Interactive_Railroad_Project/Fiction_or _Fact.html>. Accessed 10 September 2002.

UTLEY, ROBERT M.
    1960 The National Survey of Historic Sites and Buildings, Special Report on Promontory Summit, Utah (Golden Spike National Historic Site). Manuscript, United States Department of the Interior, National Park Service Region 3, Santa Fe, NM.
    1969 *Golden Spike National Historic Site, Utah.* National Park Service, Historical Handbook Series No. 40. Washington, DC.

WEYMOUTH, HEATHER M., SANDY CHYNOWETH PAGANO, AND ANGELA L. GARRISON
    2006 Archaeological Inventory of Golden Spike National Historic Site and Adjacent Bureau of Land Management Railroad Rights-of-Way Fiscal Year 2002 Interim Report, Report No. 1279. Report to RMC Consultants, Inc., Wheat Ridge, CO, and National Park Service, Lakewood, CO, from Sagebrush Consultants LLC, Ogden, UT.

WEYMOUTH, HEATHER M., SANDY CHYNOWETH PAGANO, ANDREW WILLIAMSON, AND ANGELA L. GARRISON
    2006 Golden Spike National Historic Site Systemwide Archaeological Inventory Program Fiscal Year 2003 Interim Report, Report No. 1303. Report to RMC Consultants, Inc., Wheat Ridge, CO, and National Park Service, Lakewood, CO, from Sagebrush Consultants LLC, Ogden, UT.

WEYMOUTH, HEATHER M., AND DON SOUTHWORTH
    2002 Golden Spike National Historic Site Systemwide Archaeological Inventory Program Fiscal Year 2001 Interim Report, Report No. 1225. Report to RMC Consultants, Inc., Wheat Ridge, CO, and National Park Service, Lakewood, CO, from Sagebrush Consultants LLC, Ogden, UT.

ZIER, CHARLES D.
    1985 *Archaeological Data Recovery Associated with the Mt. Hope Project, Eureka County, Nevada.* Bureau of Land Management, Cultural Resource Series, No. 8. Reno, NV.

MICHAEL R. POLK
SAGEBRUSH CONSULTANTS
3670 QUINCY AVENUE, SUITE 203
OGDEN, UT 84403

Lynn Furnis (林・法内斯)
Mary L. Maniery (玛丽・马聂里)

An Archaeological Strategy for Chinese Workers' Camps in the West: Method and Case Study
针对西方华人劳工营的考古学策略：方法与个案研究

ABSTRACT

Railroad work camps associated with Chinese laborers were often occupied for very short periods of time, leaving temporally discrete but shallow deposits of material and ephemeral features for archaeologists to explore. One methodological approach that has proved effective focuses on exposing and investigating the horizontal deposits across the sites, as opposed to more traditional vertical excavations. The use of broad areal exposure and documentation can lead to detailed spatial and functional analyses of material and features. Using a work camp associated with the Virginia & Truckee Railroad as a case study, the authors argue the validity of this approach for subsequent work on railroad-related work camps occupied by Chinese laborers in the 19th and early 20th centuries.

与中国劳工相关的铁路劳工营通常只被使用了很短一段时间。它们为考古学家的探索留下了在时间上的不连贯的表浅的物质堆积和短暂遗迹。因此，有效的方法学致力于挖掘并调查不同考古现场之间水平堆积层，与传统的垂直式发掘不同。对广大地域考掘与文献的使用，有助于对物质与遗迹进行详细的空间与功能分析。本文作者以弗吉尼亚和特拉基铁路附近的一个劳工营为个案研究，力图证实上述方法在日后有关十九世纪至二十世纪初年中国铁路劳工营的研究中的有效性。

Introduction

The second half of the 19th and early years of the 20th centuries in the western United States saw a frenzy of activity focused on resource extraction and construction projects. Workers drifted from mining camps to reclamation projects, dam construction sites to railroads, looking for employment. Camps to shelter and feed laborers near work sites comprised a significant part of the cultural landscape in the West and have been the focus of archaeologists for many years (Van Bueren 2002).

Work camps associated with some industries, such as logging, were occupied seasonally year after year. While considered temporary, these camps had a sense of permanence in their layout and design, with designated cookhouse, waste-disposal, bathing, and living areas. Railroad camps lasted only as long as the work continued along a section of the route. In flat, open land, work moved quickly. Areas that required concentrated and specialized construction efforts, such as building a line over the crest of the Sierra Nevada, gave rise to camps that were occupied for longer periods of time.

In 2013, the California Department of Transportation produced an historical context and archaeological research design for work camps in that state. The design identified four task-specific types of short-lived camps associated with railroad construction. The four sequential tasks were initial survey work, clearing and grubbing the route, grading the route, and the final laying of the rails. Chinese workers are associated with the middle two tasks (clearing/grubbing and grading) (California Department of Transportation 2013).

Building railroads required constant movement of workers and establishment of camps along the line, advancing with the construction. Tents or makeshift structures normally served as housing; there was no time to transport or build wooden shelters for an extremely mobile workforce. While contemporary accounts and company archives sometimes noted living conditions in main camps, Chinese workers often lived outside the main camp in communal shelters, eating traditional fare prepared by their own cooks. The isolated nature of their camps, poor documentation in archival records, language barriers, and short-term occupancy have resulted in a lack of detailed information about life in the camps, increasing the importance of the archaeological record (California Department of Transportation 2013). The challenge lies in ascertaining the best approach to gathering data useful for interpreting life in the camps, given the short-term and rapid movement that characterizes these types of sites.

Historical Archaeology, 2015, 49(1):71–84.
Permission to reprint required.

Methodological Approach

Archaeologists have long grappled with how to approach assessing the importance of Chinese railroad work camps. The short duration of occupancy, use of tents, and limited access to amenities and commodities resulted in shallow and often sparse deposits of materials. Using traditional excavation methods focusing on visible cultural features and vertical stratigraphy often does not result in collecting data with interpretive value.

As early as 1980, archaeologists recognized that using traditional methods of exploration at Chinese mining camps was not effective (LaLande 1981). Chinese sites are often characterized by a central U- or hairpin-shaped hearth and perhaps a tent pad. The camp sites contained surface scatters of artifacts and features, such as ash deposits from firebox cleanout activities, but lacked any substantial hollow-fill features or dense refuse deposits. In 1981 LaLande used surface scrapes and artifact collection on several camps in Oregon and found that broad areal exposure revealed additional features and artifact distribution patterns that were not evident using the traditional vertical approach.

Other researchers have since employed spatial and functional analyses for interpreting Chinese camps in the western United States and New Zealand (Richie 1983; Tordoff and Maniery 1986). They anticipated the shallowness of deposits and concluded that most archaeological data from these sites are best generated by analysis of surface artifact scatters and aboveground feature remains. The typical camp has at least one hearth or cooking feature, small earthen tent pads, and an occasional shallow depression used for refuse or ash disposal. Artifacts, particularly of domestic function, are concentrated around the hearth features, decreasing in frequency with distance from the features (Tordoff 1987).

Developing methods for investigating work camps focused on an approach that balanced maximum data recovery with reasonable labor expenditure. In 1984, Dr. Judith D. Tordoff combined systematic surface clearing, formal testing of ash deposits and hearth boxes, and metal detection surveys to explore 13 mining camps once occupied by Chinese in northern California. Her method of clearing, recording, and documenting the horizontal artifact scatter,

rather than focusing on the vertical distribution, effectively revealed activity areas and artifact distribution patterns, leading to the identification of additional site attributes (Tordoff 1987). Her approach has been used at numerous Chinese camps since that time.

Tordoff used the central hearth feature as a focal point and laid out grids around hearths and peripheral areas on the site. In general, grids measured 5 m^2. Vegetation cover was peeled back from the surface of selected grids exposing ground surface anomalies, such as small depressions, artificially flattened areas, and discrete ash deposits. Artifacts exposed during the clearing were left in place, mapped, identified by function, and collected for further analysis. Tordoff supplemented the horizontal data with firebox excavation, cross-sectioning of depressions, and collection of ash for specialized botanical studies. Her efforts generated quantitative and qualitative data from the sparse surface scatters of artifacts and subtle aboveground features that would not have been discovered with a focus on subsurface information. Her approach identified functionally distinct use areas on sites, including living, cooking, and work areas, and proved essential in gathering the maximum available information from these short-term work camps (Tordoff 1987).

Tordoff's success led others to apply her methods at other Chinese work sites, including railroad camps, which are prime examples of living situations that produced temporally discrete, surficial artifact deposits. Using Tordoff's surface-collection grid method and focusing on surface artifact and feature distributions and associations proved effective during the investigation of a camp associated with the Virginia & Truckee Railroad (V&TRR). Using the V&TRR site as a case study suggests that broad areal exposure and spatial and functional analysis of Chinese work camps is an appropriate approach to take in recovering meaningful data from similar sites.

Virginia & Truckee Railroad Workers' Camp: A Case Study

Site 26Or214, Area G is the official site number of a Nevada railroad camp, called Lakeview Camp, first recorded by archaeologists in 1994 (Figure 1). Historical records and

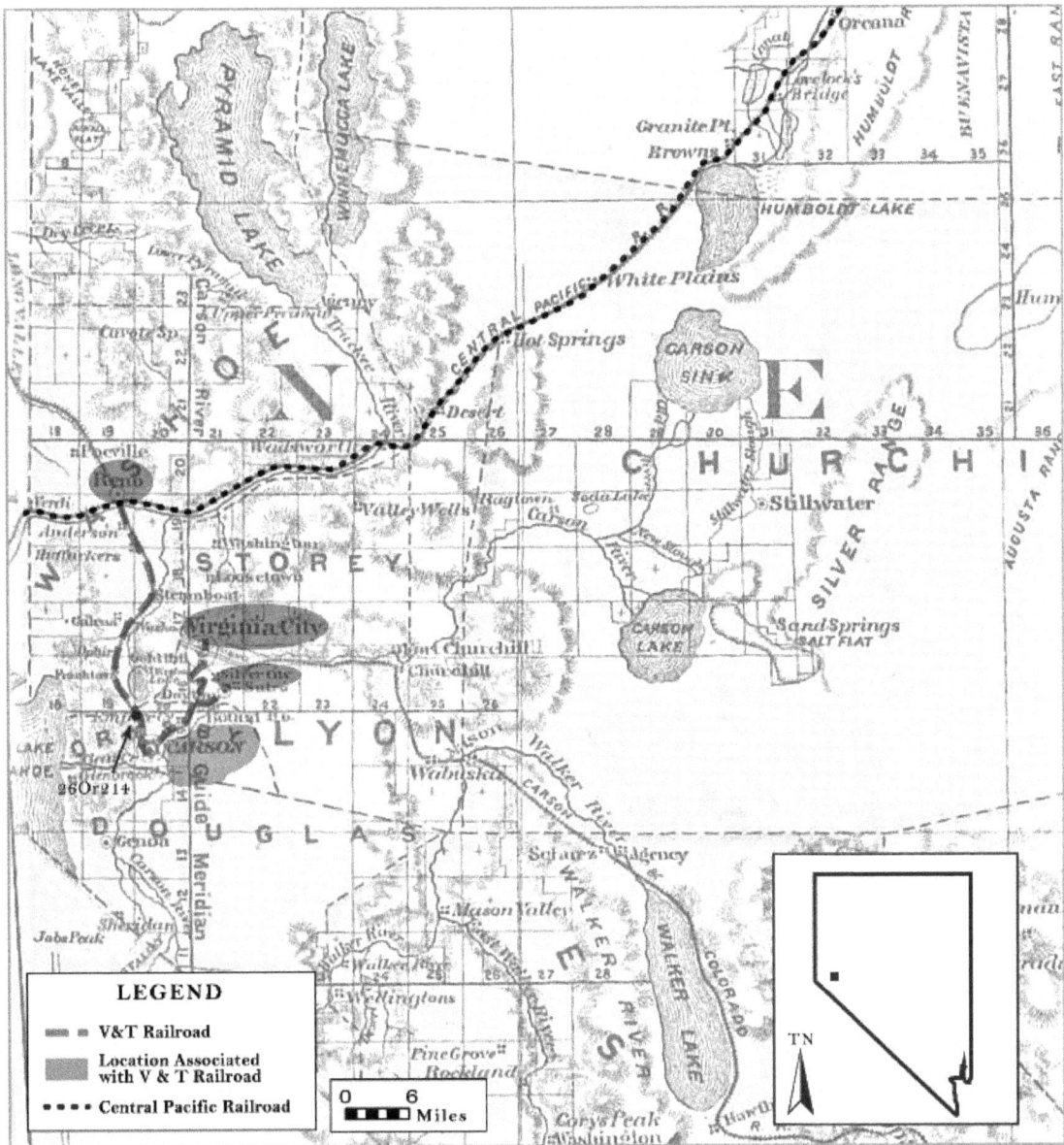

FIGURE 1. Map showing the Virginia & Truckee Railroad route between Reno and Carson City, Nevada, 1884. (Original map in possession of Lynn Furnis.)

archaeological work suggest that Lakeview Camp was occupied by Chinese workers for perhaps only a few weeks during the spring or early summer of 1872. When Lynn Furnis (formerly Lynn Rogers) had the opportunity to direct a test excavation of this sparse, mostly surface deposit through Archaeological Research Services, Inc., she designed a field strategy and data collection method only slightly modified from Tordoff's horizontal, surface-exposure approach

(Rogers 1997). It differed from Tordoff in a few ways. First, the entire site was subdivided into 69 large, 10 × 10 m collection squares, rather than limiting work to hearth feature areas (Figure 2). Subtle stone "hearth" features were found after the site had been gridded. Second, minimal project funding precluded extensive artifact curation, leading to a strategy of field-cataloging and -analysis of artifacts. Third, for comparative purposes Furnis selected

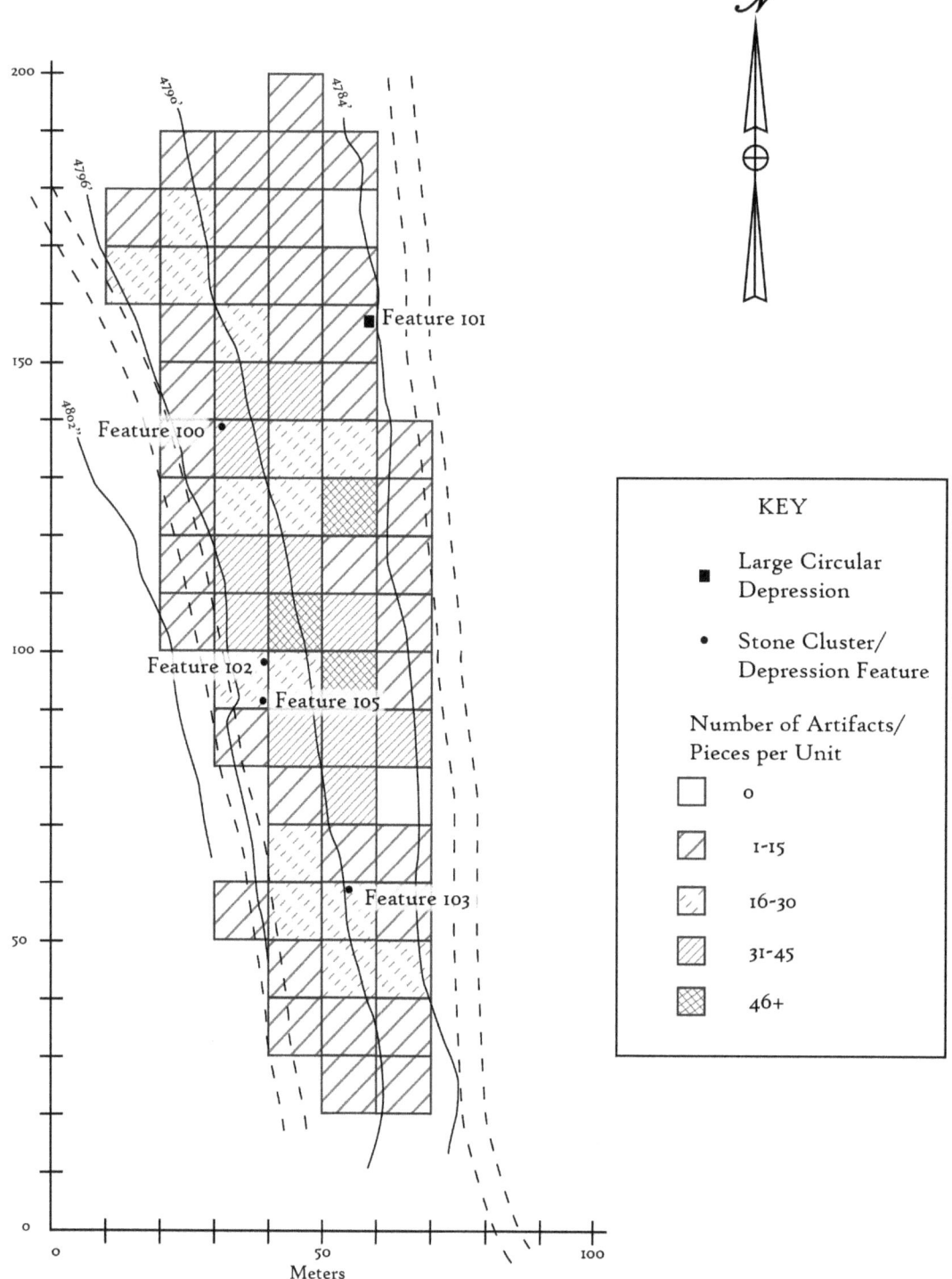

FIGURE 2. Lakeview Camp site grid, showing surface artifact densities (Rogers 1997:29).

a few collection units for surface clearing. Tordoff's method includes more extensive surface clearing. Artifacts from most squares at Lakeview Camp were located, mapped, and cataloged on an uncleared ground surface.

The Lakeview Camp field crew inspected each collection unit for surface artifacts and features. They plotted all items of Chinese origin and of European American origin known to date to the 1870s or earlier on a unit-gridded map and cataloged, described, and tallied each piece. They collected only unique or representative artifacts from the surface. The crew systematically scanned four collection squares with metal detectors and shovel scraped and screened two others to 5–10 cm below surface for recovery comparisons. Three standard 1 × 2 m excavation units were also dug at two surface features in order to determine their character, function, and artifactual associations.

The unit artifact-plot maps provided the data for the artifact distribution maps (Figure 2). These, along with artifact functional categories and fine-grained locational data entered in the database, enabled Furnis to generate distribution maps for any functional artifact group, following Tordoff's (1987) approach. Cross-tabulations of artifacts by function and location revealed spatial patterns and associations within and between groups.

Research Questions

The goal of the Lakeview Camp study was to learn about life in a railroad construction camp occupied by Chinese workers. Questions included: When was the site occupied in terms of year and season? How many people occupied the site and for how long? Who were the occupants? How was the site used? Answers to these basic questions were sought through the artifacts, their spatial and functional distributions, and historical documents.

The Site

Situated 3 mi. north of Carson City, Nevada, Lakeview Camp is one of an estimated 41 camps briefly occupied during the building of the V&TRR between Reno and Carson City (Figure 1). Mixed crews of Chinese and European Americans constructed this 31 mi.

long line between July 1871 and late August 1872, finishing at Carson City. Lakeview Camp is one of only four camps between Reno and Carson City that have been identified by archaeologists, although no systematic survey of the line has been attempted. Three additional camps have been identified along 13 mi. of the V&TRR line between Virginia City and Carson City (Wrobleski 1996). The V&TRR constructed its initial line from Virginia City to Carson City between 1869 and 1870 to transport the ore from its many mines to the processing mills along the Carson River (Myrick 1962:136–137). Bond money from Ormsby and Storey counties also influenced this decision. To connect the railroad to the new, transcontinental Central Pacific Railroad (CPRR) in Reno, the V&TRR extended the line from Carson City to Reno two years later.

Lakeview Camp site lay at the western margin of Little Ranch (operated from 1861 to 1905), away from buildings, pastures, and cultivated fields. The V&TRR grade was located 183 m west of and 70 m uphill from the camp, on a steep segment of extensive cutting and tunneling. Lakeview Camp was nearly 152 m long (north–south) and 61 m wide (east–west), at an average elevation of 1458 m above mean sea level. Spread on alluvial sediment along the eastern flank of Lakeview Hill, the site was characterized by a modest scatter of mid- to late-19th-century European American artifacts mixed with abundant imported Chinese ceramic fragments, brass and iron cans and can parts, four stone clusters, and one large depression.

In 1994 David Wrobleski (1996) conducted similar work at Site 665-6, a V&TRR Chinese workers' camp on the Virginia City segment above American Flat. Thought to be occupied during 1869 and 1870 V&TRR construction, the site has a similar artifact assemblage to that of Lakeview Camp, though its many tent platforms and several stone hearths suggest a more lengthy occupation. The site (3362 m²) is roughly one third the size of Lakeview Camp (9272 m²). Wrobleski employed similar field methods to Furnis's; he gridded the site in 5 × 5 yd. squares and mapped surface artifacts within them. Artifacts were field analyzed and tabulated. Wrobleski conducted no excavation, surface scrapes, or surface clearing.

Lakeview Camp Archaeological Features

The field crew identified four features similar to one another along the central and western portions of the site (Figure 2). Designated Features 100, 102, 103, and 105 were small and subtle in appearance. Features 100, 102, and 103 each consisted of a cluster of local, flat, schist stones, placed on the ground surface, the clusters spaced approximately 39.6 m apart, oriented in a north–south direction (Figure 2). Feature 105 consisted of a small rectangular depression devoid of stones. Feature 101 was a large depression that was excavated but yielded few artifacts and no information as to its age and function.

Originally, the four features were assumed to be fencepost supports. Feature 100 was selected for excavation to determine what it was, in hope of shedding light on all four similar features (Figure 3). The assemblage of artifacts and faunal remains there suggested use as a cooking feature, such as a pit oven or the base for a portable Chinese or American stove or brazier. The features may mark the locations of kitchens where the Chinese cooks for each work gang performed their tasks. The types of artifacts distributed near each stone feature suggest that food was prepared and consumed near them. Each had a shovel part nearby. At Feature 100, the crew found several large cans riddled with punched, square holes. Features 100 and 102 included iron wood-stove parts. A suggestion might be made that perhaps some foods were baked or steamed in the small depressions, employing stones for cooking and requiring shovels to open and close the pits, move coals and hot stones, and possibly transport cooking vessels and foods out of the pits. Feature 100 was excavated to 50 cm below surface and yielded mammal bone, fish vertebrae, machine-cut and L-head nails, charred wood, clothing buttons, shoe parts, a soy-sauce jug spout, wine- or champagne-bottle fragments, and in the lower level a small depression and more stones, some of which were stained black. As with Tordoff's hearth firebox excavations, subsurface excavation proved productive at this temporary, mostly surface site when employed alongside extensive focus on surface resources.

Archaeological Features at Site 665-6

Features at this smaller site were more numerous and far more substantial than the subtle ones identified at Lakeview Camp. Wrobleski (1996) mapped 13 domestic features consisting of 10 tent platforms, 1 tent platform with an associated stone cairn or hearth, and 2 stone cairns/hearths, as well as 2 large, partially leveled areas at one end of the site. All were close to a drainage and a spring. Food-related artifacts, wine bottles, and cut nails were associated with many of the features.

Artifacts and Their Distributions

At Lakeview Camp, surface artifacts from the 1870s were clustered in two areas, with 31 to 63 artifacts per collection square, while a light scatter graced the remainder of the space (Figure 2). Altogether, the crew recorded 1,336 whole or fragmentary artifacts from the surface (1,158 fragments), from the shovel scrapes between 0 and 5 cm below surface (158 fragments), and from scrapes between 5 and 10 cm below surface (20 fragments), representing a minimum number of items (MNI) count of 532. Another MNI of 459, in 775 pieces, was recovered from three excavation units within Features 100 and 101. The total assemblage was comprised of 2,111 fragments representing a MNI of 991. The surface artifacts are summarized in Table 1 by functional group. Organizing artifacts by their functions, as was done with this site's artifacts, is useful for interpreting site occupation and use over time. The categories of artifacts from Site 665-6, also shown in Table 1, are similar to those from Lakeview Camp, except for the modified, munitions, and multiuse categories.

Architectural Artifacts

Metal hardware, such as machine-cut nails, tacks, and brackets, and building materials, such as wooden boards and corrugated iron sheeting, comprise the architectural group at Lakeview Camp. The vast majority in this group were machine-cut nails. There were 381 size 12d nails found deposited in Feature 100, where used lumber, embedded with nails, was

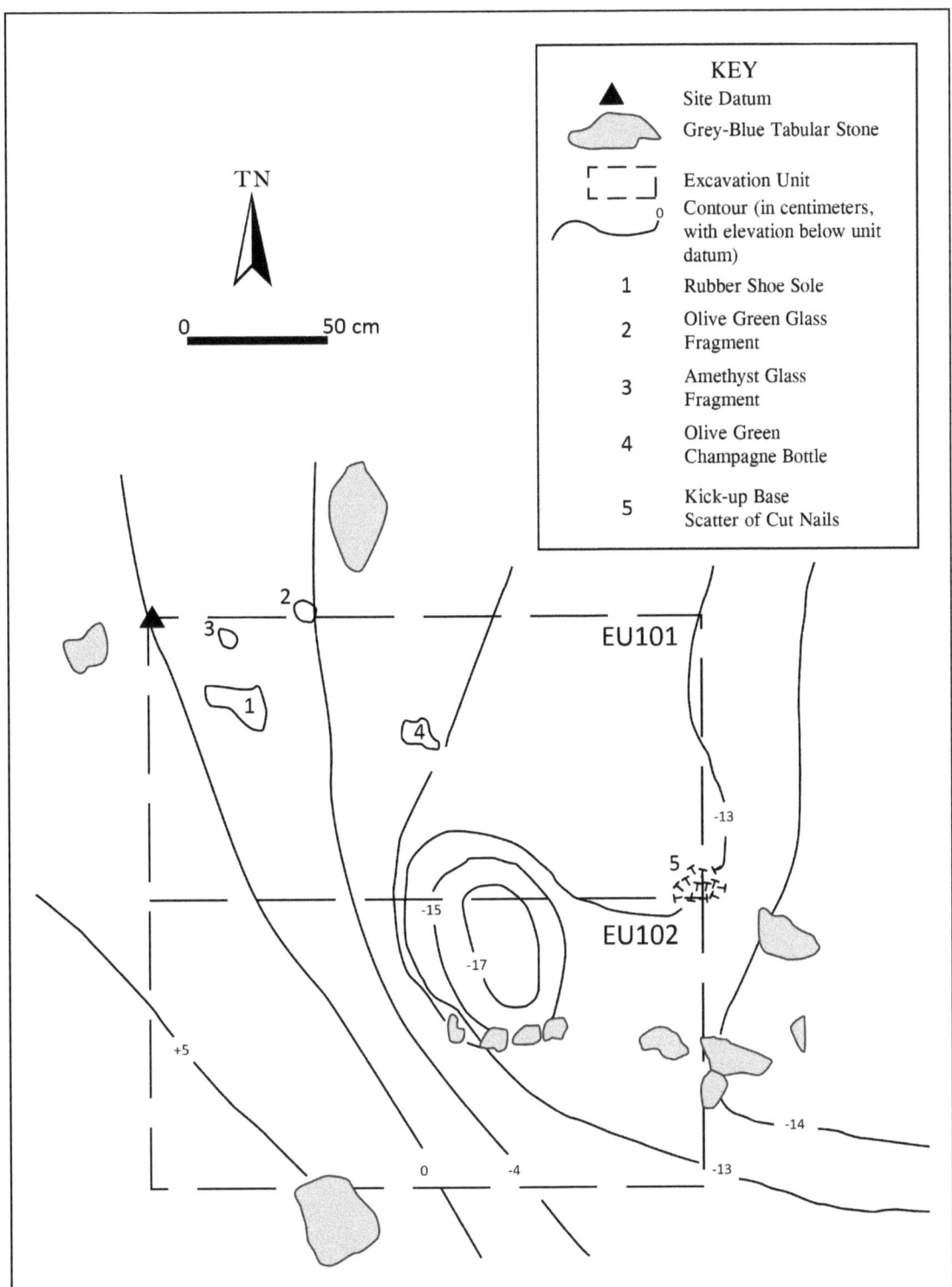

FIGURE 3. Surface plan of the Feature 100 stone cluster (Rogers 1997:11).

TABLE 1
SURFACE ARTIFACT COUNTS FROM LAKEVIEW CAMP
AND SITE 665-6

Functional Category	Lakeview Camp MNI	Lakeview Camp Fragments (Site 665-6 Fragments)	Percentage of Total MNI for Lakeview Camp
Architecture	72	83 (60)	13.53%
Domestic	2	2 (0)	0.38%
Food	122	527 (176)	22.93%
Industry/commerce	7	7 (1)	1.32%
Modified artifacts	109	114 (0)	20.49%
Munitions	14	16 (0)	2.63%
Personal	75	271 (47)	14.10%
Transportation	4	5 (1)	0.75%
Multiuse/unknown	127	311 (7)	23.87%
Total	532	1,336 (292)	100.00%

apparently burned for cooking and heating. A few of the surface nails and spikes were probably used to pierce metal fuel cans for reuse as strainers and rinsers, and repairing utensil handles, tent poles, and other objects used at the camp. Boards, nails, and hardware were found scattered across the site's surface. Architectural artifacts from Site 665-6 consisted of 60 cut nails and nail fragments.

Domestic Artifacts

Two large iron washtubs were located in the northern half of the site. The first was an oval, 4 gal. tub, suitable for watering or feeding animals, personal bathing, laundering of clothes, or washing dishes. The second tub was round, modified with numerous rectangular holes (pierced from the inside toward the outside), apparently for use as a strainer or rinser.

Food-Related Artifacts

Food-related artifacts comprised the second-largest functional group at Lakeview Camp (Table 1) and included the greatest proportion of artifacts manufactured in and imported from China. Chinese-made porcelain rice bowls, a serving bowl, and tea- and wine-cup sherds were recorded, as well as pieces of 16 dark brown-glazed stoneware spouted jugs. Bamboo (n=16) and Four Seasons (n=1) patterns were present,

as well as Winter Green (Celadon) pattern (n=8) vessels. One Winter Green serving-bowl sherd was distinguished by an unidentified character, pinpricked through the glaze, on its interior surface. Metal food containers included 16 large rectangular food (leaf tea?) and four cooking-oil cans, all manufactured in China (Figure 4). Lesser numbers of European American food containers and tablewares were present and are considered contemporary with the Chinese use of the site.

At 10 Northern Pacific Railroad (NPRR) construction sites in Montana (1882–1883), no Double Happiness bowls were observed, although Bamboo bowls are reported from 9 of the sites (Merritt et al. 2012:686,687). At Site 665-6, Chinese-manufactured bowls in Bamboo (MNI=12) and Double Happiness (MNI=4) patterns, and brown-glazed and unglazed stoneware pieces (83 fragments) comprised the largest functional group (Wrobleski 1996). No European American ceramics were noted, and only a few European American cans were present. Furnis recorded no Double Happiness bowls at Lakeview Camp. Wegars (1993:160) contends that Bamboo bowls supplanted Double Happiness vessels around 1870. Because Site 665-6 is on the V&TRR line constructed between 1869 and 1870, with Lakeview Camp likely occupied in 1872, the bowl patterns support Wegars's hypothesis.

At Lakeview Camp, artifacts for food preparation consist of large iron items, including

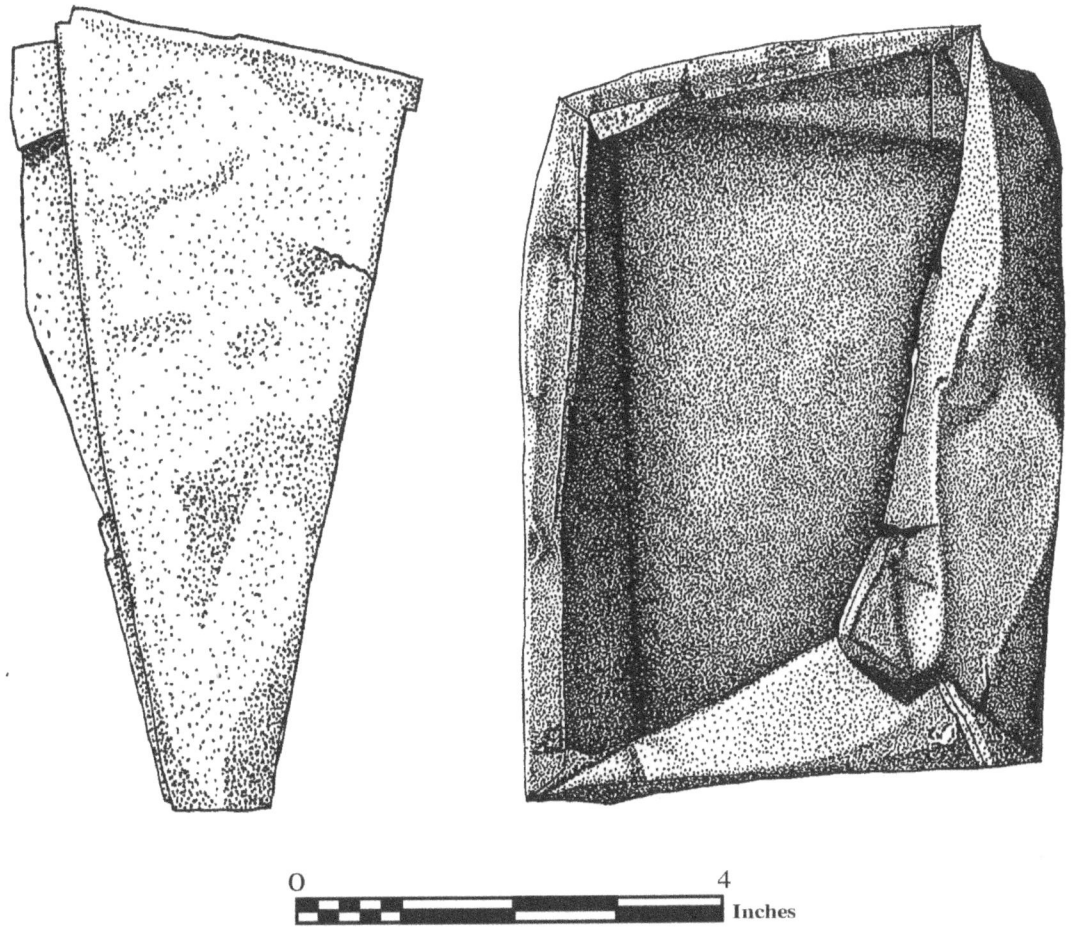

O   4
                                     Inches

FIGURE 4. Chinese-made rectangular can and funnel made from a can part (Rogers 1997:58,72).

a bowl, a rectangular can pierced with vertical slits around its lower half (possibly used for germinating bean sprouts [Wegars 1995:5]), a wood-stove cast-iron burner plate and pipe segment, and four pierced containers. A washtub, bucket, rectangular can, and cylindrical corrugated can were all modified by means of rectangular holes punched from the inside surface and may have served as food drainers, strainers, or rinsers. All five metal containers were recovered near Feature 100 in the core area of the camp, where most of the cooking took place. Clusters of Bamboo and Winter Green vessels, opium cans, and champagne bottles were also found within this space. Site 665-6 yielded no food preparation artifacts.

Food storage containers included at least 16 handmade rectangular cans, thought to have held 10–12 oz. of loose-leaf tea (Figure 4). Each

measured between 2.9 and 3.0 in. tall, between 6.1 and 6.4 in. long, and between 3.9 and 4.25 in. wide. The cans, formed from four separate rectangular sheets soldered together, were probably made in China. Similar cans have been identified on Chinese-occupied sites at Pierce, Idaho, at CPRR sites east of Wells, Nevada, at one V&TRR site in Silver City, Nevada, and along the Eureka & Palisade Railroad in central Nevada (Callaway 1979:275–276; Zeier 1985:144–145; Stapp 1990:198; Zeanah and Rogers 1990; Wrobleski 1996:42–44). Wrobleski (1996) found no tea cans at Site 665-6. Four similar cans from Lakeview Camp, but smaller and with wire-top handles, are identified as Chinese cooking-oil cans (Stapp 1990).

European American beverages, such as soda and mineral water, were represented by 19 bottles distributed across the site with no apparent patterning. Alcoholic-beverage bottles, on the other hand, differed in their distribution; see the "Personal Artifacts" discussion below.

Industry and Commerce Artifacts

Three Chinese coins were recovered from the site, and, while they are media of exchange, they were generally used as tokens, gaming pieces, or good-luck charms by immigrant Chinese in the United States (Farris 1984:147–149). These are discussed below under "Personal Artifacts."

Parts from four round- and square-nose shovels were recorded. Shovels were common and necessary camp tools and were basic railroad grade-building tools used by Chinese workers. The parts were found within 10 m of four stone cluster/depression features. The shovels were likely used in campfire building, cooking, and pit digging. Site 665-6 produced one shovel head located near a small tent pad.

Modified Artifacts

A large group of sheet-metal artifacts from Lakeview Camp are considered industrial artifacts or by-products apparently produced by the Chinese workers while camping. The artifacts include a round, dished can end, 13 fuel-can lids, 6 pieces of brass opium cans, and 114 sheet-iron pieces modified from can parts for new uses, pieces that were the by-products of such reworking and became scrap, or pieces that were saved as raw material for future use. They comprise one-fifth of the entire surface assemblage. Most have not been identified as to function. A few were recognizable as funnels and as patching material for other objects. No artifacts exhibiting such "a salvaging ethic" (Merritt et al. 2012:689) were recovered from Site 665-6.

Four sheet-metal rectangles were fashioned into handmade funnels. The sheet-metal pieces may have been salvaged from the tea and cooking-oil cans. The funnels, which vary in size, were used to fill narrow-mouth vessels, such as bottles, kerosene cans, and black-powder cans. They were located in the site's core area, where presumably cooking, eating, and socializing took place. Altogether, 61 rectangles cut from cans were distributed over the site, with a slight concentration in the core area.

One large, round can end was modified by hammering into a concave shape and pierced with one square nail hole, possibly forming a can-type charcoal brazier. It was located near Feature 100 and could have held a wok for cooking food. Lids cut from 13 kerosene cans were also found. The can bodies were apparently reused as carrying containers for water or hot tea, fitted with wire bales that could be suspended from carrying poles by camp members.

Munitions Artifacts

Whole and fragmentary munitions were recorded at Lakeview Camp, implying the use of rimfire arms and shotguns, as well as some percussion types. Most of the 14 artifacts were .22 cal. long casings and shotgun shells. They were well distributed over the site, although two clusters within the northern half were directly attributable to the scanning of sample collection units with metal detectors. The detectors demonstrated that munitions, small nails, and shoe nails are categories of artifacts rarely observed by archaeologists on the ground surface, but present within the upper 5–10 cm of site sediments. While some of the munitions may be attributable to the Chinese occupants, they also may have come from earlier hunting, varmint-killing (rabbits), or plinking activities by Little Ranch occupants.

Personal Artifacts

Artifacts categorized as personal comprised 14% of the Lakeview Camp surface assemblage (Table 1). Included were clothing buttons, shoe parts, purse and luggage parts, a brass night key, medicine bottles, grooming and personal sanitation items, pastime items such as gaming pieces, liquor and wine bottles, tobacco and opium pipes, and opium cans. All of the buttons and shoe parts were European American, common types of the time, with metal trouser buttons and Prosser porcelain shirt buttons. Wrobleski (1996) recorded one metal and one Prosser porcelain button at his site.

Two purse and luggage parts were found near Feature 100. Only two glass medicine bottles were found, both of European American origin. Two glass Go (wéiqí) game pieces, three brass Chinese coins, and tobacco and opium pipes were found in the southern part of the site. Site 665-6 yielded one patent-medicine bottle.

More than half (MNI=40) of the personal items represented indulgence activities: liquor, opium, and tobacco consumption. They were distributed somewhat differently at the site, with fragments from six European American liquor bottles clustered near the stone features. Abundant fragments (n=208) of the MNI of 25 champagne bottles and fragments from 7 brass opium cans were scattered across the site, with some clustering in the northern half. Wrobleski (1996) reported fragments from one whiskey bottle and three wine or champagne bottles, all scattered in and near the large, partially leveled site areas.

Transportation Artifacts

Lakeview Camp is flanked on its east and west sides by dirt roads that have been in use for many decades. Still, only four artifacts were found that relate to site-contemporaneous transportation. These included a square-head carriage bolt and three draft-animal trappings artifacts. At Site 665-6 one horseshoe nail was identified as the single transportation artifact.

Multiuse Artifacts and Unknown-Use Artifacts

This artifact category is the largest represented at Lakeview Camp. Most of the artifacts can be named, but they have multiple uses and have not been assigned to a specific functional group. Included are an iron bar, bolts, hooks, sheet iron, wire, metal strips, collars, unidentified bottle fragments, and barrel parts. At Site 665-6, barrel hoops, wire, sheet metal, and a metal strap were recorded. Only barrel parts will be discussed here in greater detail.

Metal hoops and wooden staves from at least 12 barrels or kegs were deposited at Lakeview Camp, with the majority (n=9) in the northern half. Barrels were handy containers, frequently used by Chinese workers for holding drinking water, hot tea, or hot bath water (Kraus 1969:111). Their slight clustering in the site's northern half, where the ground is more level and less cluttered with food artifacts, suggests this may be an area of personal space, where baths were taken, clothes were mended, and tents were pitched.

Results

Through extensive documentary research and artifact and spatial analysis of the Lakeview Camp assemblage, some of our research questions were answered.

When Was Lakeview Camp Occupied?

Although 70–80 men, including at least 40 Chinese, were working on the nearby Lakeview Tunnel from December 1871 through late April 1872, Lakeview Camp has revealed no evidence of substantial stone hearths, dugout dwellings, or other features needed to survive the particularly harsh winter of 1871–1872 (*Reno Crescent* 1872). Between February and April 1872 at least 150–200 Chinese laborers were hired to complete the line to Carson City. In late February at least 100 Chinese were working on the grade between Lakeview Tunnel and Carson City. Some of these men likely resided at Lakeview Camp. By June 600 Chinese workers were on the route, between Steamboat Hot Springs and Carson City (*Nevada State Journal* 1872). Chinese grading and tunnel crews may have camped at Lakeview Camp one or more times between late February and late August 1872, but it is most probable that grading crews inhabited the site in the warmer months of spring or early summer of that year.

What Was the Duration and Size of the Camp Occupation?

Based on the proximity of Lakeview Camp to Lakeview Tunnel and the difficult terrain, grading crews may have camped at the site for two or three weeks, while tracking crews would have stayed perhaps a night or two. An estimate of 40–70 Chinese men camped together at the site, based on the low density of artifacts and features at Lakeview Camp, and on the well-known practice of organizing Chinese workers into groups of 10, 20, or 30 men (Goodwin 1991:181). Agents typically distributed wages to the Chinese workers through English-speaking crew chiefs who represented each group of men. Each crew paid for its own cook and food, and lived together in groups in the camps, procuring supplies from Chinese merchants, who provided foodstuffs from China in addition to other supplies (Goodwin 1991:181).

The estimated number of occupants is also based on the distribution of artifacts, cooking features, and the resultant pattern of activity areas. The core area of the site, based on artifacts used for food preparation and consumption, revealed two or three dense artifact clusters, each likely representing the public space of one work group of 10–30 men. If there were three such groups at the site, then 30–90 men camped together at the site.

As noted above, Furnis estimated a narrower range of 40–70 Chinese occupants, based on a consideration of tea allotments for railroad workers in 1870. The *Railroad Gazette* of 10 September 1870 printed a list for the benefit of railroad company owners and bosses that detailed the daily rations needed to supply one Chinese railroad laborer in 1870 (Wrobleski 1996:18). For tea, an extremely important commodity to the Chinese workers, the list's author suggested that 1/3 oz. of tea daily was needed for each worker. The 26 rectangular, Chinese-made leaf-tea cans from Lakeview Camp were estimated to have held 10–12 oz. of tea each. One can supplied enough tea for 30–36 men for one day, relying on the 1/3 oz. per day suggested amount. The Lakeview Camp cans represent 26 days' worth of tea for 30–36 men, 13 days' worth of tea for 60–72 men, or 9 days' worth of tea for three work crews. Based on the distribution of workers along the V&TRR line at a given time, the number of workers employed, and the distribution of artifacts at Lakeview Camp, Furnis concluded that two crews of Chinese men occupied the camp for at least two weeks in 1872.

Who Were the Lakeview Camp Occupants?

From the beginning, archaeologists assumed the site occupants had been Chinese men working for the V&TRR during its construction. The site surface was littered with easily recognizable and common Chinese-made items and is situated close to the railroad grade. Fieldwork and analysis confirmed this initial assumption.

How Was the Site Used?

Tordoff's surface-exposure method was effective and informative in revealing activity areas, subtle features, and patterned artifact distributions at Lakeview Camp (Tordoff 1987). Artifact patterning at the Lakeview Camp suggests that two central areas, located close to each other, represent public spaces for two crews centered on the stone features, where cooking, eating, and socializing took place. Private sleeping areas were located outside the core area (Figure 2). The most level and flat areas of the site yielded the fewest artifacts and may have been unused or were reserved for sleeping, grooming, and sanitation, although remnants of tent platforms, dugouts, and small depressions were not found. The northern and southern ends of the site did yield light artifact scatters, and it is there that the workers most likely slept, perhaps with a crew at each end.

The placement of four stone cluster/depression features supports the two-crew idea. All are located along the western edge of the site and are spaced somewhat evenly from north to south. They are associated with shovel parts; the three northern features also have pierced metal containers and metal funnels fashioned from can parts. Features 100 and 102 are associated with cast-iron stove parts and large numbers of food- and beverage-related artifacts. The southern features (103 and 105) have far fewer food and beverage artifacts, and probably provided warmth for the campers and perhaps heat for bathwater. Feature 100 in the north is thought to have served as the kitchen and social space for one work group, while Feature 102 served another group. Feature 105 is 7 m from Feature 100, within the same dense artifact cluster, and probably served this same work group. A moderate to light scatter of personal and domestic artifacts surrounded the southernmost stone feature (103), suggesting a more private space.

Winter Green–pattern porcelain vessels (Celadon) and contemporaneous European American food vessels were most restricted in their distribution. The Winter Green vessels were more expensive imported wares and were found only in the northern half of the site where European American tablewares and food containers were concentrated. Other European American items associated with the northern site area were glass medicine bottles and barrel parts. Perhaps Chinese men of higher status within the groups occupied this part of the site or used it to entertain European American visitors, such as their Caucasian V&TRR supervisors, a practice documented for urban 19th-century Sacramento (Praetzellis 1997). It is also possible that the European American artifacts represent a separate short-term occupation by European Americans or others, slightly before or after the Chinese camped on site.

Conclusion

The short-term and often single-episode use of Chinese railroad workers' camps, resulting in a lack of hollow-fill features or foundations, challenges traditional archaeological practices used to extract meaningful information from sites. Using broad horizontal exposures, metal detection, detailed mapping, functional analysis of surface artifacts, and focused excavation of features has proved to be an effective strategy for these types of sites, as demonstrated by the results of research at Lakeview Camp. As archaeologists continue to investigate Chinese railroad camps, employing a similar approach to fieldwork could result in a more meaningful analysis of site activities and in a growth of the comparative dataset for these short-term sites.

Acknowledgments

Both authors were privileged to work with Dr. Tordoff in the early 1980s as she was developing her methodological approach to Chinese mining camps, and we were fortunate to direct fieldwork at similar sites at which we could use her approach. We thank her for inspiring us early in our careers. Furnis thanks Vickie Clay for giving her the opportunity to work at Lakeview Camp, as well as numerous volunteers. We thank the anonymous reviewers and Barb Voss for providing thoughtful comments and suggestions that have strengthened this article. Amber Rankin is thanked for preparing all the figures used in this article.

References

CALIFORNIA DEPARTMENT OF TRANSPORTATION
2013 *A Historical Context and Archaeological Research Design for Work Camp Properties in California.* California Department of Transportation, Cultural Resources Office, Division of Environmental Analysis, Sacramento.

CALLAWAY, CASHION
1979 Metal Artifacts from Ninth and Amherst. In *Archaeological and Historical Studies at Ninth and Amherst, Lovelock, Nevada*, Vol. 1, Eugene M. Hattori, Mary K. Rusco, and Donald R. Tuohy, editors, pp. 250–346. Nevada State Museum Archaeological Services Reports. Carson City.

FARRIS, GLENN
1984 Chinese and Annamese Coins Found at the Woodland Opera House Site. In *The Chinese Laundry on Second Street: Papers on Archeology at the Woodland Opera House Site*, David L. Felton, Frank Lortie, and Peter D. Schulz, editors, pp. 147–150. Department of Parks and Recreation, California Archeological Reports, No. 24. Sacramento.

GOODWIN, VICTOR
1991 Transportation. In *Nevada's Northeast Frontier*, Edna B. Patterson, L. A. Ulph, and Victor Goodwin, authors, pp. 133–206. University of Nevada Press and Northeastern Nevada Historical Society, Reno.

KRAUS, GEORGE
1969 *High Road to Promontory: Building the Central Pacific (Now the Southern Pacific) across the High Sierra.* American West, Palo Alto, CA.

LALANDE, JEFFREY
1981 Sojourners in the Oregon Siskiyous: Adaptation and Acculturation of the Chinese Miners in Jackson County, Oregon, 1860–1900. Master's thesis, Department of Interdisciplinary Studies, Oregon State University, Eugene.

MERRITT, CHRISTOPHER W., GARY WEISZ, AND KELLY DIXON
2012 Verily the Road was Built with Chinaman's Bones: An Archaeology of Chinese Line Camps in Montana. *International Journal of Historical Archaeology* 16(4):666–695.

MYRICK, DAVID F.
1962 *Railroads of Nevada and Eastern California*, Vol. 1. Howell-North, Berkeley, CA.

NEVADA STATE JOURNAL
1872 Railroad Progress. *Nevada State Journal* 1 June:3.

PRAETZELLIS, ADRIAN C.
1997 Historical Archaeology of an Overseas Chinese Community in Sacramento, California, Report to United States General Services Administration, Sacramento, CA, from Sonoma State University, Anthropological Studies Center, Rohnert Park, CA.

RENO CRESCENT
1872 Tunnel at Lakeview. *Reno Crescent* 20 April:2.

RICHIE, NEVILLE
1983 Archaeological Research on Nineteenth Century Chinese Settlement in the Cromwell Area. *Courier* 29:2–18. Queenstown, New Zealand.

ROGERS, C. LYNN
1997   Making Camp Chinese Style: The Archaeology of a V&T Railroad Graders' Camp, Carson City, NV. Report to Silver Oak Development Company, Carson City, NV, from Archaeological Research Services, Virginia City, NV.

STAPP, DARBY CAMPBELL
1990   *The Historic Ethnography of a Chinese Mining Community in Idaho.* Doctoral dissertation, Department of American Civilization, University of Pennsylvania, Philadelphia. University Microfilms International, Ann Arbor, MI.

TORDOFF, JUDITH D.
1987   Dutch Gulch Lake Excavation at Thirteen Historic Sites in the Cottonwood Mining District, Cottonwood Creek Project, Shasta and Tehama Counties, California, Dana McGowan Seldner, contributor. Report to United States Army Corps of Engineers, Sacramento District, CA, from California State University, Sacramento.

TORDOFF, JUDITH D., AND MARY L. MANIERY
1986   Analysis, Evaluation, Effect Determination and Mitigation Plan for Two Chinese Mining Sites in Butte County, California. Manuscript, USDA Forest Service, Lassen National Forest, Susanville, CA.

VAN BUEREN, THAD M. (EDITOR)
2002   Communities Defined by Work: Life in Western Work Camps. Thematic issue, *Historical Archaeology* 36(3).

WEGARS, PRISCILLA
1995   Miscellaneous Topics. *Asian American Comparative Collection Newsletter* 12(1):5−6.

WEGARS, PRISCILLA (EDITOR)
1993   *Hidden Heritage, Historical Archaeology of the Overseas Chinese.* Baywood, Amityville, NY.

WROBLESKI, DAVID E.
1996   The Archaeology of Chinese Work Camps on the Virginia and Truckee Railroad. Master's thesis, Dpartment of Anthropology, University of Nevada, Reno.

ZEANAH, DAVID W., AND C. LYNN ROGERS
1990   A Class III Archaeological Survey of Proposed Land Acquisitions and Transportation Corridors Associated with the Thousand Springs Power Project, Toano Draw, Elko County, NV. Manuscript, Intermountain Research, Silver City, NV.

ZEIER, CHARLES D.
1985   *Archaeological Data Recovery Associated with the Mt. Hope Project, Eureka County, Nevada.* Bureau of Land Management, Cultural Resource Series No. 8. Reno, NV.

LYNN FURNIS
14382 FLOMAR DRIVE
WHITTIER, CA 90603

MARY L. MANIERY
PAR ENVIRONMENTAL SERVICES
PO BOX 160756
SACRAMENTO, CA 95816

Charlotte K. Sunseri (夏洛特·桑瑟里)

Alliance Strategies in the Racialized Railroad Economies of the American West
美国西部种族化的铁路经济中的结盟策略

ABSTRACT

The rural railroad community of Mono Mills, California (1880–1917), was home to individuals of Chinese, Paiute, and European ancestry seeking work in the midst of the economic downturn of the West's mining region. Archaeology of the workers' households and archival evidence for the business ventures associated with their livelihoods, such as the Virginia & Truckee Railroad and the Bodie & Benton Railroad & Lumber Company, suggest that, particularly for the Chinese workers, aggregated transience and racism was a major factor in their daily lives and choices. The findings explore multiple ways in which racism biased job opportunities for Chinese laborers while it increased alliance building among marginalized groups—including intercommunity sociality, regional networks for employment, and economic cohesion—and perhaps led to increased fidelity between labor crews and powerful capitalists of the West. These dynamics had long-term impacts on the local, regional, and national socioeconomic networks in which the Chinese laborers participated.

在美国西部矿区经济低迷的时候（1880–1917），中国人、派尤特印第安人以及欧洲人后裔曾前往默诺米尔斯寻找工作，在那里的乡村铁路社区建立了新的家园。对工人们居家环境的考古研究，和相关商业风险投资的文献证据（例如，弗吉尼亚和特拉基铁路、博迪和班顿铁路和伐木公司），显示出集体流动性与种族主义极大地影响了工人们的日常生活与选择，对中国工人来说尤其如此。这些研究成果探索了种族主义对中国劳工的工作机会产生影响的多重方式；而与此同时，种族主义也在增加边缘群体之间的结盟—包括社区间的社会交往、雇佣的区域性网络以及经济凝聚力—而这种结盟也有可能促进了劳工与西部的权贵资本家们之间的相互忠诚。这些互动关系对中国工人所参与的在地的、区域性的以及全国性的社会经济网络都有着长期的影响。

Introduction

The 1859 discovery of silver in the Comstock Lode of western Nevada rekindled the rush for riches that had characterized the beginnings of the Gold Rush a decade before (Magnaghi 1981:131). As population booms brought transformative aspects of urban life to Virginia City, Nevada, and the rest of the Comstock (Figure 1), business and commerce followed in the miners' wake. One of the major efforts to integrate the region more fully into broader national commerce networks was the construction of the Central Pacific Railroad (CPRR), which retraced the trans–Sierra Nevada paths of so many early miners. A shortage of labor for the CPRR in the West—largely due to the 1864 silver and quartz bonanzas in Nevada that pulled away many European American workers and the 1865 Irish-worker strikes—led CPRR management to hire Chinese crews, experimentally, at first, then by the thousands in 1865 (Aarim-Heriot 2003:80). When the Chinese-dominated railroad crews finally crossed the Sierras to reach Reno in 1868, the most dangerous and time-consuming western portions of the line were behind them. The company response to the relative ease of creating a lower-gradient railroad bed heading east from Reno was to reduce the number of employees on those sections outside the Sierras. Many railroad workers were let go at this point. Some workers transitioned from construction to service industries for the CPRR in Reno. Others sought various work on the Comstock, including mining, service industries, and continued work as organized crews for railroad companies run by Virginia City capitalists. This work often took Chinese crews out of the urban core to the peripheries of this mining region, as smaller spur railroads and lumbering efforts permeated the landscape radially from Virginia City (Chung 1998).

The CPRR-driven flood of skilled labor into the Comstock after 1868 is contextualized by the racial hierarchy of the European American social world at this time. Historians refer to the late 19th century as the Gilded Age (coined by Mark Twain and Charles Dudley Warner in an 1873 satire), named for its exceptional scope and rate of social change, and the imagined and heavily proselytized facade of success

Historical Archaeology, 2015, 49(1):85–99.
Permission to reprint required.

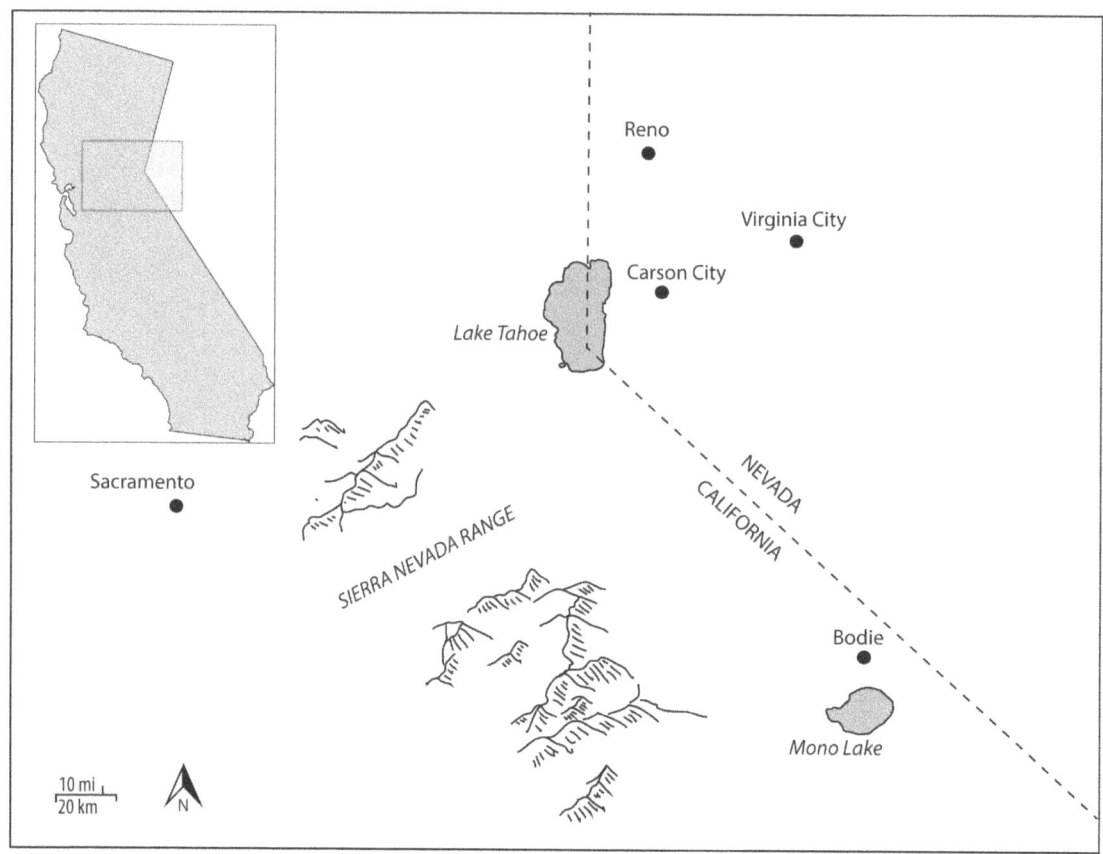

FIGURE 1. Map of late-19th-century regions of the Comstock (Nevada) around Lake Tahoe and Bodie (California) by Mono Lake. (Drawing by author, 2014.)

promised in the West. The gilding masked the corruption inherent in American political life, as well as the stark daily experience of many Americans, including the majority of miners and railroad workers whose lives were not improved by the gold or silver bonanzas. Additionally, gilding certainly ignored the racism and struggle woven into the fabric of these communities. The legacies of racialized labor dynamics suggest that a complete investigation of the lives of Chinese transcontinental railroad workers must consider the life trajectories of those who left CPRR employ to make communities in this new place.

Hsu (2000:61) argues that Chinese immigrants survived economically adverse environments in the American West through kinship networks that provided a safety net when jobs were scarce, social and economic support to offset discriminatory laws, and connections to find jobs. The stories of survival described

by historical and archaeological studies illustrate how transience, racial politics, and labor inequalities characterize many aspects of the Chinese experience. In this context, Chinese laborers may be viewed as socioeconomic strategists whose mobility across the landscape and within new communities was but one aspect of an emerging social dynamic that made them important participants in extensive networks that ranged broadly across the goldfields of the West.

Social Identity and Agency in Labor Settings

In Gilded Age sites across the West, as with other studied sites, the materiality of labor and power are present in industrial spaces (Shackel 2004; Casella 2005), work areas (Gillespie and Farrell 2002; Hardesty 2002, Van Bueren 2002; Silliman 2006), and household or domestic spaces (Baxter 2002; Maniery 2002; Wurst 2006). By considering labor simultaneously with ethnic identity, race, and gender (Wurst 1999; McGuire and Reckner 2002; Casella 2005; Silliman 2006), the power relations inherent in the commercial and mining endeavors on the Comstock and other boomtowns become apparent. Social identities, including class and ethnic affiliation, consider that group memberships are "created within the tensions of an unequal society" (Burke 1999:19) and "produced through power-laden negotiations of [these] tensions between sameness and difference" (Voss and Allen 2008:5). Capitalist alienations of community and power, such as racialization of labor categories, built tensions within and between communities in the periphery. Strategies that crosscut group boundaries, such as pluralistic solidarity, may have become significant forms of resistance for allied subaltern communities.

A relational or structural approach to class examines individuals' "relationship to the means of production and to each other" (McGuire and Reckner 2002:46) within a power-laden dynamic that defined entities of capitalist investors/owners of the means of production, managers and administrators for the company, and workers whose labor was extracted in the production of goods and wealth. By considering the "small-scale daily activities of individuals negotiating, appropriating, living in, and suffering through particular labor regimes" (Silliman 2001:381), labor may be thought of as practice that goes beyond economics as a form of social action and a vital medium of agency and resistance (Saitta 1994; Silliman 2001, 2005).

A focus on conflict and contradictions in labor settings allows investigation of the nature of underlying social relations between individuals and groups. In this way, class is seen as the "surface appearance of the complex web of social relations of production" (Wurst 2006:195). These relational perspectives focus on the totality of social relations that comprise the lived experience of groups in the past. Material approaches to class relationships as economic and social links among individuals must consider their nature as a multiscalar concept (Wurst 1999, 2006). This calls attention to the ways in which labor relations and

class structures operated at local company scales, just as they did at broad, national scales (McGuire and Reckner 2002); thus, the legacies of these labor relations were not specific to the geographical area whose needs were fed by the products of labor. In this way the peripheries of mining and milling regions of the West were integral to the existence of urban and industrial cores of San Francisco and the East Coast (McGuire and Reckner 2002). Closer contextualization of the economic contributions of Chinese railroad workers in California and Nevada shows such multiscalar and class-based dynamics and paints a rich picture of their lived experiences in these settings.

From the Central Pacific Railroad to the Periphery

Many Chinese workers in Virginia City and the Comstock may have ended up there by happenstance after losing their employment on the Central Pacific Railroad (CPRR) as the railroad reached Reno in 1868. The ways that they made opportunities for themselves in this place may highlight their agency and resistance, pushing back against the difficult labor dynamics of their situation. Because labor unions used leverage to bid against Chinese employment in mining companies, many skilled Chinese crews opted for work on the nearby Virginia & Truckee Railroad (V&TRR) line from Reno to Carson City and Virginia City (Figure 2) (Magnaghi 1981:137; James 2012:43). Unemployed Chinese from the CPRR were hired at such a rate that initially 300 Chinese were employed in 15 work camps along the line, and plans called for increasing that number to 1,000 (Magnaghi 1981:152; Furnis and Maniery, this issue).

The V&TRR Company was managed locally by Henry M. Yerington and controlled by William Ralston, Darius O. Mills, William Sharon, and Thomas Bell on behalf of the Bank of California and wealthy mining investors of the Union Mill & Mining Company (Beebe and Clegg 1950; Piatt 2003:134). Opportunities for high-return investment in this part of the West relied heavily on flexibility and agility in connecting existing infrastructure with boomtowns, as new strikes paid out. Because Yerington's new short line acted as just such a spur line

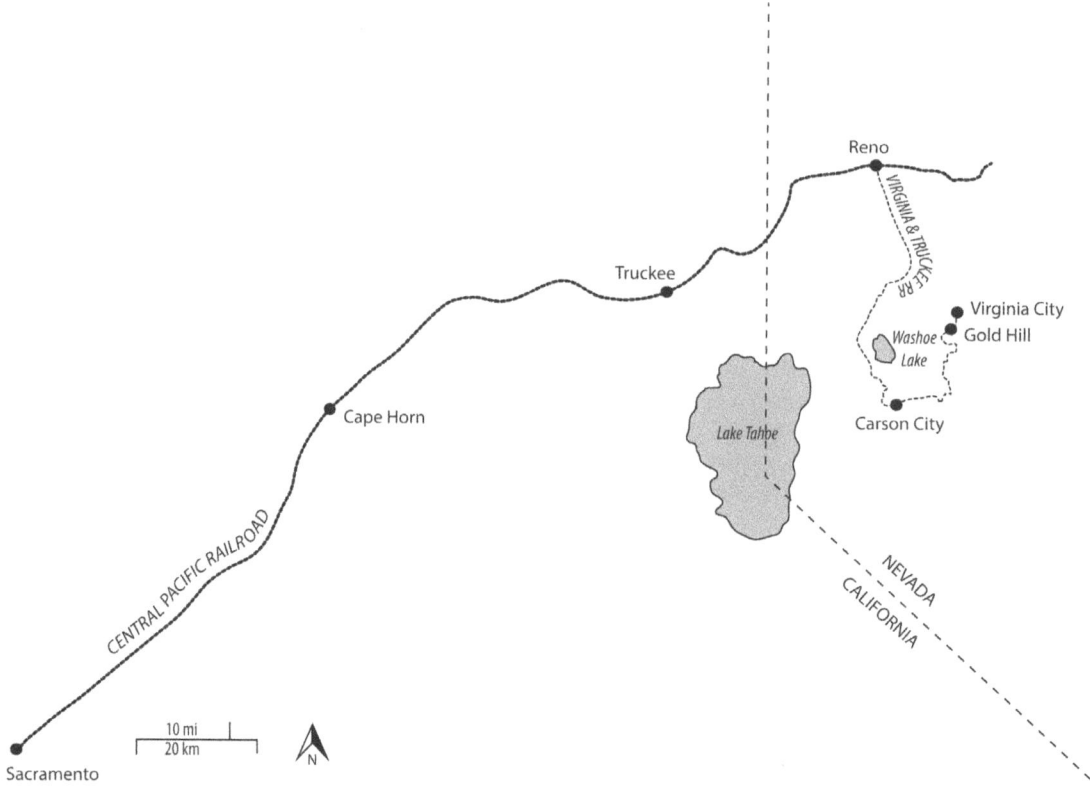

FIGURE 2. The Central Pacific Railroad and the Comstock's Virginia & Truckee Railroad. (Drawing by author, 2014.)

from the CPRR, it had tremendous payoffs on the order of $100,000 per month. The investors took those proceeds and began other projects, including the nearby Carson & Colorado Railroad (C&CRR) (Beebe and Clegg 1950:31). Due to racialized employment limitations for Chinese in the mines (James 2012:43), the strong economic ties between Yerington and the managers of former CPRR crews were likely established during this V&TRR project.

Across the Comstock, economic opportunities became more limited in 1877 as several mines failed and were shut down. Hundreds of miners and laborers were unemployed in Virginia City, Gold Hill, and Silver City around this time, and most set their sights on the boomtown of Bodie, California (Piatt 2003:53). Both economic struggles and racial violence against the Chinese around this time—culminating in 1875 in a major Chinatown fire—resulted in the departure of many Chinese from Virginia City (James 2012:44). At the same time, the growing Bodie Chinatown was reportedly smaller only than that of California's capital at

Sacramento (Cain 1961:157), as many Chinese relocated to the south.

Tracking individual Chinese laborers in historical settings can be difficult. However, the census of the Bodie region in 1900 included 26 Chinese who immigrated to the United States before the end of transcontinental railroad construction. At least 49 who arrived between passage of the Burlingame Treaty of 1868 and its amendment in 1880 are also recorded (U.S. Federal Census 1900). There are notorious inconsistencies in census enumeration of the Chinese population in this era, and nearly 90% of the Chinese counted in Bodie in 1880 are not named individually, but listed as "Chinamen." Other scholars cite the predominance of data to indicate that Bodie's Chinese population was transplanted from Virginia City in 1878 (Wedertz 1969:36). This mass migration from the Comstock to Bodie strongly suggests that some Bodie Chinese shared common histories of laboring for the CPRR and Virginia City capitalists prior to relocation to the south. An even stronger link between these places exists in the connections between those who hired Chinese laborers in Virginia City and future business ventures in Bodie and the California/Nevada Mono Basin.

Documentary Evidence for Chinese Labor in Railroads and Mills

Referred to as "Green Gold" (Chung 2003), wood was the most under-acknowledged, yet critical, resource of the West. The resource was essential for railroad ties and mining-operation support, and as fuel. Built in a location with virtually no timber to exploit, Bodie was at the mercy of overland wood freighters who charged up to $20/cord in March 1880 (Wedertz 1969:157). To satisfy this need for lumber, a company headed by Comstock lumber tycoons Duane L. Bliss and Henry M. Yerington, along with Bodie Standard Mine shareholder Robert N. Graves, employed Chinese crews to build a narrow gauge from Bodie to the forests in the south and a mill town therein (Figure 3) (Piatt 2003:134). Mono Mills, California, began operation in August 1881 and started by cutting ties for the coming railroad (Yerington 1883). Many of these same crews would maintain the rail line and work at various positions in the new community around Mono Mills (Wedertz 1969:155; Piatt 2003).

Yerington's personal business papers include payments made to Chinese individuals who worked in his service, and most likely to managers or labor organizers of Chinese railroad crews from the V&TRR work. The 1875 payments of $85.00 to Ah Gee of Carson, Nevada, for three weeks of service; $30.00 to launderer Sam King of Carson; and $59.75 to servant Jim Chou were signed with Chinese characters by these individuals (Yerington 1883). Although a relationship between individuals, such as Gee, and the crews of workers on Yerington's projects is not yet fully documented, the notes represent payments for multiple workers'

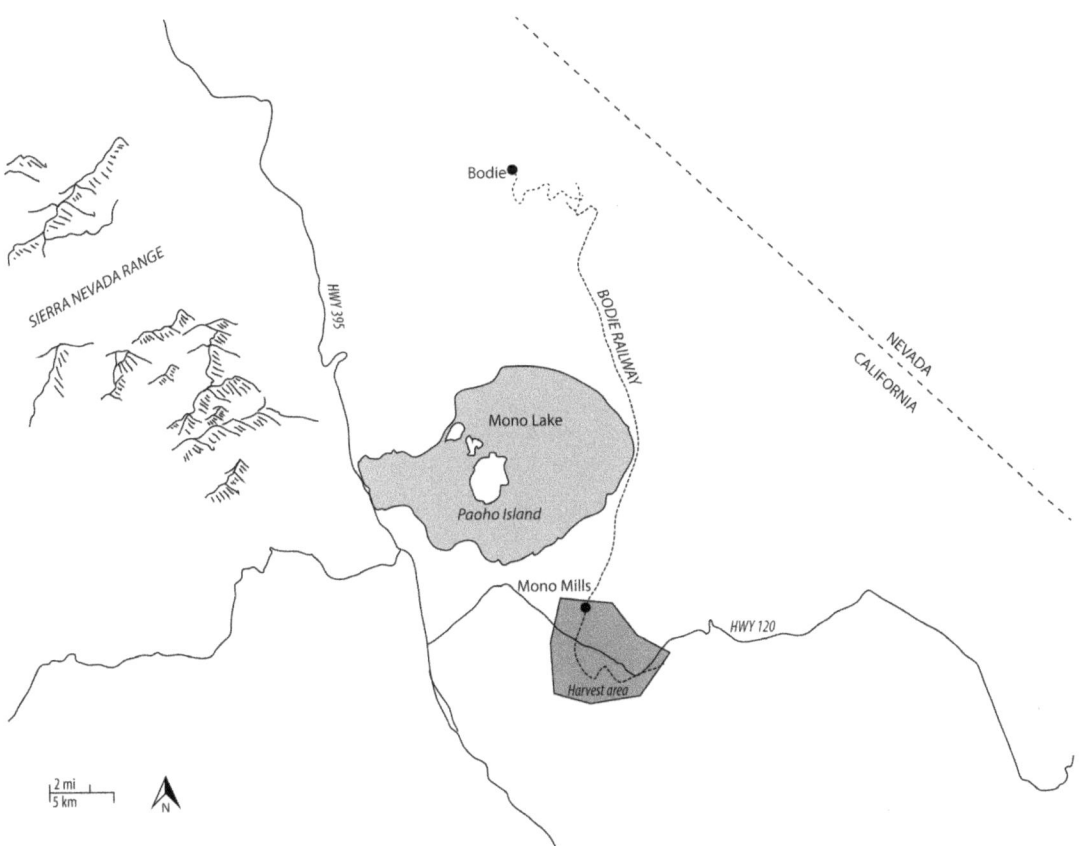

FIGURE 3. The 32 mi. Bodie Railroad from the main mines to Mono Mills in the south. (Drawing by author, 2014.)

wages over multiple days—as a comparison, an estimate of the going rate for the labor of a Chinese worker on the Bodie Railroad in 1880 was $1.25/day with board (Wedertz 1969:159). Future research may elaborate the persistence of labor structures from the CPRR to V&TRR to Mono Mills. It is expected that Yerington's preference for these workers was also in line with the general key attributes for Chinese-laborer selection on the transcontinental and other railroads more generally: their cooperation, capacity for hard work, and perseverance (McGowan 2005).

Archival evidence suggests that Yerington's regional railroads were interconnected by a shared labor force. Previous employment connections undoubtedly structured Yerington's selection of Chinese crews for the Bodie Railroad, as many of the Chinese who had made the move from Virginia City to Bodie likely had railroad experience with the V&TRR and CPRR. Chinese laborers were shared between the Bodie Railroad Company and the C&CRR in summer 1881. Despite the visibility of bringing on more Chinese workers while Bodie labor unions rioted to keep jobs in their hands, Yerington offered to send 60 more Chinese laborers from the Comstock to join the crews at Mono Mills in July 1881. Similar structuring of labor for even simple jobs, such as painting company buildings in Bodie, were handled by sending trusted laborers from Carson City (Yerington 1883). The labor needs were met by an agreement between the Bodie Railroad and Hop Sing Freight & Toll Company, which provided more Chinese laborers in exchange for freight deliveries between Hawthorne and Virginia City, Nevada, and San Francisco (Yerington 1883). For the Chinese communities, survival in an increasingly hostile national context meant strategic mobilization of their knowledge of capitalist employers with stakes in mining activities and commerce.

Yerington and his fellow investors likely intended the Bodie Railroad to function much like the V&TRR, which had extended the productivity of Virginia City by opening it to new markets and commerce via the CPRR. Bodie was expected to become a railroad town as many lines planned to make it there—including the Nevada & Oregon Railroad, California & Nevada Company, C&CRR (Wedertz 1969),

and the V&TRR (Watson and Brodie 2000)—but never did. Although isolated from other rail lines, the final 32 mi. trek from Bodie to Mono Mills provided vital jobs, as well as lumber and fuel to maintain the growth of Bodie (Yerington 1883).

The Chinese on the Periphery of Urban Life and Society

Despite their critical economic contributions and connections to long-term employers, the Chinese on the Comstock and in Bodie still occupied positions on the periphery of society. Much of the justification of racist treatment of the Chinese in this era was embedded within discourse about the state of the economy and the struggles experienced in the daily lives of European American middle and lower classes. The economic downturn in the West had as much to do with failures of some of the largest mines as it did the introduction of cheaply made goods from the eastern United States via the transcontinental railroad. These eastern U.S. goods made California companies noncompetitive, although the railroad was originally expected to introduce prosperity to California and the West (Wey 1988:114). Further, national trends in discrimination and legislation were contextualized by criticism that Chinese Americans "worked too hard ... saved too much, and spent too little" (McClain 1996:10).

As the Chinese were increasingly targeted as scapegoats for the general economic downturn, violence against their communities increased. Chinese experienced harassment and arson, such as when Virginia City's Chinatown was burned down in 1875 (James 2012:44). Similarly, Bodie's Chinese exclusion coincided with the decline of the silver and gold mines in 1881–1882 (Sprague 2003). The Chinese laborers in Bodie were assaulted and chased to the outskirts of town during a race riot in 1881. Tellingly, these individuals were rescued by Yerington's men, who ferried them to safety on Paoha Island in Mono Lake until tensions died down (Wedertz 1969:158; Wey 1988:141). Similar acts to protect Chinese employees include the payment of $69.50 by the railroad company for the release of arrested Chinese men in June 1881 (Yerington 1883). After their rescue on Paoha Island, many of the Bodie

Chinese moved their community to the grow-ing Chinatown in Mono Mills at the other end of the rail line. This transplantation to Mono Mills reveals aspects of trust between Yering-ton and his Chinese railroad crews, despite the broader context of the Chinese Exclusion Act of 1882 and the political support this law had among capitalists who hired the Chinese.

The Chinese in the Mono Basin experi-enced local exclusion and racism most heav-ily during their removal to Mono Mills from Bodie in 1881 and again in 1882, when they were denied citizenship and voting rights at a national level. Attempting to limit their eco-nomic opportunities locally, a Mono County grand jury ordered opium dens closed by law in 1885 (Watson and Brodie 2000:169). To further marginalize the Chinese in the Mono Basin, throughout the 1880s and 1890s news-papers described them as unsavory elements of society. Mono County stories were widely reported in distant newspapers when they pre-sented negative portrayals of Chinese, often depicting them as dangerous characters; e.g., the story of the mysterious death of Poker Tom after gambling at the establishment of merchant Ah Tia (*Denver Rocky Mountain News* 1891; *San Diego Union* 1891).

While anti−African American rhetoric and laws from antebellum America were duplicated within the context of California and national discriminatory legislation, the racial hierarchy of labor was not disrupted, but in fact reified by the hiring of Chinese. These laborers did jobs others were unwilling to do and accom-modated supervisory opportunities for their white counterparts (Aarim-Heriot 2003:10,80). Each part of the Mono Mills community had a specific role in the development and maintenance of the railroad. The Paiute used their knowledge of the Mono Basin land-scape to scout and plan the railroad location and maintain the line. The Chinese provided numerous trained laborers for the railroad, mill, and service industries. Chinese men were also assisted in their growing culinary reputa-tions as boardinghouse cooks (Billeb 1968) by their new community partners, the Mono Lake Paiute, who knew the local culinary resources of the region and could procure new foods for the cooks (Sunseri 2012). European Americans used their sociopolitical power to leverage racialized agendas for the economies of the West and imposed an "American" social structure.

One's job was determined as much from ethnic background as from skill or training, yet strategic alliances that crosscut those racialized categories were mobilized by all groups. In labor-based intercultural encounters, interactions between Chinese and non-Chinese were structured by skill, class, and occupation (Voss 2005). It is likely that alliance strategies worked to increase tensions between labor-ers—who were highly skilled yet discriminated against on the basis of ethnicity and race—and wealthy capitalists such as Yerington, who prof-ited from their labor while supporting legisla-tion and social pressures to diminish laborers' social and political rights. Thus, the fidelity and trust that may have been established between railroad investors like Yerington and his crews in the V&TRR or C&CRR prior to the Bodie Railway were likely influenced by these national dynamics of labor and power in which the Chinese participated.

Materiality of Daily Life and Alliances

While archival records provide Yerington's perspective on Chinese crews in his employ, researchers must look to the archaeology of their households to understand better Chinese experiences in this labor setting. The Mono Mills archaeological collection has resulted from excavations and surveys conducted by the U.S. Forest Service Passport in Time Project in 1988 and a San Jose State University field school in 2012. The latter project identified and excavated at least three distinct households and associated features for waste disposal (Figure 4). The resulting collection of cataloged arti-facts suggests that Chinese−Native American alliances at Mono Mills are materially visible through economic interactions through such items as food, ceramics, and flaked cutting edges made of obsidian and glass bottles. The evidence for tools used and foods consumed in each household provides one perspective on economies shared by ethnic groups.

Members of the field school excavated a discrete household in the Chinatown neigh-borhood (Figure 5) comprised of a mound of Bishop tuff (a local building material for

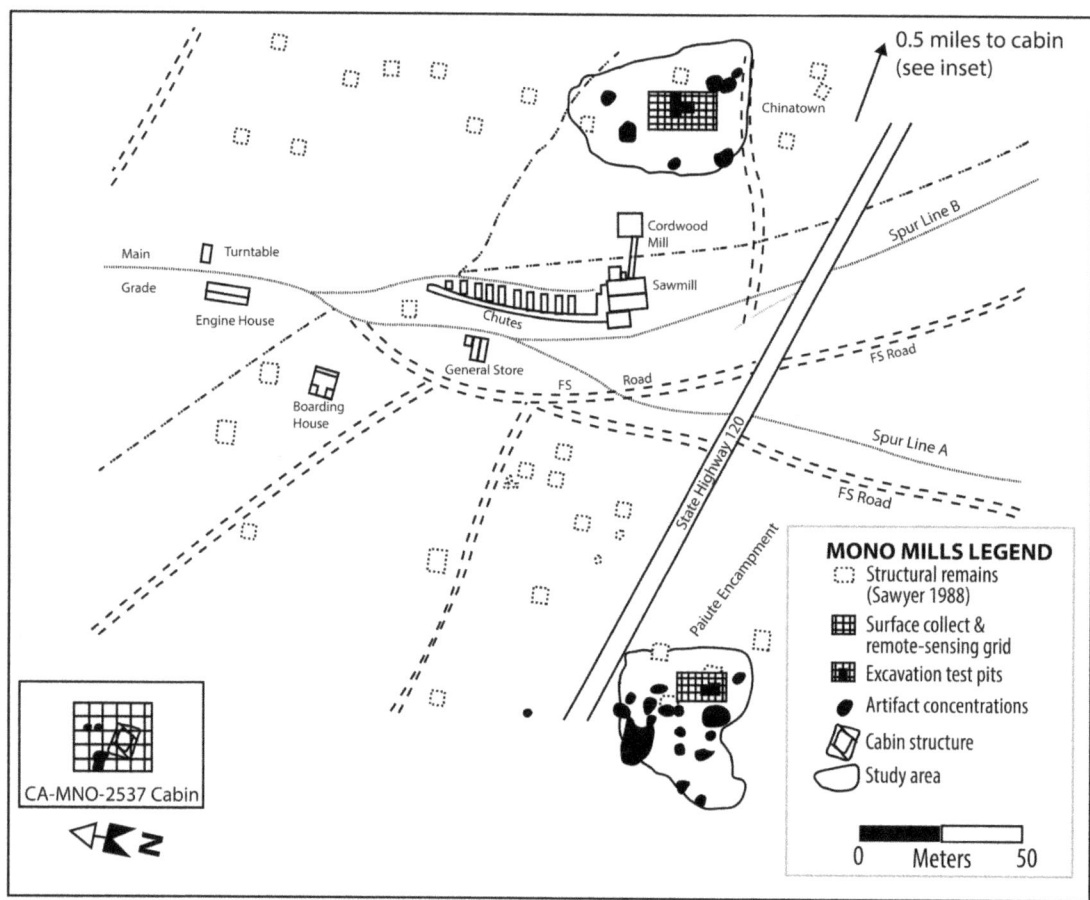

FIGURE 4. Site map of archaeological investigations during 2012 field season, adapted from Sawyer (1988). (Drawing by author, 2014.)

foundations and fireplaces or other masonry structures), window glass, milled wood, and household debris. Research focused on this locale to understand materials associated with daily life and use of space. Archaeologists and students excavated a deep privy or midden adjacent to the structure containing charcoal, faunal remains, cans, bottles, a washbasin, and a wooden barrel. This Chinatown household excavation recovered a large cache of pine nuts (Figure 6), a resource that 19th-century Paiute harvested and sold widely. Other food remains include those of cuttlefish, industrial cuts of beef, pork, and chickens, supplemented with locally available wild game, fowl, and fish. Artifacts associated with food processing and consumption include flaked bottle glass, particularly colorless forms, along with flakes and nodules of obsidian; blue-and-white

Chinese-made porcelains of Four Flowers and Bamboo designs; Celadon bowls and cups; and British-made ironstone plates. Many sherds of brown-glazed stoneware vessels were recovered. Hellman and Yang (2013) identify these as *nga hu* (spouted jar) and *tsao tsun* (liquor bottle) forms, traditionally used to transport and store soy sauce, other condiments, and liquors used in Chinese cuisine.

Participants in the field school also excavated features associated with a cabin (Figure 7) still standing toward the eastern end of the Chinatown neighborhood (Site CA-MNO-2537). This research clearly delineated interior and exterior household features. The cabin was surrounded by circular scatters of household artifacts likely resulting from looting pits previously excavated across the site. Archaeologists could not identify any discrete trash midden or privy.

FIGURE 5. Excavations at a discrete household in the Mono Mills Chinatown. (Photo by author, 2012.)

Materials recovered include *fut how nga peng* (wide-mouthed jar) vessels, traditionally associated with tofu, sweet-bean paste, beans, pickled vegetables, shrimp paste, sugar, and condiments (Hellmann and Yang 2013), along with Chinese-made porcelains, and flaked bottle glass.

The final household researched by the field school was located in the Paiute neighborhood of Mono Mills, segregated spatially from the neighborhood of Chinese townsfolk. The use of space in households of the Paiute neighborhood shows a marked difference in domestic activities and trash disposal compared to the cabin or households in the Chinatown. Archaeological investigation identified workspaces for basket making and potential house-floor features adjacent to associated concentrations of milled wood debris. The study did not identify discrete

FIGURE 6. Cache of pine nuts recovered from the Mono Mills Chinatown household. (Photo by author, 2014.)

middens or privies for household trash disposal. Much less trash and fewer artifacts characterized this site: beads for basketry, a Chinese-made porcelain spoon of Four Flowers design, ironstone vessel sherds, complete cans and bottles, and a finished tool made of bottle glass.

Textual references to material interactions between Paiute and Chinese laborers include alleged gifts of prime-cut steaks from Chinese cooks to their Paiute friends (Billeb 1968). Archaeological research also reveals exchange of locally harvested pine nuts and Chinese imported porcelain, as well as use of flaked obsidian and glass artifacts in Chinatown households. Such exchanges of food and items from daily life suggest how familiarity between the ethnic groups likely provided opportunities for shared material culture. These items from daily life suggest the ways that alliances

between Chinese and Paiute individuals were one way both groups negotiated Mono Mill's labor regime (Silliman 2001, 2005) and lived through the racism of this system. These interactions broadly exemplify the materiality of resistance to labor structures imposed on the Chinese in this era and the agency to build a community in this difficult setting. These preliminary studies show extensive similarity in the material culture of households investigated in the Paiute neighborhood and Chinatown, and suggest interethnic coalitions.

Resistance through Social and Economic Agency

Vertical relationships established between Chinese crews and capitalists who hired them, such as Yerington, were fundamental

FIGURE 7. Cabin (CA-MNO-2537) at the east end of the Mono Mills Chinatown. (Photo by author, 2012.)

to their employment and to some extent their geographic representation across the West. Alliances established horizontally with other laborers functioned to ensure longevity of their positions in emerging pluralistic societies, including those at Bodie and Mono Mills. In particular, relationships with other marginalized groups, such as Native Americans and African Americans, were established on a foundation of similar social standing, labor positions, and mutual survivorship in the European American world. Anecdotes by Jin Mun suggest that some Chinese building the railroads were protected from raids by local tribes because of the shared affinity for long braided hair, or queues (Chinn 1989:72), while other narratives explain Chinese–Native American alliances more by mutual vulnerability than similar aesthetic— such as narratives of the Karuk of the Klamath River, who protectively hid Chinese from white oppressors (Pfealzer 2008:20).

Because of the histories of migration and employment between the Comstock and Bodie, the Chinese interacted with many communities of Northern Paiute from Virginia City (including the tribes from Walker Lake, Winnemucca and Pyramid lakes, Carson Desert, and Mason and Smith valleys) to Bodie/Mono Mills (including Bridgeport and Mono Lake tribes). Marriages between Chinese men and Paiute women were not uncommon in Nevada (Chung 1998:223, 2011b:140), such as that between Sam Leon and Daisy Benton of Schurz, Nevada. Exemplifying the regional networks illustrated by these relationships, the couple resided in Bodie, and Sam later died in Reno (Chung 2011a).

Social agency to resist the roles and lives expected by their European American counterparts is a vital aspect of Chinese experience in California. While relationships were structured by national exclusionary laws limiting the immigration of Chinese women and California antimiscegenation laws outlawing Chinese/white marriage after 1880, there were existing patterns of Chinese/Paiute marriage in Nevada since at least 1870 (Chung 2011b:140). The presence of many Chinese women and children in Virginia City in 1870 (James 2012:44) indicates families on the Comstock. These Chinese were not merely sojourners, but were trying to make an immigrant community in the place (Chung 1998).

Half the Chinese women in the 1880 Bodie census were reportedly married, although no children were listed (Wey 1988:140). The presence of at least two husband/wife pairs in Bodie's 1880 Chinatown and the married status of 67% of Chinese individuals in the 1900 Bodie census—with the average duration of marriage reaching the silver anniversary—suggests the marital status of many Chinese men in this community, but does little to clarify whether their families resided in Bodie (U.S. Federal Census 1880, 1900). Other scholars suggest that many Chinese men likely left their wives and families in large urban Chinatowns, like those of Sacramento or San Jose, that were deemed safer than lawless mining towns of the Comstock or Bodie (Chung 1998:204).

Although not documented by the census, archaeology of the Mono Mills Chinatown suggests the potential for the presence of family groups and children in this labor setting. A toy tea set recovered from a Chinatown household reflects play in a working-class context (Yamin 2002), as well as types of play in which children in the Chinatown may have participated. Further studies may verify that the Bodie/ Mono Mills Chinese community has the potential to be described similarly as an immigrant community—rather than by a male-sojourner narrative—as laborers resisted the social lives and roles imposed on them by their European American neighbors.

Mining Towns' Participation in Broader Economies

The economic lives of people of the railways, Comstock, and Bodie were intimately linked in the late 19th century. The interconnected webs of Chinese labor crews, their European American and Native American counterparts, powerful capitalists who employed them, and the products of their labor are important articulations in understanding labor and class structures.

The regional economies of the Comstock included the flow of commercial goods as much as the networks of laborers. The business

papers of Henry Yerington include shipping bills that indicate a long-term business partnership between the regional railroads and Hop Sing Freight (Yerington 1883). While the goods or services purchased for Mono Mills from Hop Sing Freight are not listed, Hop Sing was a leading, wealthy merchant in the Virginia City Chinatown who sold pork and Chinese delicacies to white patrons (Magnaghi 1981:138). Correspondence with the crew manager at Bodie Railroad indicates that Hop Sing provided Chinese laborers, likely on a temporary basis, to aid in railroad construction (Yerington 1883). The purchase of goods from this vendor to supply his Chinese workers would link Yerington's capital to the broader operation of Chinese companies on the Comstock that ran stores, controlled the labor force, and facilitated the payment of debts by wealthy individuals in Virginia City's Chinatown (Magnaghi 1981:148). The provisioning of Mono Mills Chinese laborers reveals links to the broader political economy of western mining towns.

The duplication of capitalist investors (including Yerington, Bliss, Graves, and Ralston) among the V&TRR, the C&CRR, and the Bodie & Benton Railway & Lumber Company further suggests the linkages between Mono Mills and broader economies of the West and across the United States (Wedertz 1969:159; Piatt 2003:134). The products of Chinese labor are linked to regional scales of economies due to the paired nature of the relationship between railroad crews and this group of investors whose projects ranged across the West. More broadly, the financing of these railroad projects links labor on the mining periphery to powerful investors and banks in San Francisco and New York. The archaeology of the spaces lived in and labored on by the Chinese shows the social impact of national economics and immigration policy that acted at a much larger scale than the local experiences of the laborers or those whose needs were fed by the lumber and other products of their labor.

Conclusion

Considering the dynamism, range, and scale of their considerable contributions to the development of the West, it is unsuitable to describe all Chinese immigrants in the 19th century as members of "an amorphous coolie mass" (McGowan 2005:136). Not only were the experiences of these communities dissimilar across the West, but the opportunities afforded to and created by individuals on this difficult social landscape were met in various ways with agency and resistance, as well as with hardship. The texture provided by a case study of Chinese laborers on the Comstock and in Bodie provides an illustration of the paths some Central Pacific Railroad workers took as they made lives for themselves and their families in the West.

Virginia City and Bodie and their famous bonanzas were possible only because of Chinese workers and the expertise they supplied to the railroad and lumber industries. This is in stark contrast to the tensions inherent in their contributions to the growing national economy during one of the most devastating and wide-ranging eras of racialized violence and injustice (Hsu 2000). The likelihood that Yerington, a capitalist who managed the V&TRR crews, relocated some of his trusted Chinese crews to his next venture at the Bodie Railroad sets a stage for the community these laborers built at Bodie and Mono Mills. This dynamic illustrates that the labor relations and class structures experienced by these Chinese operated at broad, national scales, as well as at local company scales (McGuire and Reckner 2002), and were not only specific to the geographical area whose needs were fed by the products of their labor.

Documentary evidence for Chinese labor contexts, along with an emerging archaeological study of their materially lived experiences, is needed to flesh out fully the complexity of Chinese experiences in Bodie and Mono Mills. When it served them, the powerful capitalists who employed Chinese laborers found occasions to protect them from racialized violence. Material data from recent archaeological investigations suggest that, while labor opportunities of Chinese were structured by their ethnicity and class, their abilities to ally themselves with other marginalized groups created new and diverse social and economic opportunities. Chinese and Paiute townsfolk likely exchanged locally available foods—including pine nuts, fish, fowl, and large game—along with Chinese imported porcelain, flaked obsidian, and flaked-glass artifacts.

Cross-cultural exchanges of food and items from daily life link ethnic groups through a shared material culture. More generally, the histories of these Chinese workers with Paiute tribes on the Comstock had far-ranging impacts on their experience in this new setting. The interactions between Chinese workers and the Mono Lake Paiute changed their social and economic opportunities in what would otherwise have been a European American social world. Their agency in the face of what might seem to be insurmountable legal constraints and racialized violence of the Gilded Age provides an important perspective on the Chinese experience in this era.

Acknowledgments

Special thanks to Barbara Voss, Rebecca Allen, Jun Sunseri, and four anonymous reviewers for valuable comments on previous versions of this manuscript that greatly improved this article. Archaeological data for this article is the result of the 2012 SJSU field project conducted in collaboration with the Mono Lake Kutzadika'a Paiute Indian Community, as well as faunal-analysis research completed by Alexandra Levin.

References

AARIM-HERIOT, NAJIA
  2003   *Chinese Immigrants, African Americans, and Racial Anxiety in the United States, 1848–82*. University of Illinois Press, Urbana.

BAXTER, R. SCOTT
  2002   Industrial and Domestic Landscapes of a California Oil Field. *Historical Archaeology* 36(4):18–27.

BEEBE, LUCIUS, AND CHARLES CLEGG
  1950   *Legends of the Comstock Lode*. Stanford University Press, Stanford, CA.

BILLEB, EMIL W.
  1968   *Mining Camp Days*. Howell-North, Berkeley, CA.

BURKE, HEATHER
  1999   *Meaning and Ideology in Historical Archaeology: Style, Social Identity and Capitalism in an Australian Town*. Kulwer Academic/Plenum, New York, NY.

CAIN, ELLA M.
  1961   *The Story of Early Mono County*. Fearon, San Francisco, CA.

CASELLA, ELEANOR CONLIN
2005   "Social Workers": New Directions in Industrial
        Archaeology. In *Industrial Archaeology: Future
        Directions*, Eleanor Conlin Casella and James
        Symonds, editors, pp. 3–31. Springer, New York, NY.

CHINN, THOMAS W.
1989   *Bridging the Pacific: San Francisco Chinatown and
        Its People*. Chinese Historical Society of America,
        San Francisco, CA.

CHUNG, SUE FAWN
1998   Their Changing World: Chinese Women on the
        Comstock, 1860–1910. In *Comstock Women: The
        Making of a Mining Community*, Ronald M. James
        and C. Elizabeth Raymond, editors, pp. 203–228.
        University of Nevada Press, Reno.
2003   The Chinese and Green Gold: Lumbering in the
        Sierras. Report to Humboldt-Toiyabe National Forest,
        Carson Ranger District, Passport in Time, Carson
        City, NV, from University of Nevada, Las Vegas.
2011a   *The Chinese in Nevada*. Arcadia, Charleston, SC.
2011b   *In Pursuit of Gold: Chinese American Miners and
        Merchants in the American West*. University of Illinois
        Press, Urbana.

DENVER ROCKY MOUNTAIN NEWS
1891   No More Poker Tom. *Denver Rocky Mountain
        News* 11 June:1. GenealogyBank.com <http://
        www.genealogybank.com/gbnk/newspapers/doc/
        v2:12C601A5C4.html>. Accessed 14 August 2012.

GILLESPIE, WILLIAM B., AND MARY M. FARRELL
2002   Work Camp Settlement Patterns: Landscape-Scale
        Comparisons of Two Mining Camps in Southeastern
        Arizona. *Historical Archaeology* 36(3):59–68.

HARDESTY, DONALD
2002   Commentary: Interpreting Variability and Change
        in Western Work Camps. *Historical Archaeology*
        36(3):94–98.

HELLMANN, RAY S., AND JEANNIE K. YANG
2013   What's in the Pot? Chinese Brown-Glazed Stoneware
        Identification. In *Ceramic Identification in Historical
        Archaeology: The View from California, 1822–1940*,
        R. Allen, J. E. Huddleson, K. J. Wooten, and G. J.
        Farris, editors, pp. 227–230. Society for Historical
        Archaeology, Germantown, MD.

HSU, MADELINE Y.
2000   *Dreaming of Home, Dreaming of Gold*. Stanford
        University Press, Stanford, CA.

JAMES, RONALD M.
2012   *Virginia City: Secrets of a Western Past*. University
        of Nebraska Press, Lincoln.

MAGNAGHI, RUSSEL M.
1981   Virginia City's Chinese Community, 1860–1880.
        Nevada Historical Society Quarterly 24(2):130–157.

MANIERY, MARY L.
2002   Health, Sanitation, and Diet in a Twentieth-Century
        Dam Construction Camp: A View from Butt Valley,
        California. In *Communities Defined by Work: Life in
        Western Work Camps*, Thad M. Van Bueren, editor.
        Thematic issue, *Historical Archaeology* 36(3):69–84.

MCCLAIN, CHARLES J.
1996   *In Search of Equality*. University of California Press,
        Berkeley.

MCGOWAN, BARRY
2005   The Economics and Organisation of Chinese Mining
        in Colonial Australia. *Australian Economic History
        Review* 45(2):119–138.

MCGUIRE, RANDALL H., AND PAUL RECKNER
2002   The Unromantic West: Labor, Capital, and Struggle.
        Historical Archaeology 36(3):44–58.

PFEALZER, JEAN
2008   *Driven Out: The Forgotten War against Chinese
        Americans*. Random House, New York, NY.

PIATT, MICHAEL H.
2003   *Bodie: "The Mines Are Looking Well."* North Bay,
        El Sobrante, CA.

SAITTA, DEAN J.
1994   Agency, Class, and Archaeological Interpretation.
        Journal of Anthropological Archaeology 13:201–227.

SAN DIEGO UNION
1891   A Mono County Sensation. *San Diego Union* 18 June:3.
        GenealogyBank.com <http://www.genealogybank
        .com/gbnk/newspapers/doc/v2:136E6CD2B>.
        Accessed 14 August 2012.

SAWYER, WILLIAM A.
1988   A History and Evaluation of the Mono Mills
        Railroad Logging District, Inyo National Forest,
        California, Report No. MN-01008. Report to United
        States Department of Agriculture, Bishop, from
        Archaeological Advisory Group, Newport Beach,
        CA. Manuscript, Department of Anthropology,
        Eastern Information Center, University of California,
        Riverside.

SHACKEL, PAUL A.
2004   Labor's Heritage: Remembering the American
        Industrial Landscape. *Historical Archaeology*
        38(4):44–58.

SILLIMAN, STEPHEN W.
2001   Theoretical Perspectives on Labor and Colonialism:
        Reconsidering the California Missions. *Journal of
        Anthropological Anthropology* 20:379–407.
2005   Culture Contact or Colonialism? Challenges in the
        Archaeology of Native North America. *American
        Antiquity* 70(1):55–74.
2006   Struggling with Labor, Working with Identities. In
        Historical Archaeology, M. Hall and S. Silliman,
        editors, pp. 147–166. Blackwell, Malden, MA.

SPRAGUE, MARGUERITE
    2003 *Bodie's Gold.* University of Nevada Press, Reno.

SUNSERI, CHARLOTTE K.
    2012 Rising above Anti-Chinese Sentiment on the California Mining Frontier. Paper presented at the Annual Meeting of the American Anthropological Association, San Francisco, CA.

U.S. FEDERAL CENSUS
    1880 Mono County, CA. Microfilm publication T623, Roll 69, National Archives, San Bruno, CA.
    1900 Mono County, CA. Microfilm publication T623, Roll 94, National Archives, San Bruno, CA.

VAN BUEREN, THAD M.
    2002 Struggling with Class Relations at a Los Angeles Aqueduct Construction Camp. In *Communities Defined by Work: Life in Western Work Camps,* Thad M. Van Bueren, editor. Thematic issue, *Historical Archaeology* 36(3):28–43.

VOSS, BARBARA L.
    2005 From Casta to Californio: Social Identity and the Archaeology of Culture Contact. *American Anthropologist* 107(3):461–474.

VOSS, BARBARA L., AND REBECCA ALLEN
    2008 Overseas Chinese Archaeology: Historical Foundations, Current Reflections, and New Directions. *Historical Archaeology* 42(3):5–28.

WATSON, JAMES, AND DOUG BRODIE
    2000 *Big Bad Bodie: High Sierra Ghost Town.* Robert Reed, Bandon, OR.

WEDERTZ, FRANK S.
    1969 *Bodie 1859–1900.* Sierra Media, Bishop, CA.

WEY, NANCY
    1988 A History of Chinese Americans in California. In *Five Views: Ethnic Historic Site Survey of California,* pp. 104–158. California Department of Parks and Recreation, Office of Historic Preservation, Sacramento.

WURST, LOUANN
    1999 Internalizing Class in Historical Archaeology. *Historical Archaeology* 33(1):7–21.
    2006 A Class All Its Own: Explorations of Class Formation and Conflict. In *Historical Archaeology,* M. Hall and S. Silliman, editors, pp. 190–208. Blackwell, Malden, MA.

YAMIN, REBECCA
    2002 Children's Strikes, Parents' Rights: Paterson and Five Points. *International Journal of Historical Archaeology* 6(2):113–126.

YERINGTON, HENRY M.
    1883 Henry M. Yerington Papers. BANC MSS P-G 230, Bancroft Library, University of California, Berkeley.

CHARLOTTE K. SUNSERI
DEPARTMENT OF ANTHROPOLOGY
SAN JOSE STATE UNIVERSITY
CLARK HALL, SUITE 469
ONE WASHINGTON SQUARE
SAN JOSE, CA 95192-0113

Timothy R. Urbaniak (提摩太·乌班涅克)
Kelly J. Dixon (凯利·狄克逊)

Inscribed in Stone: Historic Inscriptions and the Cultural Heritage of Railroad Workers
石头记：铁路工人的历史碑铭与文化遗产

ABSTRACT

Historic inscriptions accompany rock art panels and sandstone cliffs throughout Montana and the North American plains. The two historic inscription locations described here emphasize the cultural and historical value of these provocative archaeological signatures. One of these includes a cliff face incised with Chinese characters near the Chicago, Milwaukee, St. Paul, & Pacific Railroad in southeastern Montana. The Chinese characters are among other historic inscriptions associated with a coal mining district established by that railroad to supply the fuel for its engines, underscoring the inherent connections between extractive industries and railroad rights-of-way. The second location includes a collection of Japanese words and names, as well as Irish and Norwegian names, incised into a sandstone cliff face adjacent to a section of the Northern Pacific Railroad. These inscribed archaeological sites represent text-aided resources that may be some of the only written accounts available to better understand the lives and identities of people in transnational work camps of railroads and associated extractive industries in the American West.

在蒙大拿州和北美平原的岩石画壁与沙岩悬崖上，历史碑铭四处可见。本文所描述的两处历史碑铭凸显了这些令人兴奋的考古学地标的文化与历史价值。其中一处碑铭刻有中文，靠近芝加哥、密尔沃基、圣保罗以及蒙大拿东南部的太平洋铁路。它们与为铁路提供燃料的煤矿相关，展现了冶金工业与铁路通行权之间的内在联系。第二处碑铭包含一系列日文、爱尔兰以及挪威的姓氏，均刻于靠近北太平洋铁路的一处沙岩悬崖上。这些考古学遗址为我们更好地理解在美国西部铁路以及相关冶金业的国际性劳工营内生活和工作的人，提供了可能是唯一的文字性资料。

Historic Inscriptions as Evidence of Labor and Identity

Historic inscriptions are a form of communication that includes names, dates, or other text, as well as images and symbolism, that are literally inscribed onto the sandstone formations that are among the iconic geographic features of the North American plains (Urbaniak 2014a). These inscriptions are often coexistent with or superimposed over communication commonly referred to as rock art. Long regarded as vandalism and graffiti, many of the historical period inscriptions are considered cultural resources under Section 106 of the National Historic Preservation Act and need to be documented in tandem with prehistoric pictographs and petroglyphs (Urbaniak and Rust 2009). These inscriptions include names and dates, and document activities in the region that encompass colonial exploration, the fur-trade industry, overland emigration, battles, homesteading, ranching, and railroad construction and maintenance. For example, William Clark's signature is one among several forms of communication carved onto the sandstone butte above the Yellowstone River in south-central Montana, at a site known today as Pompeys Pillar National Monument (Figure 1). (Most documentation for this site lacks the apostrophe, using "Pompeys" instead of "Pompey's.")

Pompeys Pillar is among the better known historic inscription sites on the North American plains. Clark's inscription: W^m. Clark, includes the date, 25 July 1806, and represents physical evidence of the Lewis and Clark expedition's route in an area where there is little evidence of the Corps of Discovery's journey through the region. There are numerous "prehistoric" petroglyphs at this site, and archaeological evidence indicates that the surrounding area has been used by humans for at least 11,000 years (MacDonald 2012). The indigenous northern-plains toponym for the sandstone pillar translates to "place where the mountain lion lies"; yet the site is known by a more modern place name given by William Clark in honor of Sacagawea's son (Jean Baptiste Charbonneau), whom Clark had nicknamed "Pomp," with the first iteration being "Pompy's Tower," later changed to "Pompey's Pillar," and now known as "Pompeys Pillar" (no apostrophe) (Aarstad et al. 2009:209).

Whether ancient or more modern, the messages and images left on the region's sandstone formations represent archaeological

Historical Archaeology, 2015, 49(1):100–109.
Permission to reprint required.

FIGURE 1. The inscription: W^m. Clark, July 25th, 1806 at Pompeys Pillar National Monument, south-central Montana. (Photo by Timothy R. Urbaniak, 2006.)

evidence of communication, and, in some cases, documentary evidence of identity, which is vital for archaeologies dedicated to people without histories. Urbaniak's (2014a) recent research represents the first systematic documentation and synthesis of the types of historical inscriptions on the North American plains and highlights the research potential of these textual and graphic archaeological resources. Although these inscriptions had undergone preliminary documentation before the authors even knew about the Chinese Railroad Workers in North America Project (CRWNAP), the CRWNAP Archaeology Network Workshop held in October 2013 at the Stanford Archaeology Center provided the inspiration and opportunity to report on two inscriptions with possible connections to railroad workers. Although not from a railroad right-of-way context, one is very likely associated with Chinese miners who worked in coal mines owned by the Pacific Coast extension of the Chicago, Milwaukee, & St. Paul Railroad, which eventually became known as the transcontinental Chicago, Milwaukee, St. Paul, & Pacific Railroad (Richards 1910:61).

The second, located on a cliff face adjacent to a Northern Pacific right-of-way, was initially reported as a Chinese inscription, but when reexamined for this project, we determined that it is actually Japanese. These Japanese inscriptions are associated with other inscriptions written by people with names that represent Irish and Norwegian heritage. When the authors learned of the scarcity of documents written by the thousands of Chinese and other railroad workers in the American West, the value of historic inscriptions for better understanding these diverse labor narratives became very apparent.

Railroads and Coal Mines

At this time, there is only one known historic inscription in Montana that includes Chinese characters (Figure 2). The initial translation suggests that these are traditional Chinese characters—as opposed to the post-1949

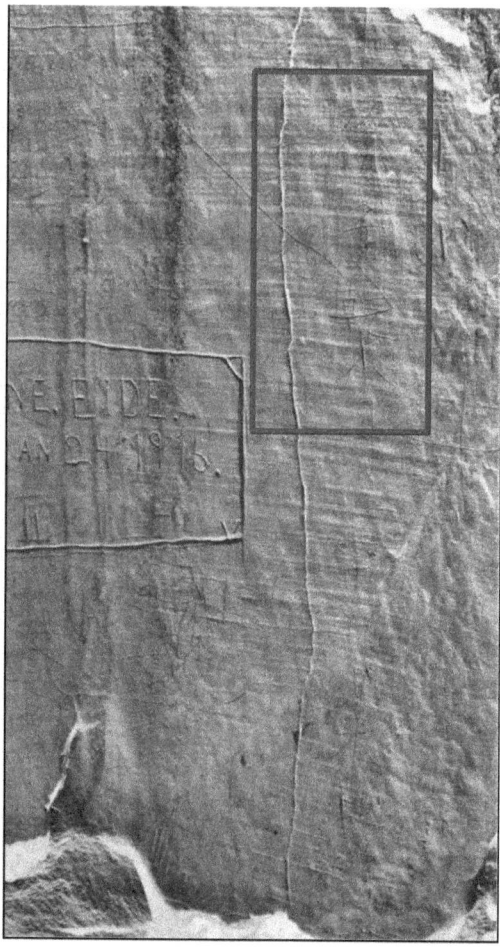

FIGURE 2. Chinese inscription on a sandstone cliff face near Roundup, Montana, dating to the area's coal-mining development, ca. 1906–1940. The image on the left is a close-up view of the Chinese inscription reading: "Sun Ziqian was here. August 29th." The image at the right shows the larger panel with neighboring, non-Chinese inscriptions; this is shown in negative image for legibility, and the Chinese characters are outlined by the rectangle. (Translation by Yanya Yang; photo and negative image by Timothy R. Urbaniak, 1999.)

simplified Chinese used in mainland China—that translate as: "Sun Ziqian was here. August 29th." "Sun" was this person's family name, and "Ziqian" was his given name (Yanya Yang 2011, pers. comm.). As to whether further research can connect this name and date with a specific Chinese individual remains to be proven. Rock art from before European contact indicates that this cliff has been used as a canvas for centuries, if not millennia. Historic inscriptions on this cliff face date from a period of coal-mining development that spanned the early 20th century (1906–1940s) in and around the community of Roundup in south-central Montana. Examples include:

Frenchie 1900 and John Lehuhmann, Germany, Bayern, Schipherdem. Among the scores of other names and dates, the cliff face also exhibits a hand-painted sign identifying one of the many coal mines in the area, suggesting that the individuals who created the historic inscriptions were involved with and likely worked in coal mines in the area.

Situated about 50 mi. (80 km) north of Billings, Montana, Roundup was given its modern place name in the 1880s when the area served as the location for an annual roundup of open-range cattle. In 1907, a coal mine and a new town, still called "Roundup," developed along the northern boundary of the old town.

Several other coal mines followed as part of a network supplying the railroads with coal (Richards 1910:80; Aarstad et al. 2009:231). The new town and coal mine developed with the arrival of the Chicago, Milwaukee, & Puget Sound Railway, which represented the Pacific Coast extension of the Chicago, Milwaukee, St. Paul, & Pacific Railroad (the Milwaukee Road) and was folded with the parent company in 1912. The Milwaukee Road ran directly through Roundup in 1908, with spur lines connecting the Republic & Roundup Coal Mining Company operations with that transcontinental railroad (Richards 1910:81; Lewis 1951:61–63); the cliff face with the inscriptions is situated approximately 11 mi. (17.7 km) from the Milwaukee Road.

The Milwaukee Road owned the coal mines, ensuring itself access to fossil fuels needed to power its engines; the surrounding Bull Mountain coalfield represented the "most promising source of coal supply for this new transcontinental road, a fact which led to its rapid development" (Richards 1910:61). The coal miners were thus working for the railroad company; very likely, many of the miners had previously worked for the same company as railroad construction workers. This is similar to the practice of the Central Pacific and Union Pacific Railroads (CPRR and UPRR) after the completion of the first transcontinental, where UPRR-owned coal mines in remote locations were staffed with workers recruited from the CPRR and UPRR construction crews (White 2011:294–295). Whether Sun Ziqian represented one of the former railroad workers hired into the mines of Roundup, Montana, remains unknown. The inscription's presence, nevertheless, draws attention to the fact that there were Chinese laborers who worked for the railroads in extractive industries that provided the fossil fuels to support the modern world's transportation requirements.

Richard White's (2011:507) point about railroads being the "epitome of the modern in the late 19th century" is important here, as it draws attention to the fact that the railroads were, technologically, "part of the move from muscle—human and animal—and wind power to steam and fossil fuels," such as coal. The railroads were also part of a "great wave of wage labor that largely eliminated slavery and indentured workers in North America and cut deeply into the ranks of independent producers" (White 2011:507). By presenting railroads as convergent with coal-mining companies and subsequently ushering in the modern world reliant on fossil fuels, the connections between extractive industrial sites and railroads cannot be overemphasized. Considering this context, the presence of Sun Ziqian in a coal-mining district is suggestive of the connections of Chinese laborers to extractive industrial satellites that were developed by and relied on railroads.

Chinese Exclusion and a Multiethnic Labor Force

The Northern Pacific Railroad (NPRR), the first railway to enter eastern Montana (Figure 3), was under construction by 1880 (Figure 4). Some of the individuals who worked along the railway carved names and dates on adjacent sandstone cliff faces, including a cliff face along the Yellowstone River (Urbaniak 2014b). Approximately 76 mi. (122 km) east of Billings, Montana, between the settlements of Big Horn and Hysham, a section of the railroad right-of-way runs between the river and a steep sandstone cliff (Figures 3 and 5). Several names and other information have been inscribed into the cliff face, including the dates 1889, 1890, 1893, 1899, 1911, and 1930. Due to the difficulty in getting to the site by any means other than the railway, these inscriptions were likely created by railroad workers, a conclusion supported by an English inscription (with an Irish name) that reads: CHAS. MACNEY\RUNN.SECTION\HERE.IN.1911 (Figure 6). In addition, there are names incised that represented a group of Norwegian railroad workers from Iowa (Roehr 1974).

Another set of inscriptions along the sandstone cliff at this site is written in kanji, a system of Japanese writing using Chinese-derived characters (Figure 7). In the first column on the right (Figure 7a) there is a date, which translates as "33rd year, April," which likely represents the Meiji period in Japan and indicates that the inscription was created between 1889 and April 1900. The Meiji period extended from September 1868 through July 1912 and corresponds to the first half of the Japanese Empire, when Japanese

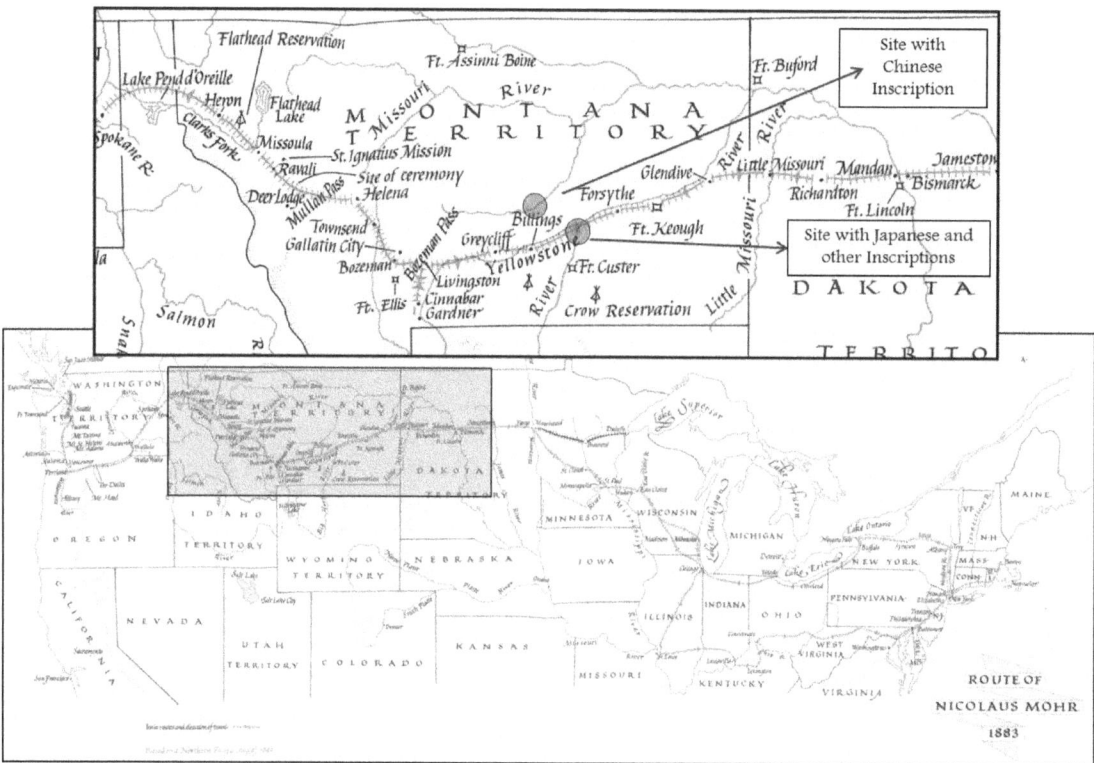

FIGURE 3. Map of NPRR route taken by Nicolaus Mohr during the 1883 Last Spike celebration (Mohr 1884). The route closely follows the NPRR line from St. Paul, Minnesota, to Seattle, Washington. The inset is an expanded view of the shaded areas, showing the NPRR in Montana in RR symbol lines and the general area of the Chicago, Milwaukee, St. Paul, & Pacific Railroad (the Milwaukee Road) in dashed lines, with the two locations of inscriptions described herein noted (Map modified by Kelly J. Dixon, 2014.)

society transitioned from a feudal system to its "modern" form. The second column from the right (Figure 7*b*) confirms this, with the characters for "Great Japan," and also for the inscriber's presumed place of origin, "Hiroshima Prefecture," a municipality or administrative district in the empire. In the third column from the right (Figure 7*c*), the same individual noted a county and village in the prefecture of Hiroshima: "Aza County, Midori [Village]." Established 1 October 1889, Midori'i Village is now part of Hiroshima City. The fourth column from the right (Figure 7*d*) includes a name, Matsutarō Toyōji. The surname Toyōji is found in Hiroshima. The column on the far left (Figure 7*e*), in the upper-left portion of the photo, includes another Japanese name: Yamato Tsuchiya (Mizuki Miyashita 2014, pers. comm.).

The Chinese Exclusion Act of 1882, along with the 1885 Alien Contract Labor Law, also known as the Foran Act, which banned all

contracts to import foreign workers for labor and service, forced labor contractors to be creative during an era when transcontinental railroad construction and operation were in desperate need of labor. Due to the exclusion of Chinese laborers during this period, these and other railroads sought laborers from other countries, including Japanese workers, who were told to lie upon entry into the United States to help the railroads keep their promise to observe the Foran Act (White 2011:303−304). Thus, the railroads worked around these legal barriers in various ways, with transcontinentals, such as the Union Pacific, the Southern Pacific, the Northern Pacific, and the Great Northern, competing for Japanese labor. This renders the Japanese inscription along the NPRR even more significant, since it provides evidence of someone from Japan documenting his place of origin in a town that was founded in 1889, after the Foran Act supposedly banned all contracts to import

FIGURE 4. NPRR work crew along the Yellowstone River in the area of the historic inscriptions containing the kanji characters shown in Figure 3, ca. 1890s. (Courtesy Western Heritage Center, Billings, Montana.)

foreign workers for labor and service. Between 1891 and 1900, over 27,000 Japanese laborers entered the United States, with more entering Canada (White 2011:304). The "33rd year" date accompanying the names and presumed home-land of the inscriber(s) suggests the inscription was created between 1889 and 1900, providing further evidence of the inscriber(s) being among those Japanese workers for whom the NPRR competed when in need of post–Chinese Exclusion Act railroad labor.

Discussion

The two inscription sites serve as remind-ers of the variety of archaeological site types related to Chinese, Irish, Japanese, Norwegian, and other laborers who created landscapes of railroad and related industries in the American West (Wegars 1991; Baxter and Allen 2008;

Merritt et al. 2012); see other articles in this thematic issue. One of the topics that came up during the October 2013 CRWNAP workshop included acknowledging the "multicultural" nature of railroad construction labor. This small collection of historic inscriptions illustrates the textual evidence of that workforce. Associated names, and, in some cases, dates, represent poignant reminders of the multivocal narratives comprising the cultural heritage of railroad workers. Although the Chinese inscription from the site in Roundup, Montana, is not directly along a railroad right-of-way, it is associated with a coal-mining area owned by a railroad. This highlights the tight connection between railroads and extractive industries, the latter of which often staffed their operations with labor-ers who initially joined the company through railroad construction work. Other coal-mining towns throughout the region also share histories

FIGURE 5. Sandstone cliff containing historic inscriptions directly adjacent to the Burlington Northern Railroad, formerly the Northern Pacific, right-of-way. (Photo by George Kucera, 2008.)

of employing Chinese laborers who were mostly former railroad construction workers. These locales, such as Rock Springs, Wyoming (the location of a brutal massacre of approximately 50 Chinese coal miners in 1885), offer "testimony to the power of the railroad to create new industries on the edges of the world economy in places where even state authority remained tenuous" (White 2011:306). The discovery of the only known Chinese inscription in Montana (and, to the best of our knowledge, in the American West) underscores the myriad ways in which Chinese labor was required to support the railroads beyond construction and operation, including extractive industrial sites located several miles away from railroad rights-of-way. It is especially significant given the fact that any written records penned by Chinese railroad construction laborers have yet to be discovered.

The cases of historic inscriptions described here represent written communication that links historical actors with specific points on the landscape and draw attention to the importance of properly documenting historic inscriptions as cultural resources that deserve the same level of documentation as prehistoric rock art (Urbaniak and Rust 2009; Urbaniak 2014a); see also Baumler and Ahlstrom (1988). While the cultural resource documentation of historic inscriptions has been acknowledged in recent years, a comprehensive record remains largely incomplete. Given the paucity of written documents created by the tens of thousands of railroad laborers, the sites described here draw attention to the need for archaeological surveys of railroad rights-of-way to locate and document additional textual evidence incised in stone, as well as to locate and document other remains of the transnational work camps of railroads and associated extractive industries in the American West.

Following the approaches of colleagues in other text-aided fields, such as Egyptology,

FIGURE 6. Historic inscription adjacent to the right-of-way of the Burlington Northern Railroad, formerly the Northern Pacific. The inscription appears to be from a railroad worker who ran the section, reading: CHAS.MACNEY\RUNN .SECTION\HERE.IN.1911. (Photo by George Kucera, 2008.)

Assyriology, and Sinology, archaeologists can incorporate historic inscriptions among the multiple lines of evidence they use to interpret the past (Hardesty 2001). As a text-based form of evidence in the archaeological record, historic inscriptions provide valuable information that can connect people and places across continents and across landscapes, and that can have powerful interpretive value for projects dedicated to the broad geographic span of a region's multivocal, transnational heritage. As such, historic inscriptions have the potential to represent the kind of "middle-range" data (Cleland 2001) that may be necessary to navigate the challenges of transnational archaeologies (Voss and Allen 2008; González-Tennant 2011).

Acknowledgments

We wholeheartedly thank Barbara Voss, Gordon Chang, Shelley Fisher Fishkin, and the students and colleagues associated with Stanford's Chinese Railroad Workers in North America Project for providing the opportunity to participate in the workshop at which this article was initially presented. We are continually grateful for Rebecca Allen's patient assistance with editorial organization and feedback. George Kucera, an employee of Burlington Northern Santa Fe Railroad, provided invaluable assistance with this project, including sharing material from his personal photo archive. We are indebted to Mizuki Miyashita, a linguist at the University of Montana's Department of Anthropology, for providing assistance with the translations of Japanese inscriptions along the NPRR. We also thank Xiaoling Liu and the Confucius Institute, as well as Yanya Yang, for taking the time to assist us with translating the Chinese inscriptions. Several years ago, Yanya Yang provided Tim Urbaniak with the first translation of the

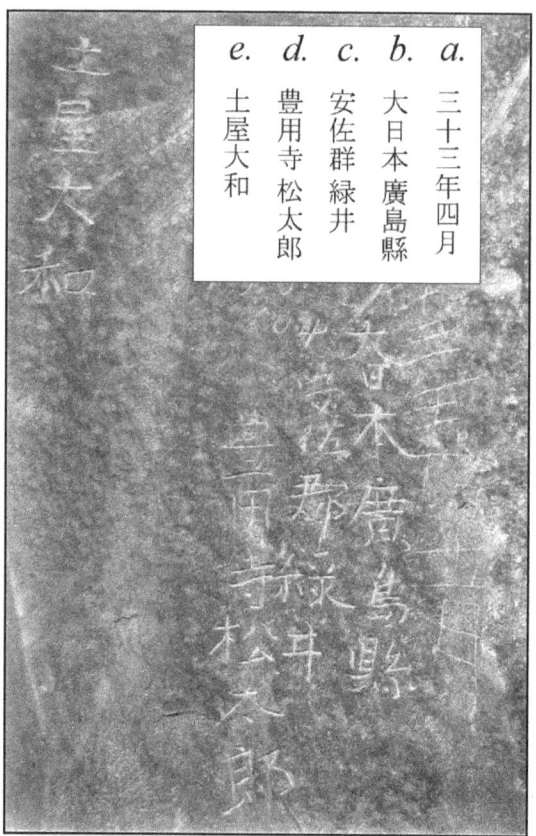

a. 33rd year, April, likely from the Meiji period in Japan, suggesting that the person who made the inscription migrated from Japan sometimes between 1889 and April 1900. Note: The Meiji period extended from September 1868 through July 1912 and represents the first period of the "Empire of Japan," when Japanese society transitioned from the feudal system to its "modern" form.

b. Great Japan, Hiroshima Prefecture.

c. Aza county, Midori'i (Village)—Aza county existed until 1973 in Hiroshima (established 1 October 1889; Midorii [Village] is now part of Hiroshima City).

d. Toyōji Matsutarō (Matsuataro, Toyoji—Toyoji is a surname found in Hiroshima).

e. Tsuchiya Yamato (Yamato Tsuchiya—probably another man's name).

FIGURE 7. Close-up view of the historic inscription panel that includes Japanese kanji characters on the sandstone cliff adjacent to the NPRR/Burlington Northern rail line between Bighorn and Hysham, Montana. The inset clarifies the kanji, and the translations are outlined to the *right* of the photo. (Translations by Mizuki Miyashita, University of Montana; photo by George Kucera, 2008.)

Sun Ziqian translation—we are grateful to her for being part of a pioneering endeavor. Finally, we thank the staff of the Western Heritage Center in Billings, Montana, as well as students and colleagues from Montana State University–Billings and the University of Montana.

References

AARSTAD, RICH, ELLIE ARGUIMBAU, ELLEN BAUMLER, CHARLENE POTSLID, AND BRIAN SHOVERS
    2009 *Montana Place Names: From Alzalda to Zortman.* Montana Historical Society, Helena.

BAUMLER, MARK, AND V. N. AHLSTROM
    1988 The Garfield Monument: An 1886 Memorial of the Buffalo Soldiers in Arizona. *Cochise County Quarterly* 18(1):3–34.

BAXTER, R. SCOTT, AND REBECCA ALLEN
    2008 National Register of Historic Places Evaluation and Damage Assessment for CA-PLA-2002/H (Summit Camp). Report to Tahoe National Forest, Truckee, CA, from Past Forward, Inc., Plymouth, CA.

CLELAND, CHARLES E.
    2001 Historical Archaeology Adrift? *Historical Archaeology* 35(2):1–8.

GONZÁLEZ-TENNANT, EDWARD
    2011 Creating a Diasporic Archaeology of Chinese Migration: Tentative Steps across Four Continents. *International Journal of Historical Archaeology* 15(3):509–532.

HARDESTY, DONALD L.
    2001 Comments on "Historical Archaeology Adrift?" *Historical Archaeology* 35(2):23–24.

LEWIS, ROBERT G.
    1951 *Handbook of American Railroads.* Simmons-Boardman, New York, NY.

MacDonald, Douglas H.
  2012 *Montana before History: 11,000 Years of Hunter-Gatherers in the Rockies and Plains*. Mountain Press, Missoula, MT.

Merritt, Christopher W., Gary Weisz, and Kelly J. Dixon
  2012 "Verily the Road Was Built with Chinaman's Bones": An Archaeology of Chinese Line Camps in Montana. *International Journal of Historical Archaeology* 16(4):666–695.

Mohr, Nicolaus
  1884 *Excursion through America*. R. R. Donnelly, Chicago, IL.

Richards, Ralph W.
  1910 The Central Bull Mountain Coal Field. In *Contributions to Economic Geology 1908, U.S. Geological Survey Bulletin 381, Volume 2, Mineral Fuels*, Marius R. Campbell, editor, pp. 60–81. U.S. Geological Survey, Washington, DC.

Roehr, Mrs. C. [Verna Roehr]
  1974 Name Carving in Montana. *St. Ansgar Enterprise* 7 February:1. St. Ansgar, IA.

Urbaniak, Timothy R.
  2014a *Historic Inscriptions of the Northern Plains: Identity and Influence in the Residual Communication Record*. Doctoral dissertation [and image archive], Department of Anthropology, University of Montana, Missoula. University Microfilms International, Ann Arbor, MI.
  2014b Site form for 24TE0128, Northern Pacific Railroad Bed (Currently Owned by the Burlington Northern Railroad) Extending between the Eastern and Western Borders of Treasure County, Montana. Manuscript, Montana State Historic Preservation Office, Helena.

Urbaniak, Timothy R., and T. Rust
  2009 The History and Preservation of a Historic Inscription from Capitol Rock National Natural Landmark. *Archaeology in Montana* 50(2):43–51.

Voss, Barbara L., and Rebecca Allen
  2008 Overseas Chinese Archaeology: Historical Foundations, Current Reflections, and New Directions. In *The Archaeology of Chinese Immigrant and Chinese American Communities*, Barbara L. Voss and Bryn Williams, editors. Thematic issue, *Historical Archaeology* 42(3):5–28.

Wegars, Priscilla
  1991 Who's Been Workin' on the Railroad? An Examination of the Construction, Distribution, and Ethnic Origins of Domed Rock Ovens on Railroad-Related Sites. *Historical Archaeology* 25(1):37–65.

White, Richard
  2011 *Railroaded: The Transcontinentals and the Making of Modern America*. W. W. Norton & Company, New York, NY.

Timothy R. Urbaniak
Montana State University–Billings
Archaeology Field Team and Drafting and Design Program
1500 University Drive
Billings, MT 59101

Kelly J. Dixon
Department of Anthropology
University of Montana
32 Campus Drive
Missoula, MT 59812

Marjorie Akin (马乔里 • 厄琴)
James C. Bard (詹姆斯 • 巴德)
Gary J. Weisz (加利 • 韦兹)

Asian Coins Recovered from Chinese Railroad Labor Camps: Evidence of Cultural Practices and Transnational Exchange
在中国铁路劳工营发掘的亚洲钱币：文化实践和跨国交流的证据

ABSTRACT

Asian coins carried and lost by Chinese workers as they lived and worked in camps along the route of the Northern Pacific Railroad can illuminate daily activities, beliefs, and the movement of people and supplies along the rail lines during their construction. A review of what is known about recovered Asian coins in Chinese work camps is compared with recently recovered examples. The role of material recovered by surface collection and the conclusions made possible with them are discussed.

在北太平洋铁路沿线劳动和生活的中国劳工携带和遗失的亚洲钱币反映了他们的日常生活、信仰以及铁路修筑过程中人口及物资的流动。本文将比较研究近期发掘的钱币和已知的中国劳工营的钱币，也将考察并讨论地表采集的文物所扮演的角色，以及我们从中得到的发现。

Introduction

Asian coins recovered in North America were part of the material culture of two great socioeconomic movements: the North American fur trade and the movement of Chinese labor to North America. We focus here on the Chinese workers and the coins they left behind at railroad labor camps along the Northern Pacific Railroad (NPRR).

Coins are frequently found where Chinese railroad workers lived and worked. Analyzing these coins can be challenging because they all changed function when they were moved across the Pacific (Akin 1992a). Understanding why these coins were shipped and carried out of China illuminates the everyday activities in the camps, religious beliefs, and related practices

of the workers. It also reveals trade patterns of goods and coinage moving out of and into southern China in the late 19th century.

Coins were developed in China about 2,600 years ago, and a multitude of Chinese words has been used to refer to various types. The most common word for the lowest-denomination brass coins in 19th-century southern China was *wen*. All the coins discussed here were often referred to in English as "cash," from a word for small copper coins used in southern India. The word "cash" was never used by the Chinese themselves, although it appears on some coins as part of English-language inscriptions.

The Asian coins most commonly found on Chinese railroad sites in North America are the Chinese *wen* and the Vietnamese *dong* (Figure 1). These coins, and the related Japanese *mon* and Korean *mun,* have a square hole in their centers and Chinese characters on one or both sides. *Dong* were modeled on the Chinese *wen*, although they were often produced from zinc instead of the various copper alloys used by the Chinese.

A full description of Asian coin types recovered in North American Chinese communities of all sizes, as well as Asian coins used by Native Americans and other communities, can be found in an earlier article in this journal (Akin 1992b). The most essential characteristics of the Asian coins that apply to this study area are:

1. They were cast of several metals, primarily copper alloys (brass) for Chinese *wen* and Japanese *mon*, and zinc for Vietnamese *dong* (that oxidize easily and deteriorate rapidly in soil);

2. They circulated in Asia for hundreds, sometimes thousands, of years, making it difficult to use them for dating except as assemblages;

3. They varied in size according to when and where they were made, with some sizes preferred for particular uses; and

Historical Archaeology, 2015, 49(1):110–121.
Permission to reprint required.

FIGURE 1. *Left*, typical *wen* obverse and reverse; *upper right*, typical *dong* obverse; *lower right*, typical *dong* reverse. (Photos by M. Akin, 2014.)

4. They were never used as money in North America, but were imported for many other uses, such as gaming pieces and talismanic items, and were employed in folk medicine.

The unusual features of Asian coins, as used in North America, provide glimpses into the daily life and the few comforts of the work camps. If the coins had been used as circulating currency (money), different things could be learned from them; yet there are aspects of daily life in the railroad camps that can be learned through these coins.

History and Archaeology of the Northern Pacific Railroad

Once completed in 1883, the NPRR extended from St. Paul, Minnesota, to Tacoma, Washington, and Portland, Oregon. Construction began in 1870, but it was many years before the NPRR had its "Golden Spike" ceremony at Gold Creek, Montana, on 8 September 1883. The railroad served a large area and provided the means to transport farm products to market and to bring goods and supplies to the Pacific Northwest.

By the spring of 1881, an army of men followed surveyors to northern Idaho and western Montana as full-scale railroad construction began. As summarized by Boswell (2014:11), waves of tree fellers, graders, and track layers did their work in northern Idaho and kept moving east to meet similar work teams moving west through Montana. Draftsmen, blacksmiths, laborers, teamsters, and carpenters comprised the force of as many as 5,000 men, nearly two-thirds of them Chinese (Figure 2).

Hired through labor contractors in San Francisco and Portland, they were often divided into gangs of 40 men under the leadership of a Chinese "boss" or foreman who received and distributed their wages. The Chinese were regarded as the hardest workers and were given many of the most dangerous tasks. In the mountainous areas near Cabinet Landing in Bonner County, Idaho, the Chinese workers navigated with ropes down steep cliffs, drilled holes, and then set dynamite charges before they were hoisted back up to safety. Some did not survive the rock blasting (Merritt et al. 2012). A detailed review of the Chinese and the NPRR is provided by Merritt (2010:154–175).

As work proceeded, new work camps were set up and became the "Front." The workers lived and staged their operations there just long enough to perform their jobs. Boswell (2014:13) noted that the Front was called "the largest moving city in the world." Some camps housed all of the labor force, but in others the Chinese were completely segregated with their own food supplies and facilities (Landreth et al. 1985).

The Chinese workers occupied work camps along the Front between 1881 and 1883 (Merritt 2009, 2010; Merritt et al. 2012; Weisz 2013, 2014; Boswell 2014). Temporary camps

FIGURE 2. Chinese railroad construction workers building the Northern Pacific Railroad grade along the Clark Fork River, ca. 1882. (Oregon Historical Society Collection, Image 002822.)

were occupied for brief periods of weeks or months and then permanently abandoned, but some long-term settlements remained in use for various purposes after the construction moved on. Several Chinese NPRR work camps have been identified in northern Idaho and western Montana (Figure 3).

Currently there are no known descriptions of camp life written by the Chinese workers themselves. The available historical documents are usually written in English. A fuller picture of the culture, lifeways, and practices of Chinese immigrant workers may be obtained elsewhere, from the sites of long-term camps, towns, and city Chinatowns. But the short-term camps offer something the long-term settlements cannot: tight dates for the loss or discard of the artifacts found there. Unlike similar short-term camps at some mines, farms, levees, and other workplaces, railroad camps are generally distributed in chronological order along a railroad line being built from one place to another, during a defined (and well-recorded) time period.

Food, liquor, medicine, and various novelties were constantly flowing from Guangdong toward America for Chinese workers who could afford

minor luxuries from home. Gaming equipment was included in the regular exports to America. Equipment for fan-tan (*fāntān*), a gambling game, included large numbers of coins that were removed from circulation in China immediately before being shipped abroad. Gambling, a popular pastime, appears to have been tolerated by the railroad authorities (Boswell 2014:14).

Surface Collecting as "Default Methodology" in Remote Settings

None of the temporary NPRR work camps has been systematically surveyed or excavated. Small, almost ethereal sites in remote locations do not attract much funding for formal survey and excavation. The same miserable weather and difficult living conditions that made the original railroad construction work so challenging also make these camp locations challenging and expensive to excavate, but these camps have attracted other types of study. Like many other similar places along the rail lines, the work camps discussed here have been visited by railroad history buffs and individuals who like to collect the material remains left behind at the

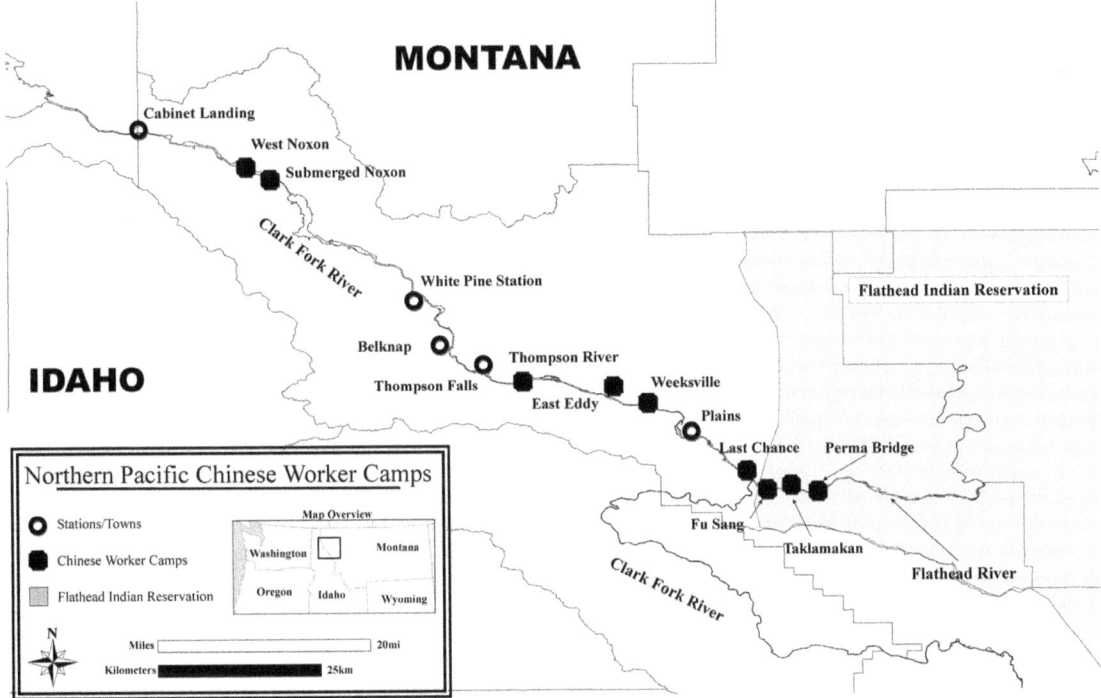

FIGURE 3. Chinese Northern Pacific Railroad work camps. (Map by Christopher Merritt, 2014.)

camps. This activity, also reported in other studies in this issue, has been going on for decades, done with a range of skill and care, depending on the collectors' knowledge, expertise, and intention to share findings.

Asian coins were recovered from several Chinese NPRR camps by amateur historian Gary Weisz. Coins were visible on the surface when he visited the sites. Weisz was formerly employed by the Northern Pacific Railway (the renamed Northern Pacific Railroad), which later became the Burlington Northern Railroad. He had access to many of the former NPRR work camps, where he collected exposed coins and other artifacts, and carefully recorded their provenience. While assisting archaeologists conducting data recovery of historical archaeological sites in Sandpoint, Idaho, he began collaboration with Dr. James C. Bard to further both public and professional appreciation of the rich numismatic history contained within these former NPRR work camps (Bard and Weisz 2012). The authors focus here on the behavior represented by the coins and what the coins can tell researchers about transnational exchange and cultural practices.

Authors Jim Bard and Gary Weisz met in 2006 during the data-recovery phase of the Idaho Transportation Department's Sandpoint Archaeology Project. Located adjacent to the tracks that belonged to the NPRR in 1882, the town of Sandpoint sprang up quickly and hosted a small Chinese settlement within the thriving mix of hotels, mercantile establishments, saloons, and restaurants. Weisz shared his knowledge of the railroad and its relationship to Sandpoint, developed over years of study and work, with Bard and the project's historical archaeologists Robert M. Weaver and Dr. Mark S. Warner. Information and photographs from Weisz's informal surveys of the work camps were shared with professional archaeologists to ensure the permanent recording of his findings and to help deepen the overall understanding of relationships between the town and the NPRR. The fruitful collaboration between Weisz and the Sandpoint team continued through the reporting phase, when it was expanded to include Dr. Margie Akin, who helped with the identification of the *wen* and *dong* recovered from Sandpoint and the railroad work camps.

Interpreting Asian Coins Found along the NPRR

Most Asian coins recovered in association with railroad camps come from two countries, China and Vietnam, with Japanese coins appearing occasionally as outliers. The non-Chinese coins were mixed with Chinese coins before leaving China.

Chinese Coins

Most *wen* recovered in North America date from the Qing Dynasty (1644–1911) and range in diameter from about 18 to 28 mm. Qing *wen* have four Chinese characters on the obverse (front) that say "circulating currency," along with the *nien hao*, or reign name of the current emperor. Each emperor, in consultation with historians, astrologers, and political advisers, chose a slogan-like name to be used instead of his personal name. An American equivalent might be a reference to the "Great Society President." No individual year of production is on the coin, but the reign name gives the range of years during which the coin was made. Standard references for Qing Dynasty *wen* include Krause and Mishler (1985), Jen (2000), and Hartill (2003, 2005).

Almost all Qing coins bear mint names on their reverses indicating where they were cast or struck. The mint name is a single syllable written in the phonetic Manchu script, or as a Chinese character, or both. Qing *wen* all have a raised rim—equal in height to the height of the characters, but varying in width—around the edge and surrounding the central square hole. Qing *wen* are composed of brass or copper in varying alloys with the exact content varying according to the location and year of production (Wang et al. 2005). Despite official standards, metallic compositions of *wen* vary widely, resulting in different types and degrees of corrosion, even in the same archaeological context.

Until 1889 all *wen* were cast in molds, with considerable weight variations. All *wen* of the standard range of sizes were accepted and used as money in late Qing China, no matter how old they were, until well after the end of the empire in 1911. These coins circulated as money throughout the 2,000 years they were produced, and this fact must be taken into account when analyzing recovered coins.

Some undersized *wen* were produced during the Taiping Rebellion (1850–1864) and are considered "counterfeits" by most Chinese numismatists. They do not appear in standard references, but archaeologists cannot ignore them. These smaller *wen* set the standard for circulation in much of southern China during the period and were the model for the Hong Kong *mil* of 1863. Some came to America and were used as gaming pieces, though apparently not for talismanic purposes, for which older and larger coins were preferred. A confusing aspect of these undersized coins is that many bore reign names from earlier periods. However, they can be assigned a production date of about 1850–1864 based on their small size, in spite of misleading reign names (Akin 1992a).

In China, *wen* were usually stored and carried in "strings" of 1,000 or multiples of 100 and were sometimes packaged in that way, but most strings were broken up once the coins shifted to nonmonetary uses. *Wen* had a value of about 1/1,000 of a silver dollar in China during the 19th century and were described in contemporary American English-language reports as being worth a tenth of a cent. In practice, the exchange rate in China often varied, from as few as 600 to as many as 2,000 *wen* to the silver dollar (Peng 1994).

In 1889 modern minting methods were introduced to China with the opening of the Canton mint. Over one billion brass *wen* were struck over the next 18 years, and in 1900 the striking of copper cents, nominally equal to 10 *wen*, commenced. These new machine-struck coins are often found on North American Chinese sites occupied after the early 1890s. They were favored for some decorative purposes because of the matching polished surfaces produced by machine striking and were often used on sewing baskets and dangling, decorative parts of coin "swords."

Vietnamese and Japanese Coins

The zinc *dong* of Vietnam were a grayish white when first cast, but they soon took on a darker color, oxidized very easily, and are considered not as attractive as the brass or copper coins (Barker 2004). They are quickly and severely damaged by fire and deteriorate rapidly in soil. *Dong* require special care when recovered from archaeological sites.

In order to analyze recovered *dong*, it is important to remember that Vietnam was occupied centuries ago by China. In Vietnamese history, there has been a tension between Vietnam's national identity and Chinese cultural forms, including the use of Chinese characters for writing, which continued for official purposes well into the period of French occupation. The Vietnamese alphabet introduced by Jesuit priest Alexandre du Rhodes (1591–1660) did not fully displace Chinese characters on coins until independence after World War II. There has often been some cross-border use of Chinese coins in Vietnam, as well as that of certain Vietnamese coins in border areas of China.

Japanese *mon*, which resembled *wen*, were not used in Japan after 1873, when the Meiji reforms replaced them with new, machine-struck *rin* and *sen*. By the mid-1870s, large numbers of *mon* (and the Chinese *wen* that had circulated together with them in pre-Meiji Japan) were loaded on ships and taken to Chinese ports to be traded for merchandise. Due to the coin shortage that began during the Taiping Rebellion, both *wen* and *mon*, all of copper alloys, were accepted in the ports of Guangdong, and some were included in coins shipped from there to Chinese living in North America (Akin 1996).

In Asia, it has not been possible to separate groups of coins from datable sites with brief occupation periods in order to determine when *dong* entered circulation in large numbers. But, in the United States, temporary settlements of Chinese workers along railroad construction projects provide just the kind of sites needed to date the introduction of zinc *dong* to China.

Examination of a large number of overseas Chinese sites has shown that zinc *dong* usually appear in assemblages deposited between the early 1880s and 1895, a result of the circulation patterns described above. Zinc *dong* have not been recovered from earlier sites, though a few brass Vietnamese coins have been found. This pattern holds true for Chinese railroad labor camps in Nevada and Texas. At the early to mid-1872 Virginia & Truckee camp near Carson City, Nevada (26-OR-214 Area

G), three *wen* were recovered (Rogers 1997). At the 1882 Southern Pacific camp near Langtry, Val Verde County, Texas (41-VV-585), four *wen* and one *mil* were recovered (Briggs 1974:95).

In Vietnam, copper-alloy coins circulated at the same time as zinc coins of similar size and design. The copper-alloy coins were preferred and traded at a higher value than the zinc coins. French colonialists moved large numbers of struck copper coins into the Vietnamese economy starting in 1879, and by 1887 tens of millions of colonial coins had become the basis of low-level transactions in Vietnam. Large numbers of zinc (but few copper-alloy) *dong* were introduced into circulation in Guangdong Province, and many were then shipped across the Pacific.

As the *mon* were copper and similar in appearance, weight, and diameter to pre-1850 *wen*, some of them circulated in China well before the Meiji period. But only after the mid-1870s did *mon* commonly circulate in China. During the fur-trade period of the 1700s and early 1800s, a few *mon* came to America among the *wen* imported to pay for furs. But at sites where more than a few of the recovered coins are *mon*, it is likely that the coins were imported from China after 1875.

The Many Uses of Asian Coins

Economic and cultural practices in China and neighboring countries are expressed archaeologically in Chinese railroad work camps. Understanding the movement of the coins and the cultural practices in which they were used helps verify dates of sites and intrasite sections of larger communities in North America. Reviewing descriptions of the noncurrency functions of these coins should help analysis when the various characteristics of the coins and the behavior connected with them are described, as they are below.

Gaming Equipment

Gaming usually involved wagering, but Asian coins were used as game pieces, not money. In the game of fan-tan, popular with the Chinese and their coworkers, coins functioned as game pieces and counters (Figure 4). Work crews often organized games in temporary camps associated with their migratory labor.

In Stuart Culin's 1891 description of fan-tan, *dong* were used as game pieces and *wen* as counters. All bets were conducted in American money. Game operators imported *wen* and sometimes *dong* specifically for use as game pieces, and there was a strong preference for uniform sets of coins (Culin 1891:5; Akin 1992b).

The dominant European American society exhibited varying degrees of tolerance for games at different times. The degree of prosecution and its severity depended on local factors. Evidence developed by Weisz (2013) suggests gaming in the segregated Chinese laborer work camps was tolerated by the NPRR and its labor contractors.

Talismanic Pieces

Talismanic pieces are material expressions of a belief system related to the spirit world and the manipulation of luck and fortune. There was wide variation in expected efficacy among people using them, and they also served as a reminder of home and "how things should be done." Examples include small groups of coins used as good-luck pieces that could be hung on walls or attached to items of personal importance, and small strings given to people departing on a long journey. They also have been found attached to keys. The coins that make up "coin swords," groups of coins tied onto a central iron rod in the shape of a sword, were used in some rituals and as offerings and gifts for special occasions (Armentrout-Ma 1984:3).

FIGURE 4. New York City—Scenes in a Chinese Gambling House (*Frank Leslie's Illustrated Newspaper* 1887).

Larger and earlier coins, such as the coins of Kāngxī (1662–1726), have long been preferred for most talismanic and religious uses (Figure 5). Vietnamese zinc *dong* were not made in China, did not carry the names of respected emperors, and were not considered to be beautiful, and so were not used for talismanic purposes.

FIGURE 5. Kāngxī *wen* modified for use in a talisman. Minted at the Wu Chang Mint (Hubei Province), recovered at Site 24SA592, the Submerged Noxon Chinese Camp. (Photo by J. Bard, 2014.)

Decoration

During the 18th and 19th centuries, the fur trade between China and ports along the coast of North America brought Chinese *wen* for exchange with aboriginal peoples who especially prized copper and brass. This introduction of Asian goods to Native Americans ended well before 1850 and was never connected with Chinese railroad worker labor camps. Sewing baskets decorated with cast and machine-struck Chinese coins were exported to the United States by the hundreds of thousands before and after 1900. These baskets were made for the American market and were not used much by the Chinese, but their presence in the towns and cities of the region must be noted.

The scant material carried by the Chinese workers from work camp to work camp did not allow for purely decorative items, but

sometimes it is difficult to separate talismanic and decorative devices. A protective coin sword hanging on a wall is both pleasant to look at and may bring protection from evil spirits. Additional holes were sometimes drilled into the coins to facilitate attaching them to other objects. Drilled holes and distinct patinas are good indications of a mixture of talismanic and decorative uses.

Medicine

Asian coins are incorporated in several traditional medicinal practices for symptomatic treatment of minor ailments. No archaeologically recovered coins have yet been found in strongly suggestive medical contexts. However, there are common practices and treatments, some still in use today, described in the literature on overseas Chinese. This kind of secondary use is hard to determine from recovered coins, but if the practices are known to archaeologists it is much more likely that some testable hypotheses can be developed to help confirm such usage.

Several medical treatments incorporated coins. The Chinese railroad workers often needed to treat themselves, using teas, massage, and ointments. For example, brass or zinc coins were boiled in water to produce a "tea" that was consumed by the patient or made into a paste for external application. Zinc in the coin was the curative agent.

Ethnic Chinese practice coin rubbing (*guā shā*) as a treatment for "hot" diseases, such as colds and flu (Nielsen 1995). It is related to acupuncture (Walterspiel et al. 1987:309; Roberts 1988) and is still very widely practiced by many Asian Americans (Yeatman and Dang 1980). The most common procedure consists of a systematic massage, using the smooth edge of a coin, of downward strokes that parallel the spine and then spread out to the sides paralleling the ribs.

It is reasonable to suggest that the Chinese railroad laborers, who had to rely on self-treatment for most medical problems, would have kept a few coins around for such purposes. Archaeologists cannot recognize this potential use unless they know about these common camp remedies.

New Observations

Timeline for Movement of Coins

The occupation dates of the NPRR Chinese railroad work camps are well known: 1881–1883 (Merritt 2009, 2010; Merritt et al. 2012; Weisz 2013). So, what new information can be gained from the archaeological evidence of the coins?

A dating problem first raised in the 1980s may be answered now within a tighter time frame. The question: When did Vietnamese zinc *dong* coins move into circulation in Guangdong Province during the coin shortage of the 1870s and 1880s? No sites in the western United States from the 1870s have shown the presence of *dong*, while sites with firm dates in the late 1880s and early 1890s all contained *dong*.

NPRR Chinese work camp site data suggest that Vietnamese zinc *dong* arrived with the workers along the railroad line by sometime in early to mid-1882 (Table 1). The sample from the single earlier site without *dong* (Dukes Island) is not large enough to conclude that no *dong* were used during late 1881, but the 1882 dates are the earliest yet known for deposition of *dong* at American sites. Communication and commerce with China was surprisingly quick,

and it is already known that imported food and other goods available in the ports of Guangdong Province appeared along the American West Coast, from Vancouver to southern California, within weeks rather than months.

Because the occupation dates for the railroad camps are known from railroad records, this table shows that the *dong* appeared by early 1882 along the shipping pipeline that ran from Guangdong to the railroad camps. This information can help to date future discoveries of small, undocumented sites or even discrete portions of complex sites occupied over several decades.

The Outliers at Last Chance

At the Last Chance Chinese Camp (26SA596), which was occupied from late 1882 to early 1883, 19 *wen*, 4 *dong*, and 5 *mon* (Figure 6) were recovered.

Weisz identified a very large tent platform that was covered with a tent—as evidenced by a handheld rock drill and a long bridge or trestle bolt driven into the ground as tent pegs—along with some smaller tent platforms. This large tent platform was possibly a former communal cooking area, and, as the largest interior space at the camp, it may also have

TABLE 1
NORTHERN PACIFIC RAILROAD CHINESE WORKER CAMPS, IDAHO AND WESTERN MONTANA,
1881–1883: OCCUPATION DATES AND ASIAN COIN FINDS

Chinese Work Camp	Occupation Dates	Asian Coins
Dukes Island 10-BR-pending	Late 1881 to early 1882	5 *wen*
Denton Slough/O'Neil Creek 10-BR-pending	Early 1882	4 *wen*, 1 *dong*
Denton Slough/ Signal 988 10-BR-546	Early 1882	14 *wen*
Twin Creek 10-BR-pending UI-BC-12-07	Early to mid-1882	7 *wen*, 1 *dong*
West Noxon 24-SA-591	Early to mid-1882	6 *wen*, 1 *dong*
Submerged Noxon 24-SA-592	Early 1882 to 1890	9 *wen*, 4 *dong*
Thompson River 24-SA-593	Late 1882	3 *wen*, 5 *dong*
East Eddy 24-SA-594	Late 1882	2 *wen*
East Weeksville 24-SA-595	Late 1882	5 *wen*, 2 *dong*
Last Chance 24-SA-596	Late 1882 to early 1883	19 *wen*, 4 *dong*, 5 *mon*
Fu Sang 24-SA-597	Late 1882 to early 1883	2 *wen* 1 *dong*
Taklamakan 24-SA-598	Late 1882 to early 1883	13 *wen*
Perma Bridge	Late 1882 to early 1883	None found

FIGURE 6. Five *mon* from Site 26SA596,the Last Chance Chinese Camp. (Photo by G. Weisz, 2014.)

been a place where gaming took place. At the edge of this large platform was found a small cache of five *mon* and a few *wen*. Why did this grouping include five *mon*? Did the owner recognize what they were, and did he intentionally retain them in this group? If so, they must have been separated from the *wen* and *dong* while in use at the camp. The known presence of *mon* in the circulating currency of the ports of Guangdong provides a full explanation of the way the Japanese coins reached the camp, since all the workers were Chinese and none were Japanese.

The Question of Reuse at Noxon Camp

The Submerged Noxon Chinese Camp (24SA592), which was occupied from early 1882 to 1890, yielded nine *wen* and four *dong*, including a Kāngxī *wen* (Figure 5). This coin, a large, well-made older coin carrying the name of a favorite emperor, exhibits two small holes on the inside edge of the rim. The

purposeful modification suggests it was used as a talisman, but did it enter the archaeological record as a strung talisman (whose string did not survive), or did the function change when the coin was used in gaming? If function and the behavior related to it changed, how can the possible uses of the coin when it entered the archaeological record be determined? At this time there are more questions than answers for this and similar finds. As more evidence is collected, we archaeologists will be able to develop useful hypotheses, generating questions that will bring us closer to understanding the behavior behind these artifacts that are used for different purposes.

Conclusion

The same practice of importing coins from neighboring countries to meet coin shortages in Guangdong is the reason why both Vietnamese and Japanese coins are found at Chinese sites in North America.

In Asia, it has not been possible to separate groups of coins from datable sites with brief periods of occupation in order to determine when *dong* entered circulation in large numbers. But in the United States, temporary settlements of Chinese workers along railroad construction projects provide just the kind of sites needed to date the entry of zinc *dong* into circulation in China—and thus into North America.

Artifacts recovered from the short-term railroad camps can be used to produce lists of food and drinks, patent medicines, and a host of liquid products that were used within a very short period of time. Artifacts assigned a use date of "the late 19th century" or "during the 1880s" may soon be assigned to much tighter time periods. This, in turn, will help date other more poorly documented sites, or specific features in use at different times, unknown to researchers until now.

When gambling equipment includes small low-value artifacts (brass and zinc coins and dice), and the gambling takes place in dark tents or buildings, above dirt surfaces, during the consumption of liquor, it takes a short time for small gambling paraphernalia to find its way into the archaeological record. Given these circumstances, it appears likely that *dong* began to enter the soil of western states no more than two or three months after they became available in quantity in Guangdong ports. If zinc *dong* reached northern Idaho and western Montana by early to mid-1882, they are likely to have entered circulation in Guangdong by early 1882.

Gaming accounts for the largest number of coins recovered from the railroad sites, with talismanic uses being next most common. Talismanic and decorative uses often overlap, so it can be difficult to ascribe one or the other function accurately for each coin or assemblage of coins. There is a possible additional use for the coins, as hardware, when coins might be used as washers, but only one such case is known to date (Briggs 1974), from a railroad camp site in Texas.

The use of the coins for medicinal purposes, although known from historical records and literature, has not yet been demonstrated at any North American overseas Chinese site. It is expected that greater knowledge and understanding of the medical practices will help archaeologists recognize such activities when they uncover the evidence.

References

AKIN, MARJORIE
  1992a *Asian Coins in the North American West: A Behavioral Studies Approach to Numismatic Analysis.* Doctoral dissertation, Department of Anthropology, University of California, Riverside. University Microfilms International, Ann Arbor, MI.
  1992b The Non-Currency Uses of the Wen in Western North America. *Historical Archaeology* 26(2):56–63.
  1996   Asian Coins: *Dong, Wen,* and *Mon.* In *Down by the Station: Los Angeles Chinatown, 1880–1933,* Roberta S. Greenwood, editor, pp. 98–104. University of California, Institute of Archaeology, Los Angeles.

ARMENTROUT-MA, EVE
  1984   *Chinese Popular Religion.* Chinese and Chinese American History Project, El Cerrito, CA.

BARD, JAMES C., AND GARY J. WEISZ
  2012   Who Has Been Working on the Railroad? A Look at the Coins from Northern Pacific Railroad Chinese Labor Camps in Idaho and Montana. Paper presented at the 39th Annual Conference of the Idaho Archaeological Society, Moscow.

BARKER, R. ALLAN
  2004   *The Historical Cash Coins of Việt Nam: Vietnam's Imperial History as Seen through Its Currency, Part I: Official and Semi-Official Coins.* COS Printers Pte., Singapore.

BOSWELL, SHARON A.
  2014   Building the Line across North Idaho: A History of Early Railroad Development. Manuscript, Idaho Transportation Department, Boise, and Bonner County Historical Museum, Sandpoint, ID.

BRIGGS, ALTON K.
  1974   The Archaeology of 1882 Labor Camps on the Southern Pacific Railroad, Val Verde County, Texas. Master's thesis, Department of Anthropology, University of Texas, Austin.

CULIN, STUART
  1891   The Gambling and Games of the Chinese in America. *University of Pennsylvania Series in Philology, Literature and Archaeology* 1(4):1–17.

FRANK LESLIE'S ILLUSTRATED NEWSPAPER
  1887   New York City—Scenes in a Chinese Gambling House. *Frank Leslie's Illustrated Newspaper* 17 December:296.

HARTILL, DAVID
  2003   *Qing Cash.* Royal Numismatic Society Special Publication No. 37. London, UK.
  2005   *Cast Chinese Coins: A Historical Catalogue.* Trafford, Victoria, BC.

JEN, DAVID
    2000 *Chinese Cash Identification and Price Guide.* Krause, Iola, WI.

KRAUSE, CHESTER L., AND CLIFFORD MISHLER
    1985 *Standard Catalog of World Coins*, 12th edition. Krause, Iola, WI.

LANDRETH, KEITH, KEO BORESON, AND MARY CONDON
    1985 *Archaeological Investigations at the Cabinet Landing Site (10BR413), Bonner County, Idaho.* Eastern Washington University, Archaeological and Historical Services, Papers in Archaeology and History 100-45. Cheney.

MERRITT, CHRISTOPHER W.
    2009 Northern Pacific Railroad Archaeological Sites in Montana. Manuscript, Department of Anthropology, University of Montana, Missoula.
    2010 *"The Coming Man from Canton": Chinese Experience in Montana (1862–1943).* Doctoral dissertation, Department of Anthropology, University of Montana, Missoula. University Microfilms International, Ann Arbor, MI.

MERRITT, CHRISTOPHER W., GARY WEISZ, AND KELLY J. DIXON
    2012 "Verily the Road was Built with Chinaman's Bones": An Archaeology of Chinese Line Camps in Montana. *International Journal of Historical Archaeology* 16(4):666–695.

NIELSEN, ARYA
    1995 *Gua Sha: Traditional Technique for Modern Practice.* Churchill Livingstone, Edinburgh, UK.

PENG XINWEI
    1994 *A Monetary History of China (Zhongguo huobi shi)*, 2 vols., Edward H. Kaplan, translator. Western Washington University, Center for East Asian Studies, Bellingham.

ROBERTS, JAMES R.
    1988 Beware: Vietnamese Coin Rubbing. *Annals of Emergency Medicine* 17(4):143.

ROGERS, C. LYNN
    1997 Making Camp Chinese Style: The Archaeology of a V&T Railroad Graders' Camp, Carson City, Nevada. Report to Silver Oak Development Company, Carson City, NV, from Archaeological Research Services, Virginia City, NV.

WALTERSPIEL, JUAN N., J. R. ROGERS, AND C. KEMP
    1987 Coin Rubbing and Acute Phase Reactants. *Australian Paediatric Journal* 23(5):309.

WANG, HELEN, MICHAEL COWELL, JOE CRIBB, AND SHERIDAN BOWMAN (EDITORS)
    2005 *Metallurgical Analysis of Chinese Coins at the British Museum.* British Museum Research Publication Number 152. London, UK.

WEISZ, GARY J.
    2013 "Stepping Light": Revisiting the Construction Camps on the Lake Pend d'Oreille Division and Clark Fork Division of the Northern Pacific Railroad, 1879–1883, 3 vols. Manuscript, Asian American Comparative Collection, Laboratory of Anthropology, University of Idaho, Moscow.
    2014 Chinese Comparative Collection, Archaeology of the Overseas Chinese, 2 vols. Manuscript, Asian American Comparative Collection, Laboratory of Anthropology, University of Idaho, Moscow.

YEATMAN, GEORGE W., AND VIET VAN DANG
    1980 Cao Gio (Coin Rubbing): Vietnamese Attitudes toward Health Care. *Journal of the American Medical Association* 244(24):2748–2749.

MARJORIE AKIN
20212 HARVARD WAY
RIVERSIDE, CA 92507-6621

JAMES C. BARD
1500 SW PARK AVENUE, NO. 424
PORTLAND, OR 97201

GARY J. WEISZ
11715 W. PINE STREET
SANDPOINT, ID 83864

J. Ryan Kennedy (莱恩·肯尼迪)

Zooarchaeology, Localization, and Chinese Railroad Workers in North America
动物考古学，在地化与北美的中国铁路工人

ABSTRACT

Analysis of zooarchaeological data from sites related to 19th-century Chinese railroad workers in the United States illustrates the variety of food choices made by these individuals and the effects of "localization" on their food practices. Due to the mobility inherent in the lives of railroad workers, data from railroad line camps and urban and rural Chinatown communities provide a fuller picture of the suite of contexts in which railroad workers made food choices. The resulting data demonstrate that, as Chinese railroad workers moved from context to context, they were able to act upon their culinary beliefs in different ways; they typically enjoyed a wide array of food options and possibilities in larger urban Chinatown communities while creatively managing local conditions to maintain some semblance of Chinese foodways, even in rural environments.

在十九世纪中国铁路工人留下的遗址中，对动物考古学资料所进行的分析显示了工人们对食物选择的多样性，以及他们饮食实践中"在地化"的特点。有鉴于铁路工人固有的流动性，本文提供了来自铁路沿线营地，矿区营地，以及城市和乡村地区的中国城社区的不同资料，以便为铁路工人进行饮食选择的一系列场景提供更完整的画面。据此得出的数据显示，在中国铁路工人游走于不同场景的过程中，他们能够以不同方式贯彻自己的烹饪原则。在城市中的中国城社区，他们顺理成章地享有广泛的饮食选择和可能性；而在乡村的环境下，他们则能够创造性地把握当地条件，保持与中国饮食的某种相似性。

Introduction

In the last half of the 19th century, nearly 380,000 Chinese people arrived in the United States (Takaki 1998:32). Many coalesced into communities known as Chinatowns, while others found themselves in rural locales as miners, agricultural workers, and, the focus of this issue, railroad workers. Like Chinese immigrants around the world, those in the United States brought their own unique food beliefs and practices from their home regions, primarily Guangdong Province in southern China. Though varied, these beliefs traditionally centered on distinction between starchy foods, such as rice or noodles (*fan*), and vegetable or meat side dishes (*tsai*) (Chang 1977: 6–7,10; Simoons 1991). Chinese food practices were characterized by flexibility and adaptability, and a wide variety of plants were consumed alongside popular meats, including pork, chicken, duck, and fish (Chang 1977:8). Beef was rarely consumed in 19th-century China. There was also a rich history of the medicinal use of foods for a variety of purposes, and the continuation of these practices in the United States is explored elsewhere (Simoons 1991; Heffner 2013; Heffner, this issue).

Scholars of Chinese cuisine note that the spread of traditional Chinese foodways usually involves initial farming of Asian staple crops, followed or paralleled by the creation and maintenance of supply networks for traditional culinary and medicinal food items, and ultimately the opening of restaurants catering to local populations of transplanted Chinese (Pilcher 2006). Superficially, such a narrative suggests attempted wholesale re-creation of traditional cuisine and does not necessarily factor in the simultaneous mixing of tradition and novelty that quite often occurs in food practices among immigrant groups (Tan 2011). Nor does this model encompass the range of experiences immigrants encountered in a single country or geographic region. Instead, this narrative is more productive when focusing on what Tan (2011) refers to as "localization," or the flexibility of Chinese and other immigrants in adapting their food practices to local economic conditions, the availability of ingredients, and exposure to new foods and cooking methods. While Tan's concept refers specifically to Chinese food practices on a national level within a broader Chinese diaspora, the concept can be productively applied to understand differences across multiple contexts within a single nation as well.

Historical Archaeology, 2015, 49(1):122–133.
Permission to reprint required.

Understanding food practices and the process of food localization among immigrant groups can provide more than a simple understanding of economic conditions at a specific site. The study of foodways is a particularly powerful way to explore daily lives of individuals within different social contexts, given the importance of food in daily routine, social bonds and boundaries, and identity marking (Hastorf and Weismantel 2007; Twiss 2007). Encountering new people, places, and foods provides immigrants opportunities and challenges, allowing creative repositioning within and between groups, while also constraining food choices to subsets of traditional food items and practices. This can lead to a middle ground between cuisine loss and maintenance, resulting in the "solidification" of food items (Janowski 2012). Often termed *soul foods*, solidified foods remain culturally important for nostalgia, memory, or group cohesion, despite often drastic changes in other aspects of traditional cuisine. Thus, it may be best not to think of an archaeological approach to foodways as the study of the maintenance or loss of traditional food practices, but instead as a series of choices, opportunities, and constraints dependent on local conditions and strategies.

The Zooarchaeology of Chinese Railroad Worker Sites

This article uses zooarchaeology, the study of animal bones in archaeological contexts, to explore the food practices of Chinese railroad workers in the United States. To interpret archaeologically recovered animal bones (Figure 1), zooarchaeologists draw on standard laboratory methods, including the identification of individual taxa and skeletal elements, as well as the generation of measures comparing species representation in past diets, such as the Number of Identified Specimens (NISP), the Minimum Number of Individuals (MNI) per species present, and the theoretical meat yield or biomass that recovered animal bones

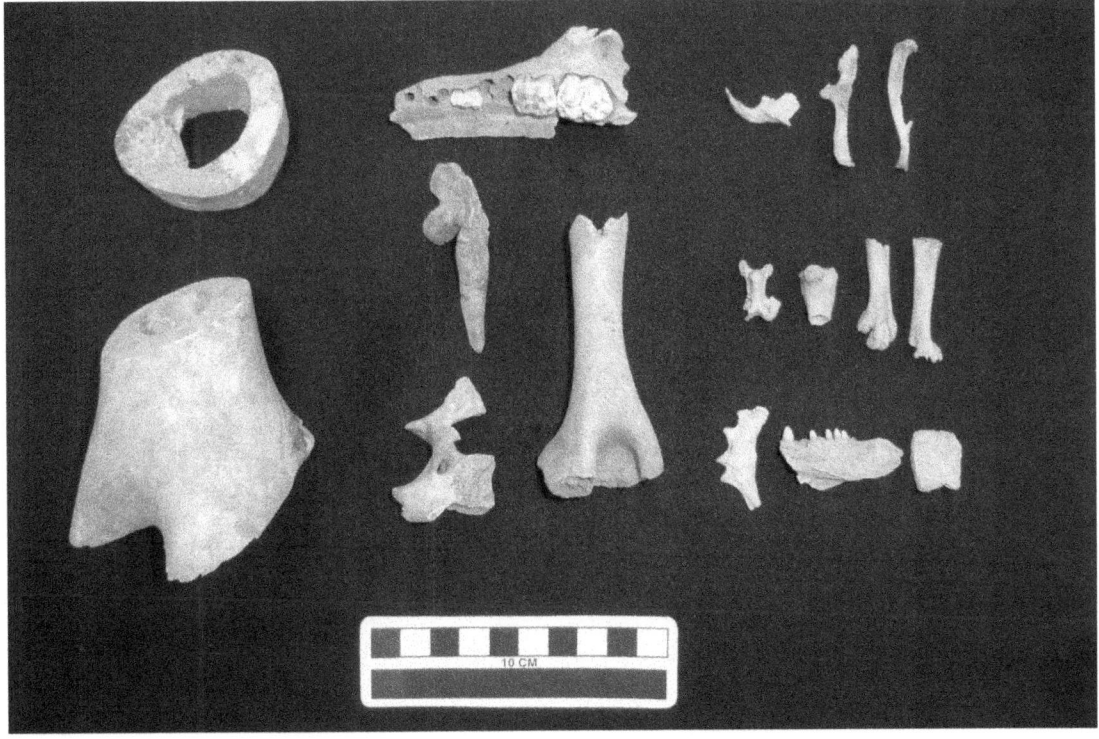

FIGURE 1. Representative faunal remains from the Market Street Chinatown, San Jose, California. *Left*: cattle long bones with saw marks; *middle*, pig maxilla, pig jugular process and occipital condyle with cut marks, pig cervical vertebra sheared in half, and a pig humerus; *upper right*: rat bones; *middle right*: bird bones, including (*far right*) two chicken tarsometatarsi sheared with a cleaver; and *bottom right*: fish bones and a turtle carapace. (Photo by author, 2014.)

represent (Reitz and Wing 2008). By comparing these measures and combining them with taphonomic and butchery modification data, zooarchaeologists can address such topics as the differential use of animal taxa and cuts of meat by past peoples, animal husbandry practices, dietary reconstruction, and the symbolism and meaning of animals. Unfortunately, cross-site comparison can be difficult if different identification standards and quantification methods are utilized, and, as is the case in this study, comparisons are often qualitative rather than quantitative in nature. Still, zooarchaeological analysis can examine the active food choices of Chinese railroad workers and the constraints they encountered based on local conditions.

Maintaining flexibility in approaching food differences among Chinese railroad workers is important for several reasons. First, since railroad construction requires continual linear movement, Chinese railroad workers encountered an ever-changing series of physical and social environments with potentially different food availability. This is useful to consider in regard to the availability of wild animals, as well as potential variability in the price of domestic meats. Second, Chinese immigrants in the United States tended to use larger Chinatowns as home bases, returning during holidays or between periods of work (Voss and Allen 2008; Voss 2013; Praetzellis and Praetzellis, this issue). Because of this, it is highly likely that many railroad workers still spent considerable time in Chinatowns away from primary railroad-related contexts. Third, Chinese railroad workers were not always railroad workers the entire time they were in the United States (Sunseri, this issue). Instead, Chinese people in the 19th-century United States found themselves transitioning among different labor roles depending on job availability, local political and economic conditions, and personal choice. Any consideration of Chinese railroad workers' foodways must address this fluidity.

Given the above reasons, this article broadly defines railroad worker–related sites by including line and lumber camps, as well as urban and rural Chinatowns. This allows exploration of food choice and localization in a number of environments experienced by, in many cases, the same individuals at different

points in their lives. The next section provides a summary of different Chinese railroad worker–related contexts and representative zooarchaeological data recovered from them. These data are examined in light of the concepts of localization, solidification, and the range of food experiences encountered by Chinese railroad workers throughout their lives. Finally, suggestions are offered for future zooarchaeological studies of Chinese railroad workers that address the ephemeral nature of data at associated sites and to produce a more robust, holistic understanding of Chinese railroad workers' food practices.

Zooarchaeological Data from Chinese Railroad Worker Sites

This section presents representative data from several site types associated with Chinese railroad workers: railroad line camps, lumber camps, and rural and urban Chinatowns (Table 1). While not comprehensive, this review allows for understanding of Chinese railroad workers' food practices and localization across a variety of site types. Future studies should consider increasing the variety of contexts to include agricultural, mining, and other sites in order to further expand understanding of food choices made by Chinese immigrants and workers in the United States.

Railroad Line and Lumber Camps

Before examining data from railroad contexts, it is important to review food supply in railroad camps. As part of labor negotiations, the Central Pacific Railroad supplied food for sale to Chinese laborers, usually through the contractor responsible for hiring Chinese work crews (Spier 1958; Krause 1969). The situation was likely similar on smaller lines as well. Crews were typically composed of no more than 30 individuals who cohabitated and pooled resources to pay for a cook and communal food supplies (Rogers 1997). Due to culinary demand by Chinese railroad workers, food was sold from mobile stores housed in railcars near the end of the tracks. As Nordhoff (1873:190) notes for the Merced Railroad, these stores were well stocked with a variety of ingredients:

TABLE 1
ZOOARCHAEOLOGICAL DATA UTILIZED IN THIS STUDY

Site Name	Type	Coll. Method	Assemblage Size	Quantification[a]
V&TRR	Line camp	Survey	Small/unknown	NISP
V&TRR	Line camp	Survey/ excavation	76	NISP
Mono Mills	Large lumber camp	Excavation	368	NISP
Spooner Summit	Small lumber camp	Excavation	36	NISP
Woodland, CA	Rural Chinatown	Excavation	717	NISP, MNI,[b] meat weight
Sandpoint, ID	Rural Chinatown	Excavation	12,785	NISP, MNI, biomass
Riverside, CA	Urban Chinatown	Excavation	40,000+	NISP, meat weight
Sacramento, CA	Urban Chinatown	Excavation	6,467	NISP, MNI,[b] meat weight

[a]Abbreviations: MNI=minimum number of individuals; NISP=number of identified specimens.
[b]MNI not calculated for large mammals.

dried oysters, dried cuttle-fish, dried fish, sweet rice crackers, dried bamboo sprouts, salted cabbage, Chinese sugar (which tastes to me very much like sorghum sugar), four kinds of dried fruits, five kinds of desiccated vegetables, vermicelli, dried sea-weed, Chinese bacon cut up into salt cutlets, dried meat of the abalone shell, pea-nut oil, dried mushrooms, tea, and rice. They also buy pork of the butcher, and on holidays they eat poultry.

Access to mobile, rail-supplied stores allowed Chinese workers, as they moved along the line during rail construction, to access more exotic food items available in larger, distant China-town communities (Gardner 2004).

Despite the large number of Chinese workers on the Central Pacific and other lines, scant zooarchaeological data exist from these sites. This is partly due to the short occupancy of railroad camps and the reliance of Chinese workers on tents rather than more permanent structures (Furnis and Maniery, this issue). Further, as discussed by Merritt et al. (2012:676), there has been little formal archaeological survey and analysis of line camp sites and their assemblages. Even for surveyed sites, faunal analysis has often not been completed.

Still, a small sample of zooarchaeological data from primary railroad sites exists and can provide insight into railroad worker food practice.

One of the few examples of zooarchaeological data from Chinese railroad workers comes from line camps along the Virginia & Truckee Railroad (V&TRR), which was constructed around 1870 (Wrobleski 1996; Rogers 1997). Wrobleski's (1996) survey of the V&TRR line between Virginia City and Mound House, Nevada, identified two camps used by Chinese workers and provides limited but important faunal data. While only a handful of specimens were recorded, Wrobleski notes the identification of pig and cattle bones within the work camp assemblages. Although the scant size of the assemblage and the few bones identified to species make quantitative analysis impossible, that both pig and cattle are present indicates Chinese workers at railroad camps consumed both traditional pork and more novel beef.

Additionally, Rogers (1997) provides data associated with an 1872 railroad camp located between Reno and Carson City, Nevada, also along the V&TRR. While no faunal remains were noted during surface survey, 94 faunal specimens were recovered from a feature likely associated with food preparation (Rogers 1997:31). Seventy-six specimens were unidentifiable mammal remains, and the remaining eighteen were vertebrae from trout or chub-sized fish. The fish bones suggest line fishing in local streams, rivers, or lakes by Chinese railroad workers, a not unheard of event. As Merritt et al. (2012) noted, Chinese laborers were observed fishing for suckers, chubs, and lake trout in the Clark Ford River while working from the Noxon Line Camp in Montana (*Spokane Falls Chronicle* 1882), and a lake near the Summit Camp in Placer County, California, is believed to have been stocked by Chinese workers to provide a ready supply of catfish (Baxter and Allen, this issue). These examples illustrate collection of wild animals to supplement foods available in railroad stores, and they suggest that fresh fish was important enough to Chinese workers to commit time toward procuring it. Additionally, Rogers's data illustrate potential differences in the ability of archaeologists to recover faunal material from surface survey vs. excavation in railroad worker contexts.

Beyond Chinese railroad line camps, zooarchaeological evidence related to railroad workers also comes from lumber operations with direct linkages to the railroad and mining industries. Lumber companies, in some cases directly owned by the railroads, frequently hired unemployed Chinese railroad workers as laborers for timbering operations supplying wood for mines, general construction, and the building of train trestles, bridges, railroad cars, and railroad ties (Chung 2003:3; Sunseri, this issue). As with railroad workers, Chinese laborers in lumber camps procured traditional food items from trade networks and nearby Chinese communities, although the level of food supply and diversity of items available likely varied based on factors such as population size.

Ongoing archaeological investigations at Mono Mills, a multiethnic town occupied from 1880 to 1915 to supply lumber to nearby Bodie, California, provides a case study illustrating foodways within a railroad-related lumber context. Owing to existing labor relationships with railway investors, Chinese workers at Mono Mills were hired to construct a rail line from nearby Bodie to Mono Mills and to maintain this line and work in the lumber mill (Sunseri, this issue).

Ongoing analysis of a faunal assemblage containing 368 specimens from a Chinese household at Mono Mills shows roughly equal NISPs for pig (n=48) and cattle (n=49) remains, along with other animals (Charlotte K. Sunseri 2014, pers. comm.). The relatively even ratio between pig and cattle suggests increased reliance on beef by Chinese residents of Mono Mills; however, the sample size makes this difficult to argue with certainty. Other animals consumed at the site include cuttlefish, chicken, and locally available wild game, fowl, and fish. Interestingly, while the identified domestic mammal remains show power-saw marks indicative of national, railroad-based distribution networks, documentary evidence from the site suggests supply of meat to Mono Mills by local ranchers and butchers. While preliminary, the faunal data from Mono Mills suggest Chinese engagement in larger trade networks to procure domestic mammals and exotic Chinese ingredients, such as cuttlefish, as well as the use of a range of wild animals to supplement diet.

Solury's (2004) analysis of a wood-camp cabin dating from the 1870s to the late 1880s on Spooner Summit in the Tahoe Basin of the eastern Sierra Nevada provides a second, limited set of zooarchaeological data from a railroad-related lumber site. Employed by the Carson & Tahoe Lumber & Fluming Company, the Chinese residents of the wood camp on Spooner Summit supplied lumber for the local mining industry and associated railroads, and they would have had access to Chinese goods and food items through their labor contractors and from other nearby Chinese communities (Solury 2004:22). Though only 36 highly fragmented bones were recovered, they provide clues to food practices at Spooner Summit. Several bones, including a large mammal femur, a pig jaw, and a handful of unidentifiable mammal bones, exhibit saw marks suggestive of nonlocal meat procurement, while at least two smaller femurs show evidence of being split lengthwise with a cleaver. Solury also identified a small mammal rib that could possibly have been from a wild animal consumed for food; however, the lack of butchery marks and species-level identification make this difficult to discern. Solury (2004:56) argues that heavy fragmentation of the faunal remains may be indicative of the preparation of soups or stews, and that the general dearth of faunal material at the site may suggest that Chinese residents ate many of their meals at a larger, nearby camp where they may have consumed more traditional foods. If true, the Spooner Summit case study demonstrates the possibility of differential faunal signatures on a local level in unique, small-scale settings. Furthermore, while in isolation the faunal data speak inconclusively to Chinese foodways at the site, other artifact classes, including botanical remains, ceramics, and metal tools, suggest a mixing of both Chinese and American practices and suggest that Chinese residents at the site adapted their foodways to local conditions.

Despite the dearth of faunal data from primary railroad-related sites, zooarchaeological analysis still provides fruitful insights into the foodways of railroad workers. Data from the camps along the V&TRR demonstrate the consumption of both traditional pork and beef, a meat not typically consumed in large quantities in 19th-century southern Chinese cuisine. The trout and chub-sized fish bones identified by Rogers (1997) corroborate documentary accounts of Chinese railroad workers consuming fresh fish. Though preliminary, the data from Mono Mills provide perhaps the most informative examination of Chinese foodways in a primary railroad context. At Mono Mills, Chinese workers consumed local and imported domestic mammals, dried cuttlefish imported from Asia, and a variety of local fowl, wild game, and fish. Although the faunal data from Spooner Summit are sparse, the possibility that workers consumed different foods at the wood camp and a nearby larger camp suggests that Chinese workers' food practices may vary drastically even between sites in close proximity to each other. Taken as a whole, these four studies illustrate some of the ways Chinese railroad workers adapted their food practices to local conditions, including their use of available domestic pork and beef, collection of fresh local fish, and the importation of exotic food items. However, none of the assemblages exhibit the variety of species described in firsthand accounts of railroad workers' foodways, such as that of Nordhoff (1873), and it is clear that additional data from other sites and material types are necessary to fully explore foodways in these rural contexts.

Rural and Urban Chinatown Sites

In addition to primary railroad contexts, zooarchaeological data from rural and urban Chinatown sites also provide evidence of Chinese railroad workers' food practices. Many small, rural Chinatowns formed along the routes of railroads, as Chinese workers stayed behind to form small communities or arrived via the newly constructed lines. Beyond being populated in part by present and former railroad workers, these smaller communities were central to the distribution of food items to Chinese laborers in nearby railroad and mining camps (Gardner 2004). Larger urban Chinatowns, on the other hand, represented major hubs of food distribution and served as home bases to Chinese laborers working in a variety of industries (Voss and Allen 2008). These communities created initial connections between new Chinese immigrants and trade networks, and instilled within them the possibility of maintaining Chinese food practices in other contexts, such as railroad line camps. Workers frequently returned to rural and urban Chinatowns for holidays and other occasions, and these visits could reconnect Chinese laborers to a broader community and provide opportunities to consume traditional items unavailable in rural contexts. The discussion below draws on data from the Woodland, Sandpoint, Riverside, and Sacramento Chinatowns.

The Woodland Chinatown, established in 1866 in Yolo County, California, was linked to the transcontinental railroad in 1869, resulting in a population increase to nearly 100 individuals by 1880 (Gust 1993:178). Excavation of a cesspool or cellar associated with a Chinese laundry or residence yielded 717 identifiable faunal remains. While pig bones (n=301) significantly outnumbered cattle bones (n=45), meat-weight calculations show that pork accounted for 40% of the total meat weight compared to 58% for beef (Gust 1993). Interestingly, while only saw marks were identified on cattle bones, a roughly equal number of saw marks and cleaver marks were observed on pig bones, suggesting Chinese residents at the site procured pork, at least in part, from European American butchers. In addition to cattle and pig, small numbers of ground squirrel (n=3), cat (n=3), and pond turtle (n=14) bones were identified, with specimens from all three species exhibiting butchery marks. Chicken represents up to 80% of the 221 identified bird bones, with duck (n=36) second, and goose, crow, quail, and dove making up the remainder. Finally, 119 bones from a dozen local fish species were identified at the site, with notable taxa including rockfish (n=8), Sacramento perch (n=18), Sacramento sucker (n=10), squawfish (n=12), and the minnow and sucker family (n=48). Taken as a whole, the Woodland Chinatown assemblage suggests that, while site residents consumed pork in some quantity, they relied more heavily on untraditional beef. They chose to supplement their diets with turtle, chicken, cat, fish, and wild animals such as ground squirrel, however, providing a range of meats in line with traditional southern Chinese cuisine.

Faunal remains from Sandpoint, Idaho, provide a case study of a much smaller rural Chinese community (Warner et al. 2014). While approximately 1,500 Chinese railroad workers were in Sandpoint in 1881 constructing the Northern Pacific Railroad, by 1900 only 9 remained in what locals referred to as "Chinatown." Despite this small population, excavation of a laundry in the Sandpoint Chinatown yielded 12,785 faunal remains. While by count pig (n=625) outnumbers cattle (n=372) in the assemblage, other measures tell a different story. According to sample biomass, a measure calculating theoretical meat weight from bone weight (Reitz and Wing 2008), beef may have made up nearly two-thirds of the meat consumed by Sandpoint's Chinese residents, compared to only one-fifth from pork. Additional taxa making up smaller portions of the diet include caprines (n=242), moose (n=1), turtles (n=27), and fish (n=24), as well as a variety of birds primarily consisting of chicken (n=52) and duck (n=18), with smaller numbers of goose (n=1), turkey (n=7), and loon (n=1) identified. Butchery marks suggest significant engagement with European American meat-distribution markets, as only 122 total chops and cuts were identified, compared to 2,335 saw marks, which are not typically associated with Chinese butchery patterns. Still, a small number of bird bones displayed typical Chinese butchering into small, bite-sized pieces. Of particular note is

that most of the Chinese residents of Sandpoint worked in local restaurants, and they may have been procuring meat from their workplaces in an effort to make do with resources at hand (Warner 2012; Warner et al. 2014:64). If this is in fact the case, Sandpoint offers an intriguing example of Chinese people at a railroad-related site consuming large quantities of beef to take advantage of local food conditions, while simultaneously maintaining other traditional practices, including the consumption of large amounts of chicken, duck, turtle, and fish.

The Riverside, California, Chinatown, established in 1885, has been the focus of extensive faunal study (Collins 1987; Goodman 1987; Langenwalter 1987). Over 40,000 vertebrate specimens were recovered from 14 features at the site, including trash pits and building basements. Pork bones (n=3,616) far outnumbered those from beef (n=365), and pork accounted for between 60% and 80% of meat weight at the site, while beef represented only 20% to 30% in most features. While most butchery of pig bones could be attributed to Chinese cleavers, cattle bones tended to show European American–style saw marks and indicate Chinese procurement of this meat from outside Chinatown. A wide variety of additional taxa were identified, including sheep (n=43), rabbit (35), deer (2), pond turtle (n=294), desert tortoise (n=8), and both butchered cat (n=11) and rat (n=7) bones, reduced into smaller pieces with a bladed instrument, such as a cleaver. Though not fully identified, 95% of the analyzed bird specimens are thought to be from chickens. House gecko (n=63) and soft-shell turtle (n=8) were also identified, both of which have Chinese medicinal uses. The fish remains from the site include local California fish, such as sheepshead (n=15), barracuda (n=59), halibut (n=20), tuna (n=18), and several species of croaker (n=17), as well as a small number of nonlocal fish, including yellow croaker (n=8) and puffer (n=32), both Chinese imports. In total, the Riverside faunal assemblage demonstrates a wider variety of animals than those from smaller sites and conforms more closely to expectations based on traditional southern Chinese cuisine (Simoons 1991) and ethnographic observation of Chinese food practices in the United States (Nordhoff 1873; Spier 1958).

Zooarchaeological analysis of material from the Sacramento Chinatown, dating to the 1850s, provides another example (Praetzellis and Praetzellis 1997). Excavation of the city's HI56 block recovered 5,562 identifiable faunal remains associated with Chinese boardinghouse residents, permanent staff, and merchants. Surprisingly, beef bones (n=1,537) outnumbered those from pork (n=512), and beef constituted upward of 80% to 90% of the assemblage by meat weight (Gust 1997). While pork accounted for much of the remainder, smaller quantities of elk (n=17), deer (n=29), and rabbit (n=4) were also present. Bird bones identified in the assemblage included chicken (n=103), turkey (n=29), goose (n=31), duck (n=54), and pheasant (n=1). While butchery patterns generally conform to European American methods, smaller animals, such as rabbits and fowl, appear to have been cut into pieces with cleavers. A total of 2,077 fish remains were identified from these contexts, and important taxa include Sacramento perch (n=1,298), suckers or minnows (n=692), Sacramento sucker (n=35), salmon (n=25), Atlantic mackerel (n=22), and several Chinese species: white herring (n=3), golden threadfin (n=15), snapper (n=13), and sea bream (n=31) (Schulz 1997). Separate analysis of 905 faunal remains from merchant contexts in the nearby IJ56 block yields conflicting results (Praetzellis and Praetzellis 1997:292–293). Here, pig bones (n=622) far outnumber those from cattle (n=21), and pork represents nearly 95% of the total meat weight. Only a limited number of bird bones were identified (n=11), and the range of fish species was similar to that of the boardinghouse contexts, with the exception of a high number of bones from yellow croaker (n=163), a highly prized Chinese food fish. Together, the Sacramento data show that, although both merchant and boardinghouse residents used a wide variety of animals in their food practices, including multiple fish and bird taxa, differences do exist. Boardinghouse residents consumed tremendous quantities of beef, whereas merchants dined on pork. Boardinghouse residents, it seems, either adapted their food practices to relatively high local pork prices (Gust 1997) or were provided beef as provision by boardinghouse staff (Praetzellis and Praetzellis 1997:286). Either way, this contrasts with the IJ56 merchants' ability to procure pork in large quantity and shows that merchants and boardinghouse residents adapted their food practices in different ways to conditions in Sacramento.

Taken as a whole, zooarchaeological analysis on Chinatown sites complements data recovered from railroad and lumber camps. Owing to longer occupations, Chinatown communities tend to produce a wider variety of taxa—closer to that observed in the documentary record—and containing more rare specimens than primary railroad contexts. As in laborer camps, however, the faunal remains from Chinatown sites vary greatly based on local conditions. The Riverside Chinatown's faunal assemblage resembles something close to a traditional southern Chinese diet, while others, such as Sandpoint, demonstrate unexpected attributes, in this case relatively high amounts of beef, likely related to residents' jobs in restaurants. Likewise, faunal data from Sacramento show how Chinese residents differentially enacted foodways based in large part on purchasing power.

Localization and the Zooarchaeological Data

The zooarchaeological data discussed above represent a range of contexts Chinese railroad workers encountered in the 19th-century United States. While varying in scale from small work camps to large Chinatowns, these locales share several traits. Of particular note is the fact that none of the sites suggest either full abandonment or retention of traditional southern Chinese food practices. Instead, individuals made strategic choices that allowed them to maintain aspects of traditional Chinese cuisine while also navigating economic, social, and environmental food constraints that at times led to necessary compromises. Overall, the faunal and documentary data from railroad camps suggest that while Chinese people often had access to a wide range of food options, including many ingredients common to traditional Chinese cooking, they also adapted their food practices to local conditions.

When examining the process of localization, several patterns ultimately emerge. Although faunal remains from primary railroad sites are sparse, they offer insight into Chinese engagement with broad food supply networks in both railroad and lumber camps. The Mono Mills case study in particular suggests that Chinese laborers procured meat from both national and local sources, while the remaining assemblages show the general consumption of both pork and beef by workers. The recovery of fish bones from a V&TRR rail camp (Rogers 1997) and wild game, fowl, and fish from Mono Mills demonstrate Chinese willingness to supplement pork and beef with readily available wild animals, a practice recorded in documentary sources describing Chinese fishing and aquaculture efforts at railroad camps. Still, ethnographic accounts of food supply to railroad workers reveal a tremendous variety of food items not seen in the archaeological record and suggest that railroad workers' food practices regularly utilized a number of traditional Chinese ingredients. Overall, railroad- and lumber-camp data suggest that Chinese laborers enacted traditional food beliefs where possible, but maintained flexibility; they readily incorporated beef into their diets, and also procured locally available animals for consumption. While economic constraints and the availability of ingredients may have had an impact on these decisions, food beliefs, such as the Chinese preference for fresh ingredients, may have motivated railroad workers to seek out wild fish and game when possible.

Even with the availability of traditional foods in Chinese railroad and lumber camps, larger Chinatown sites would still have provided residents with greater access to ingredients than in rural areas due to lengthier occupations and populations large enough to support local markets. The variety of species present in the Riverside Chinatown illustrates this, as do the comparatively high numbers of turtles, fish, fowl, and other taxa in the Sacramento, Woodland, and Sandpoint faunal assemblages. Despite commonalities in the range of taxa, zooarchaeological data suggest distinct differences in how Chinese people at each site dealt with local conditions. Riverside residents enjoyed large amounts of pork and were able to procure rare medicinal taxa, such as house geckos. Residents of Sacramento, however, ate varying amounts of pork and beef based on their purchasing power, while sharing similarly wide ranges of fish and other taxa.

Food practices in more rural communities were equally varied. Woodland Chinatown residents consumed slightly more beef than pork, alongside smaller amounts of traditionally important chicken, fish, and turtle, while Sandpoint's possibly took advantage of employment in local restaurants to procure beef, which they supplemented with available ingredients that better fit into traditional Chinese foodways. Taken together, these four Chinatown sites illustrate localization strategies across a range of sites, from a large, urban site to those in small, rural communities.

Although the above discussion attempts to demonstrate how Chinese railroad workers adapted their food practices at a local level, it must be emphasized that the different contexts discussed in this study were all encountered by railroad workers during their individual lives. When Chinese immigrants arrived in the United States, they were first exposed to large, urban Chinatowns before making their way to jobs in railroad construction and other industries. From here they would have visited Chinese communities along the railroad and at times returned to large Chinatowns for holidays and between jobs. As they moved from one context to another, they were able to act upon their culinary beliefs in different ways, typically enjoying more options in large Chinatowns, while creatively managing local conditions to maintain some semblance of Chinese foodways even in rural environments. This fluidity in Chinese labor roles in the 19th-century United States has important implications for interpreting food practice and choice when combined with the idea of localization; archaeologists must be cognizant that apparent differences between sites may be the result of individual context-specific strategies, rather than changes in identity or food beliefs.

Conclusion

This article provides an overview of zooarchaeological data from Chinese railroad worker–related sites in the United States and presents the concept of localization as a way to frame the lives of Chinese railroad workers in the past. In addition to accounting for the effects of unique conditions at any given site, localization emphasizes fluidity in the lives of

Chinese railroad workers, as they moved from urban Chinatowns to rural sites and vice versa.

Differences in food practices at any given railroad worker–related site may be determined more by local limiting factors, including economic, environmental, and social constraints, than by concrete changes in the food beliefs held by individuals inhabiting a site. This model, however, is not meant to suggest that variation and changes in foodways are always caused by external factors; instead, it implies that short-term differences perceived within zooarchaeological data may simply be evidence of the adaptation of culinary beliefs by a highly mobile group of people moving through a wide array of contexts.

While this study has shown that localization can be a useful framework, it is apparent that it can also be heavily improved upon with additional data. Of greatest importance is addressing the dearth of faunal data from railroad worker–related sites with archaeological survey and excavation. It is also imperative to utilize fine-grained collection strategies to recover remains from fish and other small animals visible in the documentary record, but often not recovered in archaeological survey and excavation. Because of the relatively small number of faunal remains recovered from rural Chinese sites, archaeologists should also consider incorporating additional data sets, including botanical remains and food-related material culture, to provide a fuller understanding of railroad workers' foodways. The understanding of the localization of Chinese food practices may also be extended by including additional site types, such as agricultural and mining camps. Ultimately, a more robust set of data and case studies will allow archaeologists to piece together the daily lives and food choices of Chinese railroad workers in a more systematic and satisfying way, and better understand changing food practices among Chinese immigrants in the United States as a whole.

Acknowledgments

Many thanks to Barbara Voss, Gordon Chang, Shelley Fisher Fishkin, and others involved in Stanford University's Chinese Railroad Workers in North America Project for providing a venue for sharing research and creating unique collaborations. I am indebted to you all for including me. I would also like to thank everyone who has shared data and information with me for this and other related projects, including Charlotte Sunseri, Mark Warner, Rebecca Allen, and Mary Maniery.

References

CHANG, KWANG-CHIH
  1977 Introduction. In *Food in Chinese Culture: Anthropological and Historical Perspectives*, K. C. Chang, editor, pp. 2–12. Yale University Press, New Haven, CT.

CHUNG, SUE FAWN
  2003 The Chinese and Green Gold: Lumbering in the Sierras. Report to Humboldt-Toiyabe National Forest, Carson Ranger District, Passport in Time, Carson City, NV, from University of Nevada, Las Vegas.

COLLINS, DONNA
  1987 Tradition and Network: Interpreting the Fish Remains from Riverside's Chinatown. In *Wong Ho Leun: An American Chinatown*, Vol. 2, pp. 121–132. Great Basin Foundation, San Diego, CA.

GARDNER, A. DUDLEY
  2004 The Chinese in Wyoming: Life in the Core and Peripheral Communities. In *Ethnic Oasis: The Chinese in the Black Hills: South Dakota History*, Lipeng Zhu and Rose Estep, editors, pp. 380–390. South Dakota Historical Society, Pierre.

GOODMAN, JOHN D.
  1987 Dragon Bones: Faunal Analysis and Its Relation to Medical Practice at Riverside's Chinatown. In *Wong Ho Leun: An American Chinatown*, Vol. 2, pp. 107–120. Great Basin Foundation, San Diego, CA.

GUST, SHERRI M.
  1993 Animal Bones from Historic Urban Chinese Sites: A Comparison of Sacramento, Woodland, Tucson, Ventura, and Lovelock. In *Hidden Heritage: Historical Archaeology of the Overseas Chinese*, Priscilla Wegars, editor, pp. 177–212. Baywood, Amityville, NY.
  1997 Analysis of Animal Bones. In Historical Archaeology of an Overseas Chinese Community in Sacramento, California, Mary Praetzellis and Adrian Praetzellis, editors, pp. 222–257. Report to U.S. General Services Administration, San Francisco, CA, from Anthropological Studies Center, Sonoma State University, Rohnert Park, CA.

HASTORF, CHRISTINE A., AND MARY WEISMANTEL
  2007 Food: Where Opposites Meet. In *The Archaeology of Food and Identity*, Katheryn C. Twiss, editor, pp. 308–331. Southern Illinois University, Center for Archaeological Investigations, Occasional Paper No. 34. Carbondale.

HEFFNER, SARAH C.
2013   Exploring Healthcare Practices of the Lovelock Chinese: An Analysis and Interpretation of Medicinal Artifacts in the Lovelock Chinatown Collection. *Nevada Archaeologist* 26:25–36.

JANOWSKI, MONICA
2012   Introduction: Consuming Memories of Home in Constructing the Present and Imagining the Future. *Food and Foodways* 20(3&4):175–186.

KRAUS, GEORGE
1969   Chinese Laborers and the Construction of the Central Pacific. *Utah Historical Quarterly* 37(1):41–57.

LANGENWALTER, PAUL E.
1987   Mammals and Reptiles as Food and Medicine in Riverside's Chinatown. In *Wong Ho Leun: An American Chinatown*, Vol. 2, pp. 53–106. Great Basin Foundation, San Diego, CA.

MERRITT, CHRISTOPHER W., GARY WEISZ, AND KELLY J. DIXON
2012   "Verily the Road was Built with Chinaman's Bones": An Archaeology of Chinese Line Camps in Montana. *International Journal of Historical Archaeology* 16(4):666–695.

NORDHOFF, CHARLES
1873   *California for Travellers and Settlers.* Ten Speed Press, Berkeley, CA.

PILCHER, JEFFREY M.
2006   *Food in World History.* Routledge, New York, NY.

PRAETZELLIS, MARY, AND ADRIAN PRAETZELLIS
1997   Historical Archaeology of an Overseas Chinese Community in Sacramento, California. Report to U.S. General Services Administration, San Francisco, CA, from Anthropological Studies Center, Sonoma State University, Rohnert Park, CA.

REITZ, ELIZABETH J., AND ELIZABETH S. WING
2008   *Zooarchaeology*, 2nd edition. Cambridge University Press, Cambridge, UK.

ROGERS, C. LYNN
1997   Making Camp Chinese Style: The Archaeology of a V&T Railroad Graders' Camp, Carson City, Nevada. Report to Silver Oak Development Company, Carson City, NV, from Archaeological Research Services, Virginia City, NV.

SCHULZ, PETER
1997   Mid-19th-century Fish Remains. In Historical Archaeology of an Overseas Chinese Community in Sacramento, California, Mary Praetzellis and Adrian Praetzellis, editors, pp. 258–268. Report to U.S. General Services Administration, San Francisco, CA, from Anthropological Studies Center, Sonoma State University, Rohnert Park, CA.

SIMOONS, FREDERICK J.
1991   *Food in China: A Cultural and Historical Inquiry.* CRC Press, Boca Raton, FL.

SOLURY, THERESA E.
2004   "Everlasting Remembrance": The Archaeology of 19th-Century Chinese Labor in the Western Lumber Industry. Master's thesis, Department of Anthropology, University of Nevada, Reno.

SPIER, ROBERT F. G.
1958   Food Habits of Nineteenth-Century California Chinese (Concluded). *California Historical Society Quarterly* 37(2):129–136.

SPOKANE FALLS CHRONICLE
1882   Life at Cabinet Landing. *Spokane Falls Chronicle* 25 July:2. Spokane Falls, WA.

TAKAKI, RONALD
1998   *Strangers from a Different Shore: A History of Asian Americans*, updated and revised edition. Little, Brown, New York, NY.

TAN CHEE-BENG
2011   Introduction. In *Chinese Food and Foodways in Southeast Asia and Beyond*, Tan Chee-Beng, editor, pp. 1–22. Nus Press, Singapore.

TWISS, KATHERYN C.
2007   We Are What We Eat. In *The Archaeology of Food and Identity*, Katheryn C. Twiss, editor, pp. 1–15. Southern Illinois University, Center for Archaeological Investigations, Occasional Paper No. 34. Carbondale.

VOSS, BARBARA L.
2013   Before and After the Transcontinental: Archaeological Reflections from San Jose's Chinatowns. Paper presented at the Archaeology Network Workshop of the Chinese Railroad Workers in North America Project, Stanford University, Palo Alto, CA.

VOSS, BARBARA L., AND REBECCA ALLEN
2008   Overseas Chinese Archaeology: Historical Foundations, Current Reflections, and New Directions. *Historical Archaeology* 42(3):5–28.

WARNER, MARK
2012   A Voice in the Wilderness: Isolation and Compromise among Overseas Chinese in Sandpoint, Idaho. Paper presented at the 111th Annual Meeting of the American Anthropological Association, San Francisco, CA.

WARNER, MARK, BREANNE KISLING, AND MOLLY SWORDS
2014   A "Community" on the Margins: Chinese Life in Turn of the Century Sandpoint. In The Other Side of Sandpoint: Early History and Archaeology beside the Tracks, the Sandpoint Archaeology Project 2006–2013, Vol. 1: Sandpoint Stories, Robert M. Weaver, editor, pp. 55–72. Report to Idaho Transportation Department, District 1, Coeur d'Alene, from SWCA Environmental Consultants, Portland, OR.

WROBLESKI, DAVID E.
  1996 The Archaeology of Chinese Work Camps on the Virginia and Truckee Railroad. Master's thesis, Department of Anthropology, University of Nevada, Reno.

J. RYAN KENNEDY
DEPARTMENT OF ANTHROPOLOGY
INDIANA UNIVERSITY
STUDENT BUILDING 130
701 EAST KIRKWOOD AVENUE
BLOOMINGTON, IN 47405-7100

Sarah Christine Heffner (莎拉·贺弗那)

Exploring Health-Care Practices of Chinese Railroad Workers in North America

试论北美中国铁路工人的医疗实践

ABSTRACT

Chinese laborers on the North American transcontinental railroads performed dangerous and labor-intensive work, and many died or were seriously injured as a result of explosions, cave-ins, and severe and unpredictable weather. These workers received meager wages and may have faced additional health risks from ethnic violence and malnutrition. Little is known about how these individuals treated their injuries and ailments and, to date, not a single document written by a Chinese railroad worker has been discovered. Analysis of medicinal artifacts, dating from 1865 to 1910, recovered from railroad sites in California, Idaho, Montana, Nevada, Texas, and Utah, combined with research on existing documentary and archaeological sources on Chinese medicine in 19th-century North America, provide a better understanding of the health-care practices employed by Chinese railroad workers. Lacking access to traditional doctors and herbal stores, workers relied on a system of informal "folk" medicine that involved using both European American and Chinese medicines.

北美横贯大陆铁路上的中国劳工从事着危险而高强度的工作。他们中有很多人都因爆炸、塌方以及严峻而变幻莫测的天气条件而死亡或重伤。这些工人的工资很低，同时还因种族暴力和营养不良而面临额外的健康威胁。这些个体是如何养伤，如何治疗疾病的？我们对此几乎一无所知。而如今也尚未找到中国铁路工人在这方面的文献记录。在加州、内华达、德克萨斯和犹他的铁路考古现场发掘的1865–1914年期间的医疗文物，连同现存的有关十九世纪北美地区中国医疗的文献及考古资料的研究，会让我们对中国铁路工人的医疗实践有更好的理解。在没有传统的医生以及中草药铺的情况下，工人们依赖于一种非正式的、"民间的"、且结合欧美与中国传统的医疗体系。

Introduction

While historians and other scholars have written with vivid detail about the accidents and injuries sustained by Chinese railroad workers on the Central Pacific, few written sources on the health-care practices of Chinese railroad workers exist. Archaeological investigations of overseas Chinese sites have tended to focus on large urban Chinatowns, while excavations of the many small nonurban labor camps scattered throughout the West are much fewer in number (Voss and Williams 2008). Even fewer archaeological investigations of Chinese railroad worker sites have been conducted. From those excavations few materials have been recovered, primarily because work camps tended to be ephemeral in nature, and railroad workers had to take all their personal belongings with them as they traveled from one camp to the next.

Despite this paucity of recovered artifacts, some conclusions can be made regarding the health-care practices of Chinese railroad workers in North America by using existing documentary and archaeological sources of information on Chinese medical practice in the United States during the 19th century, in conjunction with an analysis of artifacts—potentially related to health care—recovered from Chinese railroad sites. Framing this interpretation within the foundational background of Chinese medicine can aid in a more complete understanding of the medical practices of Chinese railroad workers.

The Theoretical Background of Chinese Medicine

A basic understanding of the theoretical underpinnings of Chinese medicine is necessary to better comprehend the health-care practices of Chinese railroad workers. The practice of Chinese medicine is based on several concepts that differ significantly from Western understandings of the human body. These include yin and yang, qi, blood, meridians, and the Five Elements/Five Phases theory, also known as *wŭ xíng*.

Yin (female) and yang (male) are two opposite but complementary forces interacting within the human body. Traditional Chinese anatomy divides the body into five yin organs (*zang*) and six yang organs (*fu*). The maintenance of a harmonious balance of these two forces is necessary to stay healthy. The yin

Historical Archaeology, 2015, 49(1):134–147.
Permission to reprint required.

organs (solid or storing organs) include the liver, heart, spleen, lungs, and kidneys, while the yang organs (hollow or eliminating organs) include the stomach, intestines, and urinary and gall bladder, as well as a system unique to Chinese medicine called the "Triple Burner" (Kaptchuk 2000:96). The yin organs perform the function of processing food and fluid, and flushing impure substances out of the body, while the yang organs store the pure substances processed by the yin organs (Maciocia 1989:8). The Triple Burner assists the yin and yang organs in their functions and helps circulate the various types of qi throughout the body (Maciocia 1989:64).

Qi refers to the thread connecting all beings, the essence of life, and is closely related to blood. Qi has two major characteristics in Chinese medicine: it is a pure substance produced by the organs and functions to nourish the body and mind, and it relates to the various functional activities of each organ. Blood functions to nourish the body, moisten the organs, and help maintain a sound mind (Maciocia 1989:37–38,50–51). Meridians are channels that carry energy, or qi, and blood through the body and serve to guide physicians in the application of external treatments, such as acupuncture and moxibustion.

The Five Elements/Five Phases theory, or *wŭ xíng*, is used to interpret the relationship between seasonal changes and the organs of the body and their various functions. Each element is associated with one of the five *zang* organs: wood with the liver, fire with the heart, earth with the spleen, metal with the lungs, and water with the kidneys (Fan 1996:11). Additionally, each element has an associated color: green for wood, red for fire, yellow for earth, white for metal, and black for water (Maciocia 1989:21). The Five Elements theory is used to diagnose illness and direct proper treatment.

Disease upsets the balance of the yin and yang elements of the body, which must be subjected to a treatment that will restore the balance between the two (Chen and Chen 1999:1). There are two primary methods of applying treatments in Chinese medicine: internal and external. Internal treatments are herbal medicines taken in the form of teas, soups, pills, powders, medicinal oils, and tonic wines. Herbal medicines are made from plants, minerals, and animal parts. Taking herbal medicine is intended to elicit one or a combination of the following effects:

perspiration, vomiting, purging of the bowels, balancing the negative effect of a disease, cooling the body, dispelling accumulated moisture, and supplementing the balance of yin and yang (Reid 1993:48–50).

External treatments include plasters, poultices, acupuncture, moxibustion, scraping (*guāshā*), massage, and cupping. Plasters and poultices are prepared by grinding and powdering herbal ingredients to form a paste or poultice that is applied to the surface of the skin.

Acupuncture involves the insertion of needles of various lengths and widths into specific points, or meridians, on the surface of the body. In moxibustion, leaves of the artemesia plant were ground into a powder, shaped into a cone or cylinder, and allowed to burn down to the skin (Barnes 2005:298). Scraping was done using a coin, soup spoon, or specialized scraping tool (Reid 1993:57). In cupping therapy, a burnt piece of cotton, cloth, herbs, or paper that has been soaked in oil or alcohol was held underneath a cup close to the skin (Palos 1971:171,173; Reid 1993:57–58).

In addition to using herbal medicines, one important method that Chinese people have used to maintain good health and treat illness is the consumption of various foods thought to have medicinal properties. Food and medicine are closely related in Chinese culture. During the European late-medieval period, Chinese physicians first began assigning medicinal properties to individual foods (Lo 2005:164). These include flavor (hot, sweet, sour, bitter, salty), thermal properties (hot, warm, cold, cool), organ networks (spleen, stomach, kidney, etc.), and direction of movement (upward, downward, floating, falling). Significant emphasis is placed on the thermal properties of food. Hot foods, such as ginger, peanuts, and chilies, can provide additional energy and are used to treat paleness and weakness. Cold foods, such as oranges, watermelon, and papaya, provide a lower amount of energy and help balance symptoms of heat excess caused by consuming too many hot foods.

Existing Sources of Information on Chinese Health-Care Practices

Although archaeological evidence of Chinese railroad workers' health-care practices is scarce, there are several existing sources of information on Chinese medicine that can aid in scholars' understanding of Chinese railroad workers' medical care and treatment. Documentary sources include newspaper and journal articles written by European Americans, advertisements placed by Chinese doctors in English newspapers, and handwritten prescriptions and ingredient lists housed in museum collections.

Though frequently biased, 19th-century European American observations of Chinese doctors and drugstores do provide important details of techniques of diagnosis and treatments employed by Chinese doctors. One such observer was ethnographer and author Stewart Culin (1887a, 1887b). Culin visited Chinese drugstores in Philadelphia and wrote detailed descriptions of the interior and exterior appearance of these stores, and how medicinal ingredients were displayed, prepared, and stored. According to his observations, the practice of Chinese medicine in the United States during the 19th century was confined to internal medicine of primarily vegetable origin, the most common preparations being in the form of teas and pills.

In larger cities, Chinese doctors placed advertisements in English newspapers and used testimonials from European American patients to market their services to a non-Chinese clientele. European Americans were attracted to the gentler, noninvasive therapies of the Chinese, which often proved more effective than Western treatments that relied on the ingestion or injection into the body of poisonous substances, such as mercury and arsenic (Shikes 1986:2). In his analysis of Chinese medical advertising in newspapers in Los Angeles, California, Bowen (1994:2) identified 26 Chinese doctors who practiced in the area from 1871 to 1913. The most commonly featured cures were for "rheumatism, lung and stomach complaints, tumors, consumption, blood disorders, asthma, and irritation of the mucus membranes" (Bowen 2002:183).

Museum collections of Chinese medicine, such as the Ah-Fong Collection and the Kam Wah Chung Collection, can also provide information on Chinese medicinal practices during the 19th century. The Ah-Fong Collection is associated with Dr. C. K. Ah-Fong, a Chinese physician who, along with his two sons and grandson, operated an herb shop in downtown Boise, Idaho, from 1889 to 1928 (Buell and Muench 1983:43–44). The contents of the Ah-Fong

apothecary were acquired in 1971 by the Idaho State Historical Society and included over 1,000 herbal specimens, as well as medical texts, herbals, medical encyclopedias, acupuncture handbooks, and medical formularies/recipe books (Buell and Muench 1983:41,42).

The Kam Wah Chung Collection is associated with Ing "Doc" Hay and Lung On, who jointly ran a general store in John Day, Oregon, from 1887 to 1940 (Edson 2003:94). On managed the grocery store, handled business transactions in Chinese and English, and arranged jobs for those in search of work. Hay ran an herbal medicine business in the front of the store and made visits to local ranchers and miners in need of his medical expertise. Restoration work on the Kam Wah Chung Building in 1967 yielded hundreds of objects, including 1,334 medicinal items, as well as dry goods and other store merchandise, furniture, and the personal belongings of On and Hay (Schierup 2007). The collection also contains handwritten prescriptions and letters to both Lung On and Ing Hay from non-Chinese individuals asking for medical advice or requesting medicine.

Archival sources such as newspaper articles and advertisements can provide information on the methods of diagnosis and treatment of disease by Chinese doctors, as well as the types of ailments treated and the medicines employed in treating those ailments. The exceptionally preserved artifacts in the Ah-Fong and Kam Wah Chung collections are superb comparative material for archaeologists studying overseas Chinese sites, including railroad camps. Research on museum collections of Chinese medicine can aid archaeologists in identifying fragments of Chinese medicinal artifacts and interpreting their original uses. Additional collections of Chinese medicine are located in the Asian American Comparative Collection at the University of Idaho, Moscow; the Wing Luke Asian Museum in Seattle, Washington; and the Chew Kee Store in Fiddletown, California.

Health Care of Chinese Railroad Workers

Living Arrangements and Diet

Chinese railroad workers were organized into teams of about a dozen, with each team assigned its own cook—who also was Chinese—and headman (Chang 2004:57). They lived in isolated camps pitched close to the tracks and were segregated from European American railroad workers (Greenwood 1980:114). In some cases, work trains were used in place of or in conjunction with work camps. Work trains were equipped with bunks and cooking facilities (Zeier 1985:138).

Services and living conditions were arranged and regulated by the supplier of labor. Labor contractors were also in charge of adjudicating disputes. One of the primary contractors of Chinese labor for the railroad was Sisson, Wallace & Company, a San Francisco–based construction company that also operated businesses at different places along the Central & Southern Pacific Railroads during the construction and operation of those tracks. Sisson, Wallace & Company provided food and clothing to the Chinese laborers, for which they were compensated by deducting a portion of the cost from railroad workers' wages (P. Ross 1913).

Chinese merchants catered specifically to the needs of their fellow countrymen, stocking imported foods and goods such as rice, dried fish, tea, opium, silk, and herbal medicines (Langenwalter 1980; Kwong and Miscevic 2005). Merchants also sold tablewares and food-storage vessels. Archaeological and documentary evidence suggests that Chinese railroad workers may have also obtained meal items from local ranchers and farmers. A nearly complete meat cleaver recovered from a line camp in Montana along the Clark Fork River suggests that railroad workers may have had access to fresh beef from local ranchers (Merritt et al. 2012:681).

The diets of Chinese laborers tended to be healthier than those of European Americans because they balanced their intake of meat, starch, and vegetables and drank boiled water or tea, while European American laborers had a steady diet of red meat, fat, and starch (Rogers 1997). Additionally, European Americans did not boil their water to remove possible contaminants. Evidence also suggests that, in addition to consuming more traditional foods, such as pork and fish, Chinese laborers incorporated beef and occasionally wild animals, such as elk and antelope, into their diet (Diehl et al. 1998; Kennedy 2013, this issue). Archaeological evidence also suggests that Chinese laborers were not different from their European American counterparts in consuming copious amounts of alcohol as well as soda water (Wrobleski 1996; D. Ross 2010).

Health-Care Treatments

Existing documentary and archaeological sources on Chinese medicine in the 19th-century United States, such as those described earlier, primarily reflect a more formal, classical system of Chinese medicine practiced by doctors who had gained their medical knowledge through university training, apprenticeship, or self-instruction. Chinese workers in remote mining and railroad camps would not have had the same level of access to the classically trained doctors and herbal medicine stores that Chinese who lived in urban Chinatowns would have had. Railroad workers would have had to rely on themselves for treatment, using less-formal "folk" medicine. This difference is reflected in the nature of the material culture related to health care that has been recovered from remote mining and railroad camps.

Most Chinese immigrants would have possessed a basic knowledge of herbal medicine, as medical knowledge was popular in Chinese society, and taking medicine was seen as an indispensable aspect of daily life. In his observations of Chinese medical practice, Culin (1887b:357) theorized that Chinese individuals were used to taking medicine since early childhood, when their mothers prescribed simple herbal remedies to relieve their childhood ailments. He also suggested that the study of Chinese medicine was not restricted to doctors, and that citizens who were not medically educated could purchase popular medical works, such as the *Golden Mirror of Medicine*, which provided specific directions for the treatment of all manner of ailments.

Archaeological evidence of Chinese railroad workers' health-care practices is sparse, in part because railroad camps were ephemeral in nature, and because few archaeological investigations of Chinese railroad worker camps have been conducted. The workers themselves were often very transient and left behind few physical remains on the surface (California Department of Transportation 2013). The remains have often been looted by bottle and relic collectors. In their documentation of railroad sites along a 90 mi. section of the Central Pacific Railroad (CPRR), Raymond and Fike (1981) noted several sites that had been extensively looted and had few surface artifacts remaining. Chinese dugouts and wells had been vandalized, and artifacts deemed undesirable by looters had been placed in piles on the surface.

Archaeological investigations of railroad sites in California, Idaho, Montana, Nevada, Texas, and Utah provide an indication of the kinds of health-care treatments that Chinese railroad workers employed. These sites date from 1865 to 1910 and include work camps, maintenance and repair shops, and settlements associated with the construction of the Central Pacific, Northern Pacific, and Southern Pacific railroads. Health-care artifacts, and those potentially related to health care, recovered from these sites include European American patent-medicine bottles, homeopathic-medicine vials, Chinese medicine vials, opium-smoking paraphernalia, barrel hoops and lids, teacups, porcelain soup spoons, and coins.

European American patent-medicine bottles have been recovered from several Chinese railroad sites. A patent medicine is a "preparation to which sole manufacturing rights are claimed by virtue of owning the formula"—rather than truly patented with the U.S. Patent Office (Bingham 1994:5). Popular types of patent medicines found at Chinese railroad sites include bitters, sarsaparillas, extracts, liniments, tonics, and veterinary medicines.

Bitters were used to treat stomach complaints, malaria, fever, and chills, and were typically composed of an alcohol-based extract derived from plants or minerals, and a small amount of bitter-tasting herbs (Torbenson et al. 2000:56). A popular brand of bitters was Dr. J. Hostetter's Stomach Bitters, bottle fragments of which were found at Lakeview Camp (26Or214) near Carson City, Nevada, and at the Cabinet Landing site (10BR413) in Bonner County, Idaho (Landreth et al. 1985; Rogers 1997). Sarsaparillas were a popular 19th- and early-20th-century cure for syphilis and typically contained root beer or birch beer with sassafras root for flavoring. Fragments of Ayer's Compound Extract Sarsaparilla and Dr. Henry's Sarsaparilla bottles were found at a labor camp associated with the Southern Pacific Railroad (SPRR) in Val Verde County, Texas (Briggs 1974). Patent-medicine

manufacturers loosely used the term "extract" to refer to any mixture of bitter-tasting herbs and alcohol in which a particular flavor or medicinal property of the herb had supposedly been extracted and preserved in alcohol. Liniments were commonly used to treat bruises, muscle aches, and headaches, and could also be applied to the chest to treat lung ailments. Archaeologists identified a bottle of Ballard Snow Liniment at the Cabinet Landing site, a medicine that claimed to cure rheumatism, nervous disorders, and lower-back pain, leaving one "as spry as a colt" (*Amador Ledger* 1909). Veterinary medicines, such as the Celebrated H. H. H. Horse Medicine, a bottle of which was found at the site of a labor camp in Val Verde County, Texas, was introduced by Daniel D. Tomlinson in 1868 and marketed for use by both man and horse (Fike 2006:147). Similar to liniments, veterinary medicines could be used to treat headaches and other muscle aches and pains.

Chinese railroad workers may have chosen to consume European American patent medicines for several reasons. European American patent medicines were convenient and affordable, and would not have required a formal doctor visit or written prescription. It is possible that the Chinese viewed European American patent medicines as a form of inexpensive liquor. For example, bitters bottles frequently contained high levels of alcohol, but were historically classified as non-potable alcohol and were excluded from high taxes placed on other spirits (Parsons 2011:12). Toulouse (1970:63) stated that "the alcoholic content [of bitters] ranged up to 40%, and the 'dosage' ran to 'three or four wine-glasses full each day.'" Bitters were often treated as a special brand of liquor and frequently sold at bars.

Homeopathic-medicine vials recovered from the Cabinet Landing site represent another convenient form of self-medication. Homeopathy was first introduced by Samuel Hahnemann in 1810 and involved administering tiny doses of medicine (Bivins 2007:89–90). Homeopathic treatments were made from a mixture of herbs, minerals, and animal parts whose chemical properties produced symptoms similar to the disease being treated. Homeopathic medicines were sold as individual vials or in kits for home use with instructions for proper administration.

Chinese medicine vials are fairly common finds on overseas Chinese sites, including railroad sites. Chinese medicine had its own version of European American patent medicines, in the form of small, single-dosage medicine vials (Figure 1). These medicines were mass-produced and did not require a written prescription from a doctor. Chinese medicine vials are popularly referred to as "opium bottles." This is a misnomer, as they did not contain opium, but instead contained single doses of medicinal pills, powder, or oil (Armstrong 1979:236). Vials were securely sealed with a wax-covered cork and had paper labels affixed to the outside of the vial, indicating their contents and the name of the manufacturer. Rarely do the labels survive in the archaeological record. An exception would be a Chinese medicine vial with a paper label

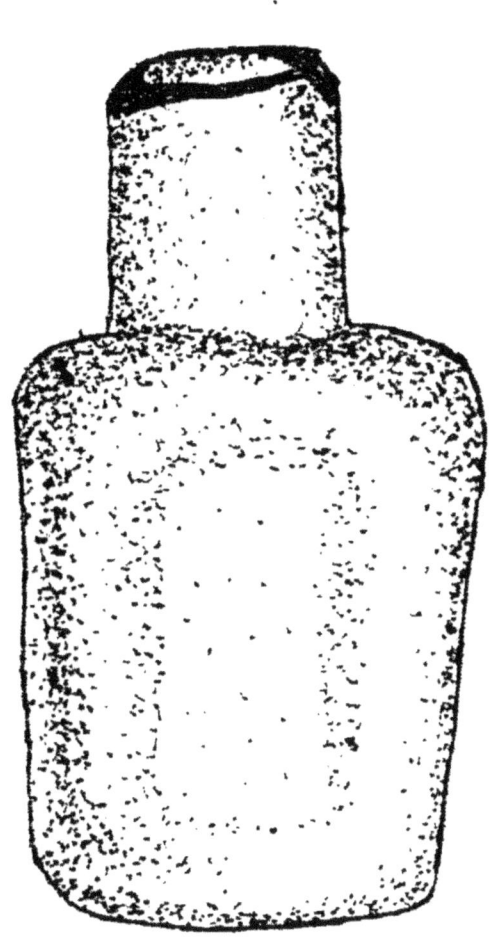

FIGURE 1. Sketch of a Chinese medicine vial from the Cabinet Landing site (Landreth et al. 1985:111).

identified at the Terrace site, a maintenance and repair headquarters along the Salt Lake Division (Wells, Nevada, to Ogden, Utah) of the transcontinental railroad (Raymond and Fike 1981) (Figure 2). The characters roughly translate to "peppermint oil specializing selling for the opening ceremony of the forge iron street" (Péng Lǐ 2014, pers. comm.). Perhaps this medicine was specially created to honor the completion of the transcontinental railroad, and that "opening ceremony of the forge iron street" was a reference to the Golden Spike ceremony at Promontory Summit, Utah.

Artifacts associated with opium smoking, including opium cans, lamps, and opium-pipe bowls, are ubiquitous on overseas Chinese sites, including railroad camps. Though most commonly associated with recreational use, the Chinese may have been using opium for medicinal purposes. The Lovelock Chinatown Collection at the Nevada State Museum contains an opium can with a red paper label affixed that indicated it contained "qīng níng wán," which translates as "clear and quiet pills" (Wiseman and Feng 1998:731) (Figure 3). According to the label, this medicine was manufactured in Guangzhou City, Guangdong Province (Péng Lǐ 2012, pers. comm.). Prepared smoking opium from China was exported in rectangular metal cans containing around 6-2/3 oz. of opium (Wylie and Fike 1993:261,287). Though typically exported in solid form, opium also came in small pellets or pills that were smoked using a short, tiny pipe (Wylie and Fike 1993:266). It is possible that these opium pills were used as a form of medicine, as the label indicates these pills could make one "pure, strong, healthy, and well" (Brown 1979:564). Opium, in the form of morphine, was used to treat acute pain, such as from an injury or chronic pain from arthritis. It was also a powerful cough suppressant and symptomatic treatment for diarrhea.

Fragments of keg-sized barrels, including barrel hoops and iron lids, that may have held whiskey or black powder, were recovered from work camps in Nevada (Zeier 1985; Rogers 1997). It has been suggested that the Chinese kept warm tea at the work site in whiskey-sized kegs and used smaller-sized black-powder kegs and cans to transport tea from the camp to the site (Zeier 1985; Rogers 1997). As

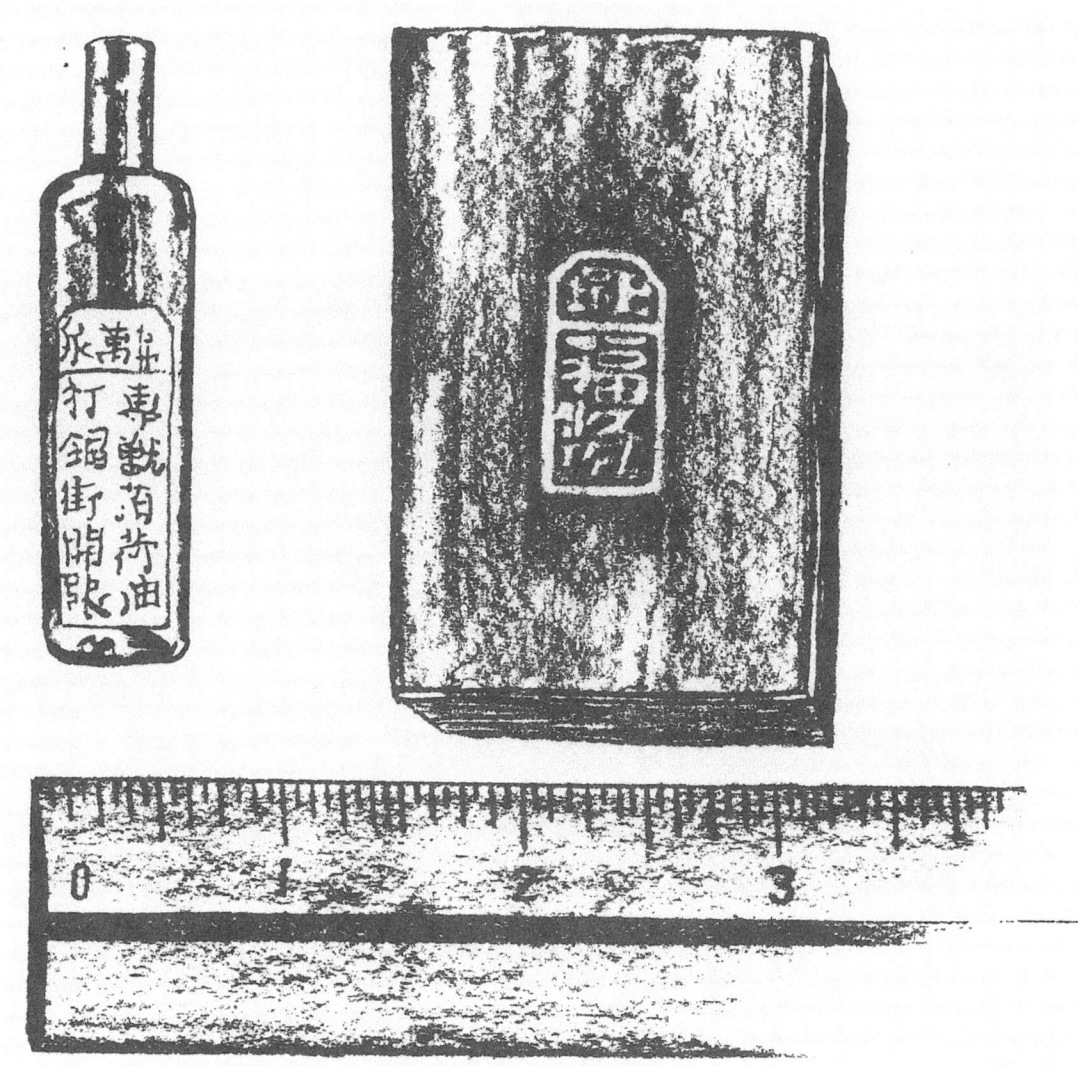

FIGURE 2. Sketch of a Chinese medicine vial with paper label and an opium tin from the Terrace site (Raymond and Fike 1981).

mentioned earlier, tea was often taken as a form of internal medicine. Chinese teacups in Celadon and Four Seasons patterns were found at Lakeview Camp and may have been used for drinking medicinal tea (Rogers 1997).

In addition to internal medicine, Chinese railroad workers may have been using external preparations. Possible evidence of the external application of Chinese medicine is brass and zinc Chinese and Vietnamese coins of low denomination that have been found at several railroad sites (Chace and Evans 1969; Zeier 1985; Rogers 1997; Merritt et al. 2012). Archaeologists have frequently interpreted these coins as

having been used as good-luck charms, magical talismans, gaming tokens, and gifts for children. Small holes were often drilled into the coins so that they could be worn as pendants or strung together and used as decorations (Farris 1979:50). It is also possible that the Chinese were using these coins to perform *guā shā*, or scraping, which involves the application of regular pressure in a stroke-like movement to areas of the body where pain, heat, and improper blood flow, or blood stagnation, are present (Reid 1993:57; Chirali 1999:45). Soup spoons were also used to perform scraping. A soup spoon with a Four Seasons design was recovered from a Chinese

FIGURE 3. Opium tin with paper label, Lovelock Chinatown Collection. (Courtesy Nevada State Museum, Carson City; photo by author, 2009.)

railroad camp in Eureka County, Nevada (Zeier 1985:139).

A final category of material culture that could potentially be associated with Chinese railroad workers' medicinal practices is faunal and floral remains. As discussed previously, food and medicine are closely related in Chinese culture. Most Chinese railroad workers had some basic understanding of the principles of hot and cold foods, and which foods could restore balance for various conditions. However, it is difficult to distinguish which food remains were being consumed for their therapeutic properties, and no

distinctively medicinal faunal or floral materials have been recovered from Chinese railroad sites.

A number of medicinal faunal and floral items have been identified at larger Chinatown sites; analysis of these items can yield information about their intended uses and therapeutic properties. Archaeological investigations at Lovelock Chinatown yielded, among other faunal and floral materials, bobcat and viper bones, a turtle carapace, cuttlefish bones, and betel nuts (Figure 4). It is likely the faunal materials were being consumed for both nutritional and medicinal purposes. Snakes were a source of

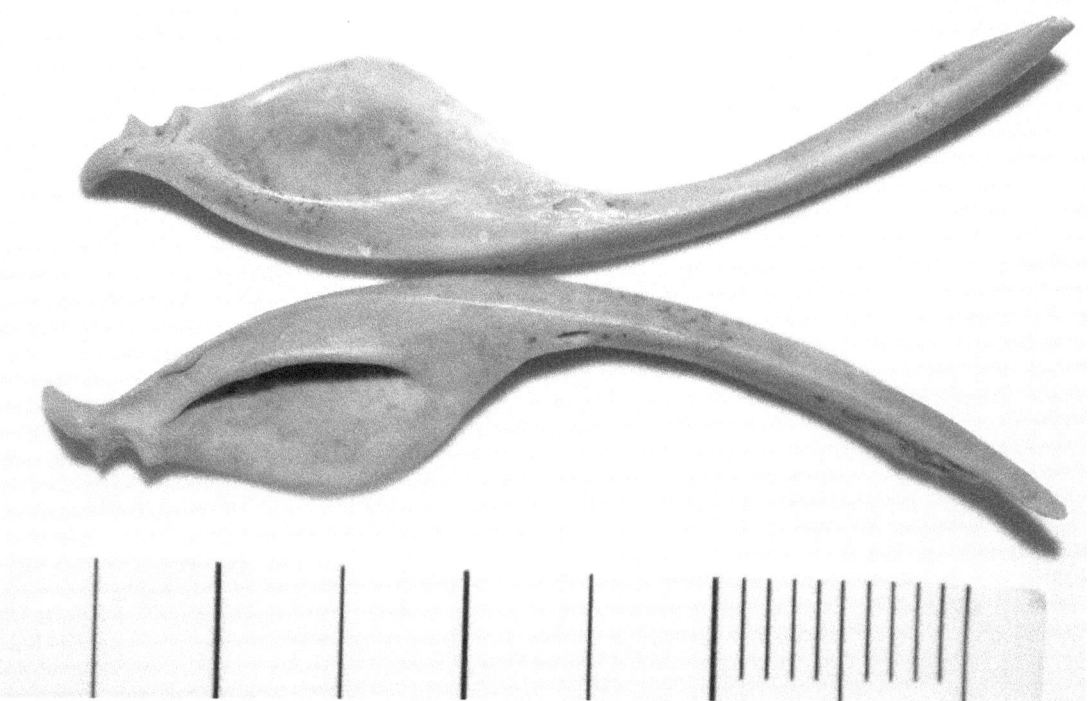

FIGURE 4. Viper bones from Lovelock Chinatown Collection. (Courtesy Nevada State Museum, Carson City; photo by author, 2009.)

wild food in China and a popular food choice of the working classes. In addition to being a food item, snakes are a sort of cure-all in Chinese medicine, and almost every part of a snake was used to treat a range of ailments, such as seizures, poor vision, colds, rheumatism, sore throat, etc. Betel nuts were used for expelling parasitic worms and treating malaria.

At the Wong Ho Leung Chinatown in Riverside, California, archaeologists uncovered 69 specimens of dried house gecko. Dried house geckos were imported into North America from China or the Malaysian Archipelago and sold in Chinese apothecary shops. The lizard's insides were removed, and the lizard was stretched and dried on a stick. The house gecko would be boiled with herbs for a medicinal soup and was thought to help improve kidney function (Langenwalter 1987:69) (Figure 5).

Exploring How Medicines Were Acquired

Chinese railroad workers obtained medicinal items, such as those discussed above, through various means. Chinese immigrants brought

herbal medicines in their luggage on their shipboard journey to the United States. In 1964, the Chinese Historical Society of America in San Francisco, California, analyzed personal belongings of Chinese pioneers from three subbasements of the Son Loy Company and discovered that most of the containers held Chinese herbs and medicines (Liu 1998:138). In addition, Chinese immigrants may have carried seeds of medicinal plants with them. The tree of heaven, *Ailanthus altissima*, also known as Chinese sumac, was introduced to California in 1850 by Chinese immigrants and is now considered an invasive species. It has a variety of medicinal properties and is used as an astringent, antispasmodic, and anthelmintic (Fryer 2010).

Chinese doctors also established successful mail-order businesses that allowed individuals who could not see the doctor in person to receive necessary medical treatment. The Kam Wah Chung Collection contains several letters, dating to the early 1900s, from non-Chinese patrons to Ing Hay and businessman Lung On. The letters contain questions regarding

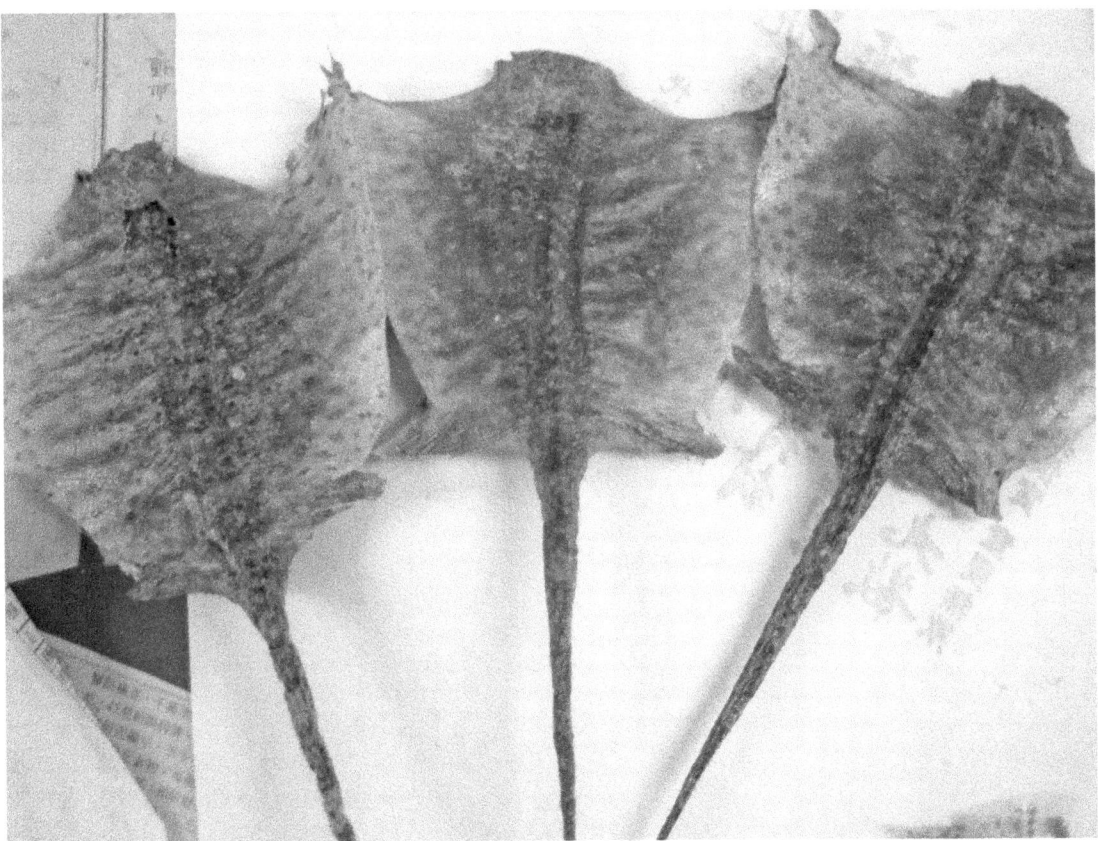

FIGURE 5. Dried geckos on sticks, Taipei, Taiwan. (Photo by author, 2011.)

particular symptoms or courses of treatment, or requests for additional medicine.

Chinese railroad workers may have gotten traditional medicines from merchants based in San Francisco and Sacramento, California, who shipped their goods to suppliers along the railroad via railcar, stagecoach, or freight wagon. In his account of "Medical Art in the Chinese Quarter [of San Francisco]," Augustus Ward Loomis (1869:496) stated that "scarcely an invoice of goods can go to the trader in the most distant mining settlements, or to the sutlers who follow up the camps of the railroad laborers, but medicines will occupy a prominent place in it." Loomis reported that there were over a dozen establishments that prepared and sold Chinese medicine. By 1878, there were 18 wholesale herb companies operating in San Francisco's Chinatown that imported herbs from China and distributed them to Chinese herbalists throughout the United States (Liu 2005:47).

Although records of items purchased and supplied to Chinese railroad workers by Sisson,

Wallace & Company are not available, inventories of items shipped to mining towns with Chinese populations may shed some light on the kinds of health-care items that the Chinese were purchasing. One such example is records of items purchased for the Cortez Mine to supply the company store located at Old Cortez, Lander County, Nevada. Old Cortez was part of the Old Cortez Mining District, an ethnically diverse neighborhood of Chinese, Mexicans, African Americans, and European Americans, and was a silver mining boomtown from 1863 to the 1930s (Hardesty 1988:82; Yancey 1998:36). Langley & Michaels Co. was a wholesale druggist-supply store in San Francisco that frequently supplied medicines to the Cortez Mine store. Examples of items purchased include Vaseline, Syrup of Figs, Mustang Liniment, antipyrine, alum, Florida Water, and Cuticura Salve (Churchill County Museum 1891). Syrup of Figs was a laxative that contained alcohol and senna, a plant with purgative properties, but actually did not contain figs (American Medical Association 1912:672).

While difficult to prove archaeologically, it is possible that Chinese doctors made visits to the railroad camps to treat more-serious illnesses. Ing "Doc" Hay became famous among residents of eastern Oregon for his role in treating laborers affected by influenza during an outbreak in area labor camps in the winter of 1919 to 1920. Hay and Lung On drove to the labor camps and delivered herbs and medicinal tea to the workers (Portland State University and Chinese Consolidated Benevolent Association 2007:47). Though not within the temporal context of the construction of the transcontinental railroads, the example of Ing Hay and Lung On indicates that traditional Chinese doctors traveled to remote areas to deliver much-needed medical care. Chinese railroad workers may have also traveled to established Chinatowns to be treated for more-serious illnesses or to purchase medicines. Hospital records, doctors' notes and journals, and store ledgers may contain information on whether Chinese railroad workers sought medical care in more populated areas.

A final means by which Chinese railroad workers may have obtained herbal medicines is through gathering local plants and capturing small animals. Types of plants similar to those found in China that may have been substituted for use in medicine include bindweed, cocklebur, cattail, pine, and willow (Bowen 2002:176). The Lem brothers, Hung Li and Hong Lee, operated a general store in the remote mining community of Island Mountain, Nevada, from 1873 to 1918 (Hunt-Jones 2006:i). According to Hunt-Jones (2006:82), the Lem brothers had local children collect lizards and toads in exchange for candy, and the brothers sent the animals back to China pickled in jars for use in medicine.

Conclusion

Certain overall patterns in relation to Chinese railroad workers' health-care practices can be delineated when analyzing the entirety of the archaeological evidence discussed above. One of the most noticeable patterns is the general scarcity of Chinese medicinal artifacts. This is in contrast to the large number of Chinese medicinal artifacts recovered from excavations

in urban Chinatowns. The remote locations of railroad camps and the transient nature of the work meant that workers would not have brought much with them. Those items that they did carry with them would have to be relatively lightweight and portable. Perhaps this is why Chinese medicine vials have been found at several railroad camps—they were small and easily portable. Due to the isolated nature of railroad camps, workers would not have had easy access to a traditional Chinese doctor, nor to the herb stores that were so prevalent in the cities of San Francisco and Los Angeles. Chinese railroad workers would have relied on an informal system of medicine, self-treating with Chinese medicines and European American patent medicines that did not require a doctor's diagnosis and prescription. In addition, workers may have gathered local plants and captured small animals to use in medicinal teas and soups. Most Chinese railroad workers would have had some basic knowledge of Chinese medical theory and would have been able to distinguish between hot and cold foods and their primary therapeutic properties.

Acknowledgments

This article stemmed from the first meeting of the Chinese Railroad Workers in North America Archaeology Network held at Stanford University in October 2013. First and foremost, I would like to thank Barbara L. Voss for inviting me to contribute to this thematic issue of *Historical Archaeology*. Additionally, I would like to thank my fellow presenters and the attendees of the October 2013 conference for their insights and additional knowledge that they have contributed to my research on health-care practices of Chinese railroad workers. I am grateful to Péng Lǐ, postdoctoral student, Beijing University, who translated Chinese characters on the medicinal artifacts discussed here. Other individuals who have assisted me in tracking down resources for this article are Eugene Hattori (Nevada State Museum), Priscilla Wegars (Asian American Comparative Collection), Robert Leavitt (University of Nevada, Reno Historical Archaeology Laboratory), and Rob McQueen (Summit Envirosolutions).

References

AMADOR LEDGER
1909   Ballard Snow Liniment: Advertisement. *Amador Ledger* 30 April:5. Jackson, CA.

AMERICAN MEDICAL ASSOCIATION
1912   *Nostrums and Quackery*, 2nd edition, Vol. 1. American Medical Association Press, Chicago, IL.

ARMSTRONG, JANE
1979   The Lovelock Bottles. In *Archaeological and Historical Studies at Ninth and Amherst, Lovelock, Nevada*, Gene M. Hattori, Mary K. Rusco, and Donald Tuohy, editors, pp. 199–250. Nevada State Museum, Carson City.

BARNES, LINDA
2005   *Needles, Herbs, Gods, and Ghosts: China, Healing, and the West to 1848.* Harvard University Press, Cambridge, MA.

BINGHAM, A. WALKER
1994   *The Snake-Oil Syndrome: Patent Medicine Advertising.* Christopher, Hanover, MA.

BIVINS, ROBERTA E.
2007   *Alternative Medicine?: A History.* Oxford University Press, New York, NY.

BOWEN, WILLIAM M.
1994   Early Chinese Medicine in Southern California. *Gum Saan Journal* 17(1):5–6.
2002   The Five Eras of Chinese Medicine in California. In *The Chinese in America: A History from Gold Mountain to the New Millennium*, Susie L. Cassel, editor, pp. 174–192. AltaMira Press, Walnut Creek, CA.

BRIGGS, ALTON KING
1974   The Archeology of 1882 Labor Camps on the Southern Pacific Railroad, Val Verde County, Texas. Master's thesis, Department of Anthropology, University of Texas, Austin. Manuscript, Asian American Comparative Collection, Moscow, ID.

BROWN, BONITA
1979   Artifacts from the Loft. In *Archaeological and Historical Studies at Ninth and Amherst, Lovelock, Nevada*, Gene M. Hattori, Mary K. Rusco, and Donald Tuohy, editors, pp. 549–595. Nevada State Museum, Carson City.

BUELL, PAUL D., AND CHRISTOPHER MUENCH
1983   A Chinese Apothecary in Frontier Idaho. *Annals of the Chinese Historical Society of the Pacific Northwest* 1:39–48.

CALIFORNIA DEPARTMENT OF TRANSPORTATION
2013   A Historical Context and Archaeological Research Design for Work Camp Properties in California. California Department of Transportation <http://www.dot.ca.gov/ser/downloads/cultural/work_camps_final.pdf>. Accessed 5 April 2014.

CHACE, PAUL, AND WILLIAM S. EVANS, JR.
1969   Celestial Sojourners in the High Sierras: The Ethno-Archaeology of Chinese Railroad Workers (1865–1868). Paper presented at the Second Conference on Historical and Underwater Archaeology, Tucson, AZ.

CHANG, IRIS
2004   *The Chinese in America: A Narrative History.* Penguin, New York, NY.

CHEN, ZE-LIN, AND MEI-FANG CHEN
1999   *A Comprehensive Guide to Chinese Herbal Medicine.* Castle, Edison, NJ.

CHIRALI, ILKAY ZIHNI
1999   *Traditional Chinese Medicine: Cupping Therapy.* Churchill Livingstone, New York, NY.

CHURCHILL COUNTY MUSEUM
1891   Invoice of Purchases from Langley & Michaels Co. by Cortez Mines Ltd. Store, 9 June. Manuscript, Churchill County Museum, Fallon, NV.

CULIN, STEWART
1887a Chinese Drug Stores in America. *Journal of Pharmacy* 59(12):1–6.
1887b The Practice of Medicine by the Chinese in America. *Medical and Surgical Reporter* 19 March:355–357.

DIEHL, MICHAEL, JENNIFER A. WATERS, AND J. HOMER THIEL
1998   Acculturation and the Composition of the Diet of Tucson's Overseas Chinese Gardener at the Turn of the Century. *Historical Archaeology* 32(4):19–33.

EDSON, CHRISTOPHER HOWARD
2003   Excerpts from The Chinese in Eastern Oregon, 1860–1890. In *Chinese on the American Frontier*, Arif Dirlik and Malcolm Yeung, editors, pp. 185–197. Rowman & Littlefield, Lanham, MD.

FAN, WARNER J-W.
1996   *A Manual of Chinese Herbal Medicine: Principles and Practice for Easy Reference.* Shambhala, Boston, MA.

FARRIS, GLEN J.
1979   "Cash" as Currency: Coins and Tokens from Yreka Chinatown. *Historical Archaeology* 13:48–52.

FIKE, RICHARD E.
2006   *The Bottle Book: A Comprehensive Guide to Historic Embossed Medicine Bottles.* Blackburn Press, Caldwell, NJ.

FRYER, JANET L.
  2010 Fire Effects Information System. U.S. Forest Service, Rocky Mountain Research Station, Fire Sciences Laboratory <http://www.fs.fed.us/database/feis/plants/tree/ailalt/all.html>. Accessed 30 May 2014.

GREENWOOD, ROBERTA S.
  1980 The Chinese on Main Street. In *Archaeological Perspectives on Ethnicity in America*, Robert L. Schuyler, editor, pp. 113–123. Baywood, Farmingdale, NY.

HARDESTY, DON
  1988 *The Archaeology of Mining and Miners: A View from the Silver State*. Society for Historical Archaeology, Ann Arbor, MI.

HUNT-JONES, PATRICIA
  2006 The Heart of a Community: An Archaeological and Historical Study of Island Mountain's Chinese General Store. Master's thesis, Department of Anthropology, University of Nevada, Reno.

KAPTCHUK, TED J.
  2000 *The Web that Has No Weaver: Understanding Chinese Medicine*. Contemporary, Chicago, IL.

KENNEDY, RYAN
  2013 Zooarchaeology and Food in Chinese Railroad Sites. Paper presented at the First Meeting of the Chinese Railroad Workers in North America Archaeology Network, Stanford, CA.

KWONG, PETER, AND DUSANKA MISCEVIC
  2005 *Chinese America: The Untold Story of America's Oldest New Community*. New Press/W. W. Norton, New York, NY.

LANDRETH, KEITH, KEO BURESON, AND MARY CONDON
  1985 *Archeological Investigations at the Cabinet Landing Site (10BR413), Bonner County, Idaho*. Eastern Washington University Reports in Archeology and History No. 100-45. Cheney.

LANGENWALTER, PAUL E. II
  1980 The Archaeology of 19th Century Chinese Subsistence at Lower China Store, Madera County, California. In *Archaeological Perspectives on Ethnicity in America*, R. L. Schuyler, editor, pp. 102–112. Baywood, Farmingdale, NY.
  1987 Mammals and Reptiles as Food and Medicine in Riverside's Chinatown. In *Wong Ho Leun: An American Chinatown*, Vol. 2, pp. 53–106. Great Basin Foundation, San Diego, CA.

LIU, HAIMING
  1998 The Resilience of Ethnic Culture: Chinese Herbalists in the American Medical Profession. *Journal of Asian American Studies* 1(2):173–191.
  2005 *The Transnational History of a Chinese Family: Immigrant Letters, Family Business, and Reverse Migration*. Rutgers University Press, Rutgers, NJ.

LO, VIVIENNE
  2005 Pleasure, Prohibition, and Pain: Food and Medicine in Traditional China. In *Of Tripod and Palate: Food, Politics, and Religion in Traditional China*, Roel Sterckx, editor, pp. 163–185. Palgrave Macmillan, New York, NY.

LOOMIS, AUGUSTUS WARD
  1869 Medical Art in the Chinese Quarter. *Overland Monthly and Out West Magazine* 2(6):496–596. San Francisco, CA.

MACIOCIA, GIOVANNI
  1989 *The Foundations of Chinese Medicine: A Comprehensive Text for Acupuncturists and Herbalists*. Churchill Livingstone, Edinburgh, UK.

MERRITT, CHRISTOPHER H., GARY WEISZ, AND KELLY J. DIXON
  2012 "Verily the Road Was Built with Chinaman's Bones": An Archaeology of Chinese Line Camps in Montana. *International Journal of Historical Archaeology* 16(4):666–695.

PALOS, STEPHAN
  1971 *The Chinese Art of Healing*. Herder and Herder, New York, NY.

PARSONS, BRAD T.
  2011 *Bitters: A Spirited History of a Classic Cure-All with Cocktails, Recipes, and Formulas*. Ten Speed Press, Berkeley, CA.

PORTLAND STATE UNIVERSITY AND CHINESE CONSOLIDATED BENEVOLENT ASSOCIATION
  2007 *Dreams of the West: A History of the Chinese in Oregon, 1850–1950*. Ooligan Press, Portland, OR.

RAYMOND, ANAN S., AND RICHARD E. FIKE
  1981 *Rails East to Promontory: The Utah Stations*. Utah State Office Bureau of Land Management, Cultural Resource Series No. 8. Salt Lake City. Reprinted 1997 by Pioneer Enterprises, Livingston, TX.

REID, DANIEL P.
  1993 *Chinese Herbal Medicine*. Shambhala, Boston, MA.

ROGERS, C. LYNN
  1997 Making Camp Chinese Style: The Archaeology of a V&T Railroad Graders' Camp, Carson City, Nevada. Report to Silver Oak Development Company, Carson City, NV, from Archaeological Research Services, Virginia City, NV.

ROSS, DOUGLAS E.
  2010 Comparing the Material Lives of Asian Transmigrants through the Lens of Alcohol Consumption. *Journal of Social Archaeology* 10(2):230–254.

ROSS, PETER V. (EDITOR)
  1913 Wallace et al. vs. Sisson et al. 1893. In *California Unreported Court Cases*, Vol. 4, Peter V. Ross, editor, pp. 34–47. Bender-Moss, San Francisco, CA. Google Books <http://books.google.com/books/>. Accessed 11 November 2014.

SCHIERUP, CHRIS
  2007 Kam Wah Chung & Co. Collection. Electronic catalog, Kam Wah Chung & Company Museum, John Day, OR.

SHIKES, RANDALL H.
  1986 *Rocky Mountain Medicine: Doctors, Drugs, and Disease in Early Colorado*. Johnson, Boulder, CO.

TORBENSON, MICHAEL, ROBERT H. KELLY, JONATHON ERLEN, LORNA CROPCHO, MICHAEL MORACA, BONNIE BEILER, K. N. RAO, AND MOHAMED VIRJI
  2000 Lash's: A Bitter Medicine: Biochemical Analysis of an Historical Proprietary Medicine. *Historical Archaeology* 34(2):56–64.

TOULOUSE, JULIAN H.
  1970 High on the Hawg or How the Western Miner Lived, as Told by Bottles He Left Behind. *Historical Archaeology* 4:59–69.

VOSS, BARBARA L., AND BRYN WILLIAMS
  2008 The Archaeology of Chinese Immigrant and Chinese American Communities. *Historical Archaeology* 42(3):1–4.

WISEMAN, NIGEL, AND YE FENG
  1998 *A Practical Dictionary of Chinese Medicine*, 2nd edition. Paradigm, Brookline, MA.

WROBLESKI, DAVID E.
  1996 The Archaeology of Chinese Work Camps on the Virginia and Truckee Railroad. Master's thesis, Department of Anthropology, University of Nevada, Reno.

WYLIE, JENNIFER, AND RICHARD E. FIKE
  1993 Chinese Opium Smoking Techniques and Paraphernalia. In *Hidden Heritage: Historical Archaeology of the Overseas Chinese*, P. S. Wegars, editor, pp. 255–303. Baywood, Amityville, NY.

YANCEY, JOHN
  1998 The Last Family in Cortez. *Northeastern Nevada Historical Society Quarterly* 98(2):30–42.

ZEIER, CHARLES D.
  1985 *Archaeological Data Recovery Associated with the Mt. Hope Project, Eureka County, Nevada*. Bureau of Land Management, Cultural Resource Series, No. 8. Reno, NV.

SARAH CHRISTINE HEFFNER
PAR ENVIRONMENTAL SERVICES, INC.
1906 21ST STREET
SACRAMENTO, CA 95811

Ryan P. Harrod (瑞安・哈罗德)
John J. Crandall (约翰・克朗达)

Rails Built of the Ancestors' Bones: The Bioarchaeology of the Overseas Chinese Experience
祖先白骨建成的铁轨：对海外华人生活经验的生物考古学

ABSTRACT

Between 1865 and 1869, thousands of Chinese immigrants came to the United States to construct the transcontinental railroad. Their impact went beyond labor and helped to develop the social and economic landscape of the country through their ingenuity. Archaeological analyses are especially important for understanding the Chinese in historical America because of the lack of written records. Bioarchaeology can contribute by providing a glimpse into the lives of these resourceful and diverse laborers who toiled to contribute to the development of the railways in the 19th century. The reanalysis of the remains of 13 Chinese men recovered from a cemetery in Carlin, Nevada, reveals that most individuals exhibited widespread musculoskeletal development suggesting frequent, repeated bodily strain. Additionally, all 13 individuals exhibited skeletal trauma or pathologies. The men recovered from Carlin reveal the extent to which Chinese railroad workers endured exploitative oppression and racism, while simultaneously embodying resilience.

在1865至1869年间，成千上万的中国移民来到美国修建横贯大陆铁路。他们所带来的影响远不止其劳动力。他们的创造力促进了整个美国社会与经济的发展。由于缺少文字记载，考古学分析对我们理解这些中国工人十分重要。生物考古学则尤为重要，因为它可以展现这些工人的足智多谋、多样化的生活。本文对内华达州卡林镇一处公墓中发掘的13具中国工人遗骸进行了重新分析。分析结果显示，这些人的肌骨骼发展暗示了频繁和重复性的身体劳损。除此之外，这13个人都显示出骨骼的损伤与病兆。卡林工人的遗骸揭示了中国铁路工人所受的剥削性压迫和种族歧视的程度，却也同时展现了他们不屈不挠的精神。

Introduction

In the 19th century, hundreds of thousands of people left their homelands in and around Guangdong Province in China to find work and build more prosperous lives. This mass emigration of laborers from China would have a profound impact on the rest of the world, as these individuals facilitated development in the Americas, Caribbean, Australia, New Zealand, and Asia. In the United States, the importance of the labor performed by these individuals is most readily apparent in the construction of the first transcontinental railroad between 1865 and 1869.

The reality is that these Chinese immigrants, or overseas Chinese, were not simply laborers, but individuals that, beginning in the early to mid-1800s, would transform the social, economic, and political landscape of the United States countless times (Chan 1991; Takaki 1998; McKeown 1999; Chang 2003). Often characterized as a single group, this vast diaspora was complex. Historical research has found that some individuals would stay in the countries to which they had migrated, but others often returned to China (Chen 2000). Regardless of how long individuals lived in the United States, their presence helped to shape and transform Sino-American relations for generations to come. Yet historians and archaeologists know relatively little about the individual lived experiences of these laborers.

One of the main reasons so little is known about Chinese laborers in the United States is because researchers have only recovered traces of their lives in this foreign land. Beyond the material culture they left behind, historians and others have had, in general, only the records and perspectives of non-Chinese Americans to rely on. Unfortunately, these accounts often offer a biased, superficial account from which to reconstruct the lives of Chinese laborers.

Recently, a number of archaeologists have increasingly sought to bring all Asian immigrant laborers, including the Chinese, into focus in their research on a wide variety of topics and using a variety of lines of evidence (Voss and Allen 2008; Ross 2013). The focus of this special issue is a specific demographic of Chinese immigrant laborers, the men who helped to build the transcontinental railroad and its tributaries. The contribution of this article is to explore the ways in which data derived from the skeletal remains of the laborers themselves can provide

Historical Archaeology, 2015, 49(1):148–161.
Permission to reprint required.

some insight into the lives of Chinese laborers working on the construction of the railroads in the historical American West.

A review of the bioarchaeological research conducted on Chinese railroad workers to date reveals that data derived from contextualized analyses of the human remains have played a minimal role in the efforts to understand the importance of the Chinese in the development of the United States during the 19th century. In fact, most of what is known about Chinese immigrants is based on only 13 burials, recovered from a cemetery in the town of Carlin, in Elko County, Nevada (Figure 1).

According to Chung et al. (2005:107), several of the burials were accidentally discovered by the landowner during construction of a new home. The archaeological analysis of the site and mortuary context was carried out by Eugene Hattori and Fred Frampton (Chung et al. 2005:107), while the initial osteological analysis of the bodies was conducted by a team from the National Museum of Natural History that included Douglas Owsley, Kari Bruwelheide, Juliet Brundige, David Hunt, Chip Clark, and Rebecca Redmond (Owsley et al. 1997). Currently, the remains are housed in the Sheilagh Brooks Laboratory in the Department of Anthropology at the University of Nevada, Las Vegas. Given the important nature of the burials, in terms of what they can reveal about Chinese railroad workers, the skeletal remains have been analyzed previously by several other researchers, including the authors. The focus of these past research projects has been on enhancing understanding of cultural retention and transformation among Chinese Americans (Chung et al. 2005), the assessment of the geographic origin in China and biological affinities of the individuals (Schmidt 2006; Schmidt et al. 2011), and, most recently, the identification of systems of inequality and violence (Harrod et al. 2013).

This article reviews the findings obtained from these analyses of the remains of the 13 burials excavated from Carlin. Relying on the detailed historical reconstructions established by Chung et al. (2005) and expanding on the

FIGURE 1. Map of Carlin, Nevada, in relation to the railroads of the American West. Image adapted from a map of the Central Pacific Railroad of California (Crofutt 1872:193). (Map by Ryan P. Harrod, 2014.)

work done by Harrod et al. (2013), the goal is to provide a more complete picture of the lives of these individuals. The focus is on analyses of skeletal injuries, muscle strain, osteoarthritis or degenerative joint disease, dental health, and mortuary treatment, because these skeletal markers provide an indication of the overall health and well-being of these men who spent a portion of their lives as railroad workers. The findings from the skeletal analysis are contextualized against historical and archival research, and the extent of muscle strain, widespread trauma, and disease testify to the cycles of suffering faced by early Chinese immigrants to America.

Historical Context

After learning of the discovery of gold in California, Chinese immigrated to the western United States by the thousands. According to archival work by Chung et al. (2005:108), the *Virginia City Territorial Enterprise* from 1871 suggests that, from the placer mines in California in the 1850s, Chinese traveled eastward into Nevada and worked near Gold Hill. Chinese immigration to Nevada only increased with the discovery of the Comstock Lode in 1859, which led to Chinese laborers engaging in a number of occupations throughout the state (Chung et al. 2005).

The construction of the Central Pacific Railroad (CPRR) began in 1868. With many Chinese in the state already, and more immigrating across the West as railroad construction rose and fell, many Chinese worked the rails and stayed into the 20th century to form immigrant communities in Nevada. Chung et al. (2005:108) noted that at least 10,000, and up to 17,000, Chinese were hired to lay track across northern Nevada. It was these Chinese who encountered the land that became Carlin, Nevada, in Elko County. After the completion of the transcontinental railroad in 1869, many of the railroad laborers stayed in Nevada as maintenance men and construction workers.

Chung et al. (2005:109) discussed some of the other occupations in which Chinese laborers engaged after the construction of the railroad was completed, including crop farmers, restaurant and laundry owners, miners, and laborers in the lumber and mining industries. All of these occupations were related to the railroad to some degree, as they often provided services for the people still working on the railroad or were subsidized directly by the railroad companies. In an interview by Chung in 2000, John Fong recollects operating, in the late 1800s, a restaurant in Carlin that was subsidized by the CPRR and used produce grown by Chinese farmers/gardeners whose plots of land were along the rail line (Chung et al. 2005:109). His oral testimony, as well as the documentary record (Carter 1976), provided testimony of the presence of the Chinese in a number of industries in Carlin after May 1869, when the railroads in the region had been completed. Carlin had a Chinatown, complete with merchants and networks tying the local Chinese community into the larger district and benevolent associations. The associations were responsible for moving remittance and the bones of the dead back to the provincial community, while bringing Chinese wares to Nevada (Chung et al. 2005). Thus, the cemetery sample discussed in this article represents a subsection of the Chinese who lived in Carlin in the 19th century. First, these men survived railroad work and were buried in a small segregated cemetery away from the European American cemetery in town. Second, they represent men who lived in Carlin after the railways were completed. Third, they were, curiously and for unknown reasons, not shipped back to their provincial community by district associations. While they likely worked on the railways and thus ended up in Carlin, the life histories of these individuals likely do not represent the full diversity of the experiences Chinese railway workers had. The information collected from these human remains offers a data set that will help to enhance what is known of railroad workers from China.

It is important to understand that, in general, the men who labored to construct the railroads in the United States during the 19th century were at greater risk of poor health and early death. Labor statistics about industrial accidents recorded by regional bureaus reveals that being a railroad worker in the mid-19th century was a dangerous job. Friedman and Ladinsky (1967:60), investigating historical industrial accidents in Wisconsin, found that during the 1800s injury incidence among rail line workers was higher than for any other industry, including mining and manufacturing-related occupations.

They also found that the number of individuals injured laboring on the railroad increased over time, and, by 1906, 5 out of every 100 workers had an accident at work (Friedman and Ladinsky 1967:60).

The assumption that being a railroad worker in the 19th century was hard and potentially lethal is corroborated by the few records Chinese laborers left behind in other countries where railways were developed in the 19th and 20th centuries. Wong Hau-hon, writing in 1926 from Canada, provided testimony to the terrors of railway construction (Yung et al. 2006). Working on the Canadian Pacific Railroad in the 1880s, Wong came from Guangdong Province, like the men from Carlin, Nevada, and discussed his experience in great detail. This man's account of his experiences working the rails in Canada informs reconstructions of the experiences of Chinese laborers in the United States. He writes:

> The work was very dangerous. ... Dynamite was used to blast a rock cave. Twenty charges were placed and ignited, but only eighteen blasts went off. However, the white foreman, thinking that all of the dynamite had gone off, ordered the Chinese workers to enter the cave to resume work. Just at that moment the remaining two charges suddenly exploded. Chinese bodies flew from the cave as if shot from a cannon. Blood and flesh were mixed in a horrible mess. On this occasion about ten or twenty workers were killed. (Yung et al. 2006:39–42)

If these same dangerous conditions existed for railroad laborers in the 19th-century United States, then risks of accidents and death were intimately tied to the building of the CPRR. The risks would have included more than just accidents along the rail line, but also death and suffering resulting from surveying the land, cutting the trees, and maintaining the railway. Eleven tunnel projects were also part of the Central Pacific railway (Baxter and Allen, this issue), and Chinese workers were the majority of those who worked the most dangerous tasks of blasting and drilling these tunnels. Fatalities and injuries no doubt abounded in such situations, as Wong's account illustrates.

Death and direct occupational injury were not the only risks facing the Chinese who built the railways running through northern Nevada. They would have also experienced fatigue, food shortages, dehydration, and exposure due to cold weather. While not all of these stressors can be inferred from bones directly, putting human skeletal remains in their larger archaeological and cultural context can help reveal if the stressors did, in fact, have an impact on the lives of Chinese railroad workers. Evidence of starvation, inferred from the degree of processing seen in the animal remains recovered from archaeological contexts, such as rail camps in Montana (Ellis et al. 2011), indicates that there were times when people appeared to be attempting to obtain as many nutrients from food sources as possible. In terms of parasites, research on the prevalence of the bacterium *Helicobacter pylori* among modern Chinese immigrants in Australia reveals that there was a differential exposure to this bacteria. The authors found that the risks were primarily cultural, and included factors such as socioeconomic status and, surprisingly, the use of chopsticks (Chow et al. 1995). The authors suggest that the use of chopsticks increased the risk of transmitting the bacteria through communal eating and sharing of chopsticks. The cultural practice of sharing utensils was common enough among Chinese in the 1930s that a health program to combat tuberculosis was started to promote ideas of individuality in eating and sleeping, including more hygienic practices at table (Lei 2010). Given that communal food practice still existed in the 1930s, it is likely that it was also common among Chinese immigrant laborers in the late 1800s.

To make up for the scarcity of written records concerning the hazards Chinese workers faced on railways in the United States, one approach is to look at the effects of hard labor and the health of contemporaneous workers involved in similar tasks. Tüchsen et al. (2005) evaluated the hospital records of 5,123 bridge and tunnel laborers and 109,383 other types of construction workers in Denmark. The researchers looked at workers who were involved in a large multiphase project, called the Green Belt Fixed Link, between 1989 and 1998. The median employment length for these workers was about two years (Tüchsen et al. 2005:24), so the workers only performed intensive labor for a relatively short period of time. Similar to their Chinese counterparts who built the transcontinental railroad over 100 years earlier, these workers were organized into labor gangs, worked strenuous and long hours, lived in camps, and were exposed to poor weather conditions. Based on hospital records, these workers had a risk of poor health and death similar to other construction workers, but were admitted to the hospital more often. They were hospitalized for a wide range of ailments, including musculoskeletal injuries, infections, parasites, cardiovascular disease, and digestive issues (Tüchsen et al. 2005:22,25–26). The indication of this study is that the relatively short period of intensely hard labor resulted in long-term consequences to the bodies of these Danish bridge and tunnel laborers that resembled, and in some ways exceeded, the consequences for workers who had done hard labor over a much longer period. Thus, the short period that the Chinese railroad workers labored to build the transcontinental railroad would most likely have significantly affected their health, and the impact should be evident on their bodies. The reality is that the Chinese men working on the railroads were at risk, not only during their relatively short times as laborers, but also long after the work on the railroads was completed.

Bioarchaeological Reanalysis of the Carlin Chinese

The value of a bioarchaeological approach to the 13 Chinese men recovered from Carlin, Nevada, is that a comparative, situated analysis of skeletal data sheds light on the dynamic relationship that human health plays with the environment, both social and natural (Table 1).

Investigating the bodies of these men provides a direct window through which to assess many of these stressors and to understand how they affected survivors, who would likely be buried later at Carlin's Chinese cemetery. Shifting ecologies, which can include changing international policy, racial sentiment, changes in the local ecology, seasonality, or changes in diet, can all alter one's skeletal health, growth, development, and risk of injury. Thus, when used creatively, skeletal data can illuminate anthropological understandings of a wide variety of biosocial processes, such as urbanization, immigration, trade, shifts in social hierarchy, increasing sociopolitical inequality, racism, and other processes that would all have affected the Chinese differently.

Mortuary Context and Demography

The first step of any analysis of burials is to reconstruct the context in which the burials were located and the demographic profile of the sample, creating the "bioarchaeological profile" (Harrod 2013:65). The 1870 U.S. census notes that about 25% of Chinese in Carlin were railroad workers, and the period the cemetery was in use includes the time of the census. Chung et al. (2005) also suggested that transient Chinese were buried elsewhere, supporting our claim that these men likely represent railroad workers who made Carlin their home after the rails were finished in 1869. The cemetery was in use in Carlin from 1885 until 1924. Thus, these remains record both injury and survival after the end of labor on, at least, the Central Pacific Railroad, and likely in other hard industries, such as logging or mining.

Located approximately two city blocks away from the public cemetery of Carlin, Nevada (Chung et al. 2005:107), the mortuary context of Carlin is not well documented historically, but a great deal of information is known about the site as a result of the detailed archaeological reconstructions by Hattori and Frampton, and historical research conducted by Chung. Burial 1 is the only exception to this, as it was removed during the construction of a new house, and the landscape was altered (Chung et al. 2005:120). A chapter in *Chinese American Death Rituals: Respecting the Ancestors* by Chung et al. (2005) provides an exhaustive account of the mortuary context of these burials that goes beyond the scope of this article. What is important to note here is that the coffin type and material, along with the associated grave goods, show that, although there was some degree of homogeneity among the Chinese men living in Carlin, there were also distinct differences, including but not limited to evidence of varying degrees of social status within the community.

The demographic profile of the men buried at Carlin, Nevada, illuminates the risks Chinese males underwent during the late 1800s and early 1900s in the American West. That Chinese men suffered marginalization, increased risks of injury, and early death in historical northern Nevada is supported by local newspaper articles (Chung et al. 2005:115–116), the establishment,

TABLE 1

SUMMARY OF AGE, PATHOLOGY, DEGENERATION, AND TRAUMA FROM 13 BURIALS RECOVERED FROM CARLIN, NEVADA

Demography		Pathological Conditions		Stress-Related Degenerative Changes		Trauma and Injury	
Burial	Age	Skeletal Pathologies	Dental Pathologies	Entheseal Development	Osteoarthritis	Antemortem Trauma	Perimortem Trauma
1	45–50+	N/A	Periodontal disease, 2 caries, and 1 abscess[a]	Moderate to robust development of upper limb, moderate development of lower limb	Slight to moderate degenerative joint and disk disease and several Schmorl's nodes on thoaracic vertebrae	1 small cranial depression fracture	N/A
2	30+	Periosteal reaction on tibia (L/R)[b]	Not scored	Not scored	Osteolitic lesions on lumbar vertebrae and iliac crest (L)[b]	Broken humerus (L), radius (L), rib (R), and metatarsal (L)[b]	N/A
3	35–45	Periosteal reaction on cranium	Periodontal disease[a]	Robust development of upper limb, robust development of lower limb	Fused sacroiliac joint and moderate degenerative disk disease	Facial fracture and broken rib (R)	N/A
4	50+	N/A	N/A	Moderate to robust development of upper limb, moderate to robust development of lower limb	Slight to moderate degenerative disk disease and several Schmorl's nodes on thoracic and lumbar vertebrae	2 large cranial depression fractures and broken tibia and fibula (L)	N/A
5	35–45	N/A	5 caries and 5 abscesses[a]	Moderate development of upper limb, moderate development of lower limb	Slight degenerative disk disease and moderate degenerative joint disease of the humerus (L/R)	2 small cranial depression fractures and broken humerus (L)	N/A

TABLE 1 (CONTINUED)

SUMMARY OF AGE, PATHOLOGY, DEGENERATION, AND TRAUMA FROM 13 BURIALS RECOVERED FROM CARLIN, NEVADA

Demography		Pathological Conditions		Stress-Related Degenerative Changes		Trauma and Injury	
Burial	Age	Skeletal Pathologies	Dental Pathologies	Entheseal Development	Osteoarthritis	Antemortem Trauma	Perimortem Trauma
6	30–40	N/A	13 caries and 7 abscesses[a]	Moderate to robust development of upper limb, moderate to robust development of lower limb	Spondylolysis (L5) and osteoarthritic changes and shortening of the clavicle (R)	2 large linear fractures of the cranium and 1 facial fracture	N/A
7	40–50	Slight to moderate porotic hyperostosis	Enamel hypoplasia, 9 caries, and 4 abscesses[a]	Moderate development of upper limb, moderate development of lower limb	Slight degenerative disk disease	1 large cranial depression fracture with reactive bone around it	N/A
8	30–40	N/A	Periodontal disease[a]	Robust development of upper limb, moderate development of lower limb	N/A	1 small cranial depression fracture, a facial fracture, and broken ribs (L/R), metatarsals (L)	Broken ribs (L/R), sternum, lumbar (L-5), sacrum, and os coxae (L/R)
9	20–30	Slight to moderate porotic hyperostosis	Periodontal disease, enamel hypoplasia, and two caries[a]	Moderate development of upper limb, moderate development of lower limb	N/A	1 large linear fracture of the cranium	N/A
10	40–50	Slight to moderate porotic hyperostosis, severe periosteal reaction on femur, tibia and fibula (L/R)	Periodontal disease, 5 caries, and one abscess[a]	Robust development of upper limb, robust development of lower limb	Slight to moderate degenerative joint disease, moderate degenerative disk disease, and several Schmorl's nodes on thoracic and lumbar	1 small and 1 medium cranial depression fracture	A severe panfacial fracture involving multiple cranial bones, rib (L/R), sternum, and cervical vertebrae (C6–C7)

TABLE 1 (CONTINUED)
SUMMARY OF AGE, PATHOLOGY, DEGENERATION, AND TRAUMA FROM 13 BURIALS RECOVERED FROM CARLIN, NEVADA

Demography		Pathological Conditions		Stress-Related Degenerative Changes		Trauma and Injury	
Burial	Age	Skeletal Pathologies	Dental Pathologies	Entheseal Development	Osteoarthritis	Antemortem Trauma	Perimortem Trauma
11	40–50	N/A	2 abscesses[a]	Moderate to robust development of upper limb, moderate to robust development of lower limb	Slight degenerative joint disease, slight to moderate degenerative disk disease, several Schmorl's nodes on thoracic and lumbar vertebrae	1 small and 1 large cranial depression fracture	N/A
12	50+	Slight to moderate porotic hyperostosis and periosteal reaction on femur, tibia, and fibula (L/R)	N/A	Moderate development of upper limb, slight to moderate development of lower limb	Slight to moderate degenerative disk disease, several Schmorl's nodes on thoracic and lumbar vertebrae	2 small cranial depression fractures	N/A
13		N/A	4 caries[a]	Moderate to robust development of upper limb, robust development of lower limb	N/A	1 small and medium cranial depression fracture and broken rib with lytic lesion	N/A

Note: Data based on the analysis by Harrod et al. (2013), Vilos et al. (2010), and Thompson et al. (2002). The findings presented support prior research by Owsley et al. (1997) and Schmidt (2006, 2009).
[a]Vilos et al. (2010).
[b]Thompson et al. (2002).

in the nearby town of Virginia City, of an anti-Chinese league that wanted to close Chinese laundries (James et al. 1994:170), and the vote in 1880 that was 17,259 to 183 in support of banning Chinese immigration (Wren 1904:82).

Analysis of demography indicates each individual is an adult male ranging in age from 20 to over 50 years, which matches the profile of the individuals who would have been living in the area at this time. The young age of some individuals at time of death suggests that these men faced hardships that were common among men who, in the United States by 1880, were typically living only into their 30s or 40s (Infoplease 2012).

With this in mind, bioarchaeological analysis goes beyond demographic data and looks at "biocultural identity" (Harrod 2013:70), which involves reconstructing disruptions in growth and development, or identifying the overall well-being of an individual, identifying stress-related degenerative changes to the body, and summarizing trauma and injury patterns (Figure 2). The value of incorporating these other markers on the bones is that they provide a way to overcome the limitations of relying on mortuary context, which is often a reflection of the people who buried an individual and not the person who was buried. Additionally, reconstructing the biocultural identity of each burial allows a better interpretation of the demographic trends seen in this unfortunately small skeletal assemblage.

Overall Well-Being

All the individuals have indicators on their bones that reveal widespread health stress. Four individuals (Burial 7, Burial 9, Burial 10, and Burial 12; 4 of 13, 30.7%) have some form of porotic hyperostosis, which has been consistently shown to develop in childhood (Stuart-Macadam 1985; Walker et al. 2009; J. Morgan 2014). The importance of porotic hyperostosis is that it indicates some form of nutritional stress during childhood that left a lasting impact on the body. This can be seen into adulthood, but can also develop in adulthood (Walker et al. 2009; Crandall and Martin 2012). This suggests that, prior to coming to work on the railroad in America, these men had already experienced some degree of physical stress in their lives. Three individuals

(Burial 2, Burial 10, and Burial 12; 3 of 13, 23.1%) have some form of periosteal reaction, which is a nonspecific indicator of bony irritation. This type of reaction generally arises due to infection and can be seen as a measure of immunocompetence. The fact that 3 of 13 individuals (Burial 2, Burial 10, and Burial 12) exhibit periosteal reaction indicates the likelihood of infection among the Carlin men during a time when tuberculosis was the leading cause of death in the United States. Finally, one individual (Burial 5; 1 of 13, 7.6%) has degenerative changes throughout the body consistent with joint breakdown due to hard labor.

Focusing on nutrition, it appears that, in terms of height, the men at Carlin were shorter than average. This is based on a recent study of the height of people in China between 1880 and 1929 (S. Morgan 2004:210). What Morgan found was that male height averaged between 166.0 and 167.5 cm; in contrast, the average height of individuals from Carlin was 162.8 cm. The difference is interesting, however, because when Morgan looked at subsets of the population, he found that men working in occupations that required less skill but more labor, such as railroad workers, had a stature that was on average 1.1 cm shorter (S. Morgan 2004:211). Stature is largely a function of childhood health. Looking at data collected during a longitudinal study of a cohort of 2,879 people in Great Britain all born in 1946, Wadsworth et al. (2002) found that leg length and, as a result, stature, were positively correlated with nutrition and overall health during the early years of childhood. Taken alongside the evidence of nutritional stress indicated by porotic hyperostosis, the reduced stature of the individuals from Carlin supports the theory that these men had had rough childhoods in China. The importance of evidence of poor health during the earliest years of life is that it may lend support to the historical evidence that people were migrating to the developing world, including the United States, in order to flee the hardship and strife that engulfed Guangdong in the late 1800s.

Stress-Related Degenerative Changes

Ancient skeletal remains provide evidence of degenerative diseases, such as osteoarthritis, or excess development of muscle attachments

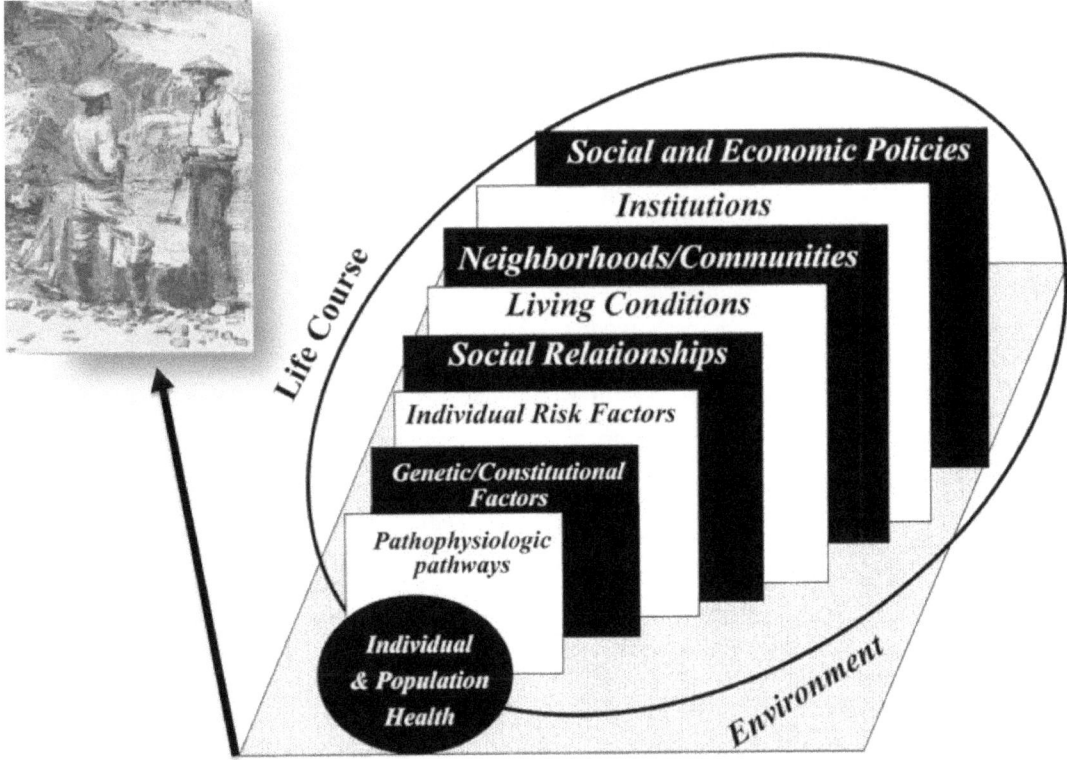

FIGURE 2. Reconstructing the biocultural identity of a Chinese railroad worker. Images modified from *Harper's Weekly* (1867) and Kaplan (2000:43). (Figure by Ryan P. Harrod, 2014.)

(entheses) that commonly affects humans, especially laborers. Analyses of degenerative joint disease, the collapse of vertebrae in the spine, or the buildup of abnormal bone at muscle attachment sites throughout the body can all shed light on the biomechanical stressors faced by past humans (Woo and Pak 2013). When contextualized, these data can be used to understand how subsistence changes, economic shifts, or transformations in industry differentially affect communities (Henderson and Cardoso 2013). The remains can also be useful for identifying patterns of violence and repeated exposure to injury, either accidental or as a result of occupational activities.

Measures of activity at Carlin are also interesting because, in general, the bones of the individuals were not more robust when compared to the mean robusticity of a sample of modern Chinese males. Yet the development of entheses among these individuals was fairly pronounced, which suggests that they were not necessarily engaged in more weight-bearing

activities, but doing different, or at least more, activities that put strain on attachment sites in the limbs. This is consistent with the historical accounts of labor endured by the Chinese in a variety of industries, including railroad construction and tunnel mining.

Trauma and Injury

There is evidence of some form of antemortem trauma on each individual from the Carlin cemetery. These injuries range in severity from small divots on the surface of the cranial vault to the complete fracture of both the tibia and fibula. The presence of even slight trauma is significant, as it illustrates that these individuals were a population that was at greater risk of injury due to accidents and violence.

Two of the thirteen buried individuals (Burial 8 and Burial 10; 2 of 13, 15.4%) show evidence of suffering injuries that were severe enough to have caused their deaths. These two burials were the focus of Schmidt's (2009) article about interpersonal violence. Burial 8 has extensive perimortem trauma, but lacks trauma to the head, which led Schmidt (2009), as well as Chung et al. (2005), to conclude that the injuries were likely related to occupational trauma. Burial 10, however, has perimortem trauma to both the body and the head that appears more likely to be the result of violence. The cranial trauma is especially indicative of violence because there is a severe panfacial fracture or trauma that involves numerous bones of the face. Additionally, research on contemporary coroner's reports, conducted by Chung et al. (2005:136–137), discovered an individual of the same approximate age as Burial 10, named Yee Hong Shing, who the coroner reported as killed by a blow to the head.

Overall Quality of Life

The analysis of health, in addition to the nutritional and activity-related findings, suggests that the Chinese men living in Carlin were working hard and, as a result, showed signs of stress and strain on their bones. They grew up in communities facing nutritional strife and left only to find more hardship, albeit of a different kind. These men had improved diets in the United States; however, trauma and musculoskeletal development data suggest that they were vulnerable to the strains of hard labor and the risk of violent injury, and likely suffered violence as racial minorities during a time of great racial tension.

Particularly interesting are the individuals who have either multiple pathological conditions or a pathology with associated traumatic injuries. For example, Burial 10 and Burial 12 have both porotic hyperostosis and periosteal reactions. The combination of childhood nutritional stress with evidence of adult infection and trauma may not be incidental, as prior developmental pathologies may increase an individual's vulnerability to infection as an adult (Clark et al. 1986; Danese et al. 2007). In terms of the co-occurrence of trauma and pathology, Harrod et al. (2013) found that three burials (3 of 13, 23.1%) had both a pathological condition that likely occurred during their adult lives and some form of traumatic injury that was more likely also to have occurred when they were adults. Burial 5 had osteoarthritis and cranial trauma, while

Burial 10 and Burial 12 had cranial trauma in association with periosteal reactions.

Harrod et al.'s (2013) recent analysis provides evidence that the pattern of skeletal injuries and stress seen among the Carlin men is similar to other ethnographic and historical cases of racialized labor exploitation, the most contemporary example being the greater risk of trauma and inequalities faced by Mexican migrant laborers in the United States today (Holmes 2013). The findings also support the fact that not all Chinese immigrants had the same experience, a finding that Chung et al. (2005) clearly showed in the historical reconstruction.

Conclusion and Future Prospects

Revealing the lived experience of the Chinese men who helped to build the railroad networks in the American West is an ongoing project that relies on multiple perspectives and a wealth of interdisciplinary data, including that from the analysis of other Chinese remains. Future bioarchaeological research will continue to contribute to this growing body of knowledge. Author Crandall is currently working on a more holistic project that incorporates a larger regional perspective and cross-cultural data to analyze the overall well-being of these laborers. His research compares the Carlin individuals with data from other Chinese migrant populations, as well as European American individuals from that same general period. The goal of the project is to put health in context, continue examining labor exploitation, and understand how diverse and different life was for Chinese laborers in the United States compared to that of other Americans. Additionally, both authors Crandall and Harrod are interested in looking at burials of individuals who remained in their home communities or whose bodies were sent home to China. Examination of the bones that made it back to China can reveal much about shifting health and identity, and the importance of funerary rituals in maintaining the transnational community across the Pacific.

Outside the research performed by the authors, there is a need for bioarchaeologists interested in asking other questions, including those revealing the more nuanced indications of sociopolitical identity, gender roles, and family relationships among the Chinese men who immigrated to the

United States and other industrialized countries in the 19th century. The focus of this article has been on the experiences of the adult men who contributed to the labor force, and, while this is important, our research only scratches the surface. To understand the lived experience of these Chinese workers it is imperative that the research incorporate more historical records and family stories passed down to descendants. Historical bioarchaeologies, in conjunction with data derived from the human remains, would expand the questions that we archaeologists are able to ask. Perhaps this could allow studies of social differences in labor camps and between merchants who supplied railroad workers with food and the workers themselves. Some potential avenues of research include ascertaining how certain occupations (mining and the use of explosives) compare to more generalized labor, determining whether some individuals did indeed hold higher status than others, and assessing whether the status a person held shifted over time. Perhaps health was bad and trauma severe for all men early on, but their status shifted as permanent communities were established. Bioarchaeological analysis often obscures rapid social transformation, making the incorporation of historical documentation more crucial to understanding whether social status was enough to buffer some individuals from poor health and traumatic injury.

The importance of women and children is woefully under-examined in this project because the burials from Carlin do not include skeletal remains from female Chinese immigrants and their children. While women and children are not often represented in documentary evidence of this period, they still played an important role in Asian American history. Additionally, with the establishment of communities like the one in Carlin came the development of families. Bioarchaeological analyses of childhood and family structure would enable discussions of kinship and U.S. "race" formation to be enriched with empirical data.

The value of continued bioarchaeological research is that it will help to illustrate the complex and often fluid nature of Chinese migration to and labor in the United States at the turn of the century. It will also provide one more line of evidence for reconstructing the history of Chinese immigrants, including understanding how and why they engaged and incorporated American cultural practices as they settled in the United States.

There are still a lot of unanswered questions regarding the Chinese who emigrated from Guangdong Province, particularly railroad workers. Did they all experience the kinds of injury and violence seen at Carlin? How did laborers experience exploitation differently among labor industries? Did merchants or different types of laborers have different experiences? Where did laborers come from, and how did they move across the United States? What about drug use (e.g., opium) and the use of medications (e.g., mercury)? We argue that bioarchaeology can, at minimum, help answer all of these questions. Research produced thus far has already revealed the lives of this poorly understood group. Future skeletal analyses can only enhance the picture of life on (and off) the rails that is emerging from the work in this issue.

Acknowledgments

The authors would like to thank the organizers of this issue and all the participants at the Chinese Railroad Workers in North America Project Conference held in October 2013. The research and wisdom of the other participants have been invaluable in shaping our research.

References

CARTER, GREGG L.
    1976   Social Demography of the Chinese in Nevada: 1870–1880. *Nevada Historical Society Quarterly* 18(3):85–86.

CHAN, SUSCHENG
    1991   *Asian Americans: An Interpretive History*. Twayne, New York, NY.

CHANG, IRIS
    2003   *The Chinese in America: A Narrative History*. Penguin, New York, NY.

CHEN, YONG
    2000   *Chinese San Francisco, 1850–1943: A Trans-Pacific Community*. Stanford University Press, Stanford, CA.

CHOW, TONY K., JOHN R. LAMBERT, MARK L. WAHLQVIST, AND BRIDGET H. HSU-HAGE
    1995   *Helicobacter pylori* in Melbourne Chinese Immigrants: Evidence for Oral–Oral Transmission via Chopsticks. *Journal of Gastroenterology and Hepatology* 10(5):562–569.

CHUNG, SUE F., FRED P. FRAMPTON,
AND TIMOTHY W. MURPHY
2005 Venerate These Bones: Chinese American Funerary
and Burial Practices as Seen in Carlin, Elko County,
Nevada. In *Chinese American Death Rituals:
Respecting the Ancestors*, Sue F. Chung and Pricilla
Wegars, editors, pp. 107–146. AltaMira Press,
Lanham, MD.

CLARK, GEORGE A., NICHOLAS R. HALL,
GEORGE J. ARMELAGOS, GARY A. BORKAN,
MANOHAR M. PANJABI, AND F. TODD WETZEL
1986 Poor Growth Prior to Early Childhood: Decreased
Health and Life-Span in the Adult. *American Journal
of Physical Anthropology* 70(2):145–160.

COHEN, MARK N., AND GEORGE J. ARMELAGOS (EDITORS)
1984 *Paleopathology at the Origins of Agriculture.*
Academic Press, Orlando, FL.

CRANDALL, JOHN J., AND DEBRA L. MARTIN
2012 On Porotic Hyperostosis and the Interpretation of
Hominin Diets, 9 October. PLOS ONE <http://plosone.
org/annotation/listThread.action?root=55385>.
Accessed 18 February 2015.

CROFUTT, GEORGE A.
1872 *Crofutt's Trans-Continental Tourist's Guide.* Geo. A.
Crofutt, New York, NY.

DANESE, ANDREA, CARMINE M. PARIANTE, AVSHALOM
CASPI, ALAN TAYLOR, AND RICHIE POULTON
2007 Childhood Maltreatment Predicts Adult Inflammation
in a Life-Course Study. *Proceedings of the National
Academy of Sciences* 104(4):1325–1330.

ELLIS, MEREDITH A. B., CHRISTOPHER W. MERRITT,
SHANNON A. NOVAK, AND KELLY J. DIXON
2011 The Signature of Starvation: A Comparision of Bone
Processing at a Chinese Encampment in Montana
and the Donner Party Camp in California. *Historical
Archaeology* 45(2):97–112.

FRIEDMAN, LAWRENCE M., AND JACK LADINSKY
1967 Social Change and the Law of Industrial Accidents.
Columbia Law Review 67(1):50–82.

HARPER'S WEEKLY
1867 Central Pacific Railroad—Chinese Laborers at Work.
Harper's Weekly 7 December:772.

HARROD, RYAN P.
2013 *Chronologies of Pain and Power: Violence, Inequality,
and Social Control among Ancestral Pueblo
Populations (AD 850–1300).* Doctoral dissertation,
Department of Anthropology, University of Nevada,
Las Vegas. University Microfilms International, Ann
Arbor, MI.

HARROD, RYAN P., JENNIFER L. THOMPSON,
AND DEBRA L. MARTIN
2013 Hard Labor and Hostile Encounters: What Human
Remains Reveal about Institutional Violence and
Chinese Immigrants Living in Carlin, Nevada
(1885–1923). *Historical Archaeology* 46(4):85–111.

HENDERSON, CHARLOTTE Y., AND F. ALVES CARDOSO
2013 Entheseal Changes and Occupation: Technical
and Theoretical Advances and Their Applications.
International Journal of Osteoarchaeology
23(2):127–134.

HOLMES, SETH M.
2013 *Fresh Fruit, Broken Bodies: Migrant Farmworkers
in the United States.* University of California Press,
Berkeley.

INFOPLEASE
2012 Life Expectancy by Age, 1850–2011. Infoplease
<http://www.infoplease.com/ipa/A0005140.html>.
Accessed 28 May 2014.

JAMES, RONALD M., RICHARD D. ADKINS,
AND RACHEL J. HARTIGAN
1994 Competition and Coexistence in the Laundry: A
View of the Comstock. *Western Historical Quarterly*
25(2):164–184.

KAPLAN, DAVID
2000 The Darker Side of the "Original Affluent Society."
Journal of Anthropological Research 56(3):301–324.

LEI, SEAN HSIANG-LIN
2010 Habituating Individuality: The Framing of
Tuberculosis and Its Material Solutions in Republican
China. *Bulletin of the History of Medicine*
84(2):248–279.

McKEOWN, ASHLEY
1999 Conceptualing Chinese Diasporas, 1984 to 1949.
Journal of Asian Studies 58(2):306–337.

MORGAN, JENNIFER A.
2014 The Methodological and Diagnostic Applications
of Micro-CT to Paleopathology: A Quantitative
Study of Porotic Hyperostosis. Doctoral dissertation,
Department of Anthropology, University of Western
Ontario, London.

MORGAN, STEPHEN L.
2004 Economic Growth and the Biological Standard of
Living in China, 1880–1930. *Economics and Human
Biology* 2(2):197–218.

OWSLEY, DOUGLAS W., KARI BRUWELHEIDE,
JULIET BRUNDIGE, DAVID HUNT, CHIP CLARK,
AND REBECCA REDMOND
1997 Preliminary Report: Osteology and Paleopathology of
the Carlin Chinese Cemetery. Manuscript, National
Museum of Natural History, Smithsonian Institution,
Washington, DC.

ROSS, DOUGLAS E.
2013 Overseas Chinese Archaeology. In *Encyclopedia
of Global Archaeology*, Claire Smith, editor, pp.
5675–5686. Springer, New York, NY.

SCHMIDT, RYAN W.
2006 The Forgotten Chinese Cemetery of Carlin, Nevada: A Bioanthropological Assessment. Master's thesis, Department of Anthropology, University of Nevada, Las Vegas.
2009 Perimortem Injury in a Chinese American Cemetery: Two Cases of Occupational Hazard or Interpersonal Violence. *Internet Journal of Biological Anthropology* 3(2). Internet Scientific Publications <https://ispub.com/IJBA/3/2/13579>. Accessed 19 February 2015.

SCHMIDT, RYAN W., NORIKO SEGUCHI, AND JENNIFER L. THOMPSON
2011 Chinese Immigrant Population History in North America Based on Craniometric Diversity. *Anthropological Science* 119(1):9–19.

STUART-MACADAM, PATRICIA
1985 Porotic Hyperostosis: Representative of a Childhood Condition. *American Journal of Physical Anthropology* 66(4):391–398.

TAKAKI, RONALD
1998 *Strangers from a Different Shore: A History of Asian Americans.* Back Bay, New York, NY.

THOMPSON, JENNIFER L., BERNARDO T. ARRIAZA, A. GALLEGOS, SUE F. CHUNG, VICKI CASSMAN, J. CONLOGUE, AND R. BECKETT
2002 A Preliminary Report on the Chinese Immigrants from Carlin, Nevada. Paper presented at the Annual Meeting of the Nevada Archaeological Association, Reno.

TÜCHSEN, FINN, HARALD HANNERZ, AND SØREN SPANGENBERG
2005 Mortality and Mobidity among Bridge and Tunnel Construction Workers Who Worked Long Hours and Long Days Constructing the Great Belt Fixed Link. *Scandinavian Journal of Work, Environment, and Health* 31(S2):22–26.

VILOS, JAMIE D., JENNIFER L. THOMPSON, AND DEBRA L. MARTIN
2010 Dental Morphology and Pathologies of Chinese Immigrants from Historic Carlin, Nevada. *American Journal of Physical Anthropology* 14(S50):236.

VOSS, BARBARA L., AND REBECCA ALLEN
2008 Overseas Chinese Archaeology: Historical Foundations, Current Reflections, and New Directions. *Historical Archaeology* 42(3):5–28.

WADSWORTH, MICHAEL E. J., R. J. HARDY, A. A. PAUL, S. F. MARSHALL, AND T. J. COLE
2002 Leg and Trunk Length at 43 Years in Relation to Childhood Health, Diet and Family Circumstances; Evidence from the 1946 National Birth Cohort. *International Journal of Epidemiology* 31(2):383–390.

WALKER, PHILLIP L., RHONDA R. BATHURST, REBECCA RICHMAN, THOR GJERDRUM, AND VALERIE A. ANDRUSHKO
2009 The Causes of Porotic Hyperstosis and Cribra Orbitalia: A Reappraisal of the Iron-Deficiency-Anemia Hypothesis. *American Journal of Physical Anthropology* 139(2):109–125.

WOO, EUN J., AND SUNYOUNG PAK
2013 Degenerative Joint Diseases and Enthesopathies in a Joseon Dynasty Population from Korea. *HOMO—Journal of Comparative Human Biology* 64(2):104–119.

WREN, THOMAS (EDITOR)
1904 *A History of the State of Nevada: Its Resources and People.* Lewis, New York, NY.

YUNG, JUDY, GORDON H. CHANG, AND HIM M. LAI (EDITORS)
2006 *Chinese American Voices: From the Gold Rush to the Present.* University of California Press, Berkeley.

RYAN PATRICK HARROD
DEPARTMENT OF ANTHROPOLOGY,
UNIVERSITY OF ALASKA ANCHORAGE
3211 PROVIDENCE DRIVE
ANCHORAGE, AK 99508

JOHN JOSEPH CRANDALL
DEPARTMENT OF ANTHROPOLOGY
UNIVERSITY OF NEVADA, LAS VEGAS
4505 S. MARYLAND PARKWAY, MAILSTOP 455003
LAS VEGAS, NV 89154-5003

Mary Praetzellis (玛丽·普莱策利)
Adrian Praetzellis (阿德里安·普莱策利)

Commentary on the Archaeology of Chinese Railroad Workers in North America: Where Do We Go from Here?
北美地区中国铁路工人的考古学研究：我们该由此走向何方？

ABSTRACT

Archaeologists have spent nearly five decades excavating sites associated with Chinese immigrants to the American West. They have studied hundreds of places and millions of artifacts and compiled enormous amounts of information. It is time for synthesis; it is time for sharing beyond the narrow archaeological community. The material is too rich, too important, to bury in technical reports and obscure jargon. It can connect contemporary American and Chinese communities in a common quest for an understanding of the past in the interests of the future.

考古学家已经对美国西部的中国移民遗址进行了将近五十年的发掘。他们已经了研究了成百上千的地点与数不胜数的文物，并积累了大量信息资料。现在是我们应该进行综合的时候，也是我们应该跨出狭窄的考古学领域，分享成果的时候。这些材料太丰富、太重要，不应该被埋没在技术性的报告与含混的术语之中。它们可以使当代美国和中国社区通过对理解过去和展望未来的共同追求而更紧密地连结在一起。

Assignment from the Chinese Railroad Workers in North America Project

Barbara Voss formed the Archaeology Network in 2012 as an adjunct to the much larger Chinese Railroad Workers in North America Project (CRWNAP), a multiyear venture between American and Chinese scholars to commemorate the 150th anniversary of the arrival of large numbers of Chinese to work on the transcontinental railroad. Chinese immigrants participated in the earlier California Gold Rush and subsequent mining booms throughout the American West; they helped create the infrastructure that built the state. For nearly 50 years, archaeologists have studied the cultural landscapes and material remains left by the Chinese and can now enable and enliven an understanding of the lives of the workers themselves.

Stanford University hosted a workshop for the Archaeology Network in October 2013, requesting that participants assess the potential of their evidence to provide material to re-create the lives and lifeways of Chinese immigrants in America. CRWNAP requested that the network explore some very basic questions regarding the daily experiences, social and economic lives, and connectedness of Chinese railroad workers in the West. As the railroad provided but a single station in the larger lives of these individuals, many in the network expanded the discussion to include the wider experiences of Chinese throughout the West, providing geographic and historical perspective. Chinese immigrants to California were linked far more by who they were, to whom they were related, and by their day-to-day experiences than by the locations of their employment. The railroad can be seen as a vector for settlement. Not just Chinese, but immigrants from around the world followed the new railroad and planted their hopes for a future in the budding towns and cities along its route. This thematic issue includes many of the papers developed for that workshop.

Backdrop and Beginnings

Paul Chace set the stage for both the workshop and this special issue with a reenactment of a presentation given by himself and William Evans, Jr., at the 1969 Society for Historical Archaeology (SHA) conference. This innovative paper covered what was then known about Donner Summit Chinese railroad workers' material culture and proposed that these materials represented an archaeological horizon that could be used as a dating tool by archaeologists who were then discovering Chinese worker sites around the world. The SHA's Overseas Chinese Research Group was formed at that meeting. Chace bravely presented this theoretically dated paper at the network meeting,

Historical Archaeology, 2015, 49(1):162–174.
Permission to reprint required.

showing both how much and how little progress archaeologists have made in the succeeding decades (Chace and Evans, this issue).

The 1969 SHA meeting was only the second of that newly formed society. At the time, historical archaeology focused primarily on the below-ground remains of historic buildings. Historical reconstruction and the recovery of early collections by the U.S. National Park Service and university archaeologists fueled the awakening discipline. An interest in the mid-19th-century West was novel in itself, and Chace and Evans's multidisciplinary approach foreshadowed great possibilities for broadening both history and archaeology.

U.S. historical archaeology exploded in the mid-1970s with the U.S. bicentennial, new environmental laws, and the redevelopment of urban "blight." Environmental laws requiring archaeological mitigation for the effects of development came into force, and the national bicentennial spawned an interest in the various immigrant groups that make up U.S. national heritage. The civil rights and third-world college movements of the 1960s had a profound influence on the way this patriotic event was celebrated; diversity became respectable. The fledgling discipline of historical archaeology contributed evocative studies of the lives of Chinese in the West and other disenfranchised groups, carving out a role for itself in the historical study of ethnicity and nation formation.

Most of this research was done in the cultural resource management (CRM) context. At the time, few universities had historical archaeology programs. While academics kicked around ideas and developed theoretical perspectives, CRM practitioners did most of the fieldwork. Most cities in the West had 19th-century Chinatowns in areas that by the mid-20th century were considered "blighted." Work in the 1970s and 1980s centered on these urban sites—Napa, Riverside, Sacramento, San Francisco, San Jose, San Luis Obispo, Santa Rosa, Ventura, Walnut Grove, and Woodland, California; Phoenix and Tucson, Arizona; Boise, Idaho; El Paso, Texas; and Lovelock, Nevada. Chinese railroad camps, by definition, are more remote and obscure. Early work centered on Truckee (Chace and Evans, this issue), Texas (Briggs 1974), and the Carson City vicinity (Furnis and Maniery, this issue).

Moving Along

The archaeology of Chinese in America developed in parallel to the discipline of historical archaeology as practiced in the western United States from the 1970s. The articles in this thematic issue can be viewed as representative of the contemporary practice of U.S. historical archaeology.

Archaeologists thrive on fieldwork in all kinds of venues. Fieldwork can be rough, but in return, archaeologists experience the past firsthand, or at least where it took place. Three articles lead tours of the archaeological manifestations of Chinese railroad worker camps as viewed by fieldworkers. R. Scott Baxter and Rebecca Allen revisit Chace and Evans's Donner Summit Camp 40 years later to prepare a damage assessment and National Register of Historic Places nomination for the Tahoe National Forest. They provide many important details of camp layout and construction, linking present features to historic photos. While they note the sheer power of the place, some of its emotional appeal is lost in the obligatory National Register jargon. Lynn Furnis and Mary Maniery take us over the summit to an early 1870s Virginia & Truckee Railroad camp in the Carson Valley. Their straightforward approach teases the maximum information from the small surface collection and provides a picture of the lives of the workers stationed there.

Finally, Michael Polk transports us nearly 600 mi. farther east, across the vast reaches of Nevada, through the desert and the Great Salt Lake, to Promontory Summit, Utah, where the Union Pacific Railroad (UPRR) and the Central Pacific Railroad (CPRR) met in 1869. This was literally the end of the line for an estimated 25,000 workers who raced to complete the job from both east (UPRR) and west (CPRR). The area is now the Golden Spike National Historic Site, the study of which has been funded over the years by the National Park Service. Archaeologists recorded 19 railroad construction campsites, 4 of which were associated with Chinese workers, showing how this diverse workforce was divided along ethnic lines.

Archaeologists love artifacts and the thrill of the find. Two articles explore artifact types. Marjorie Akin, James Bard, and Gary Weisz provide important information on Asian coins and discuss coins found at Chinese worker camps in Idaho and Montana. These coins—from China, Japan, and Vietnam—were not used as currency, but were specifically for games (fan-tan), good luck, medicine, and decoration. Using historical documents, museum collections, and archaeological evidence, Sarah Heffner explores the health-care practices of the Chinese workers, including their theoretical underpinnings, socioeconomic setting, ingredients, and material manifestations. A third article, by Timothy Urbaniak and Kelly J. Dixon, explores another trace of the past—the rock-face inscription—that provides evidence of how individuals deliberately transformed the landscape, leaving traces of a multiethnic workforce that persist to the present day.

Bones are frequently used in the study of the past. Ryan Kennedy looks at faunal remains from the spectrum of Chinese sites in the West to reconstruct food practices and how these may have varied by locale. Ryan Harrod and John Crandall study the remains of 13 Chinese men buried in Carlin, Nevada, between 1885 and 1923, to explore questions of diet, health, physical stresses, and life experiences through the techniques of bioarchaeology.

Archaeologists use their material to apply and test social theory. Both John Molenda and Charlotte Sunseri explore the process of ethnic and class resistance in the workplace. Returning to railroad worker camps in the High Sierra, Molenda seeks to explain the apparent absence of evidence of class struggle in the Chinese worker camps. To do this, he contrasts the Western ideology of possessive individualism and the spirit of capitalism, as exemplified by railroad magnate Charles Crocker, with the ideology of relational personhood and filiality of the Chinese laborer. Sunseri also covers resistance among Chinese railroad workers who settled in the Mono Basin after the railroad was completed. She describes alliances between the Chinese workers, capitalist investors, African Americans, and Paiute.

Missing Pieces and the Role of Cultural Resource Management

This issue shows that, although students, academics, and CRM practitioners all write

about the archaeology of Chinese in the West, the excavated data are almost exclusively from CRM projects. As each piece of CRM work is funded and reported separately, relying on these reports has hampered progress, as new practitioners retrace the steps of those who came before them. This observation brings up a fundamental question: How should one do synthetic research in a CRM framework?

Chinese sites' exotic appearance and abundance of artifacts made them relatively easy to identify and to justify as worthy of legally mandated investigation—at least initially. And while property developers do not want to pay for more work than is necessary, the law requires that a site's "information potential" be realized for the public benefit before it is destroyed. How can this be achieved?

Urban Chinese sites generate huge quantities of artifacts (Figure 1). Archaeologists love the excitement of the excavation: the thrill of discovery. Some excavate with no guarantee that a report will be forthcoming or that the artifacts and notes will be curated. This is particularly egregious in relation to urban Chinese sites. Archaeologists over-excavate and underreport. For every 10 or so reports on Chinese sites in the West, there may be an orphaned collection waiting in a basement or storage facility.

While others may disagree, we—the authors—feel the responsibility to offer the following stern critique in the hopes of provoking thoughtful change. Blinded by a wealth of exotic artifacts and hampered by the competitive commercial environment of development-driven archaeology, we archaeologists have created an unsatisfactory template for Chinese archaeology: repeat established research questions, add historical context, illustrate nifty artifacts, slap on tried and now-trite conclusions. The abundance of data has somehow weakened the motivation for deeper understanding. Contextual analyses focused on time and place with a racist backdrop abound. Missing are the people, their culture, their family histories, their voices, and the voices of their descendants. The authors know this is true, for we do the same thing. In summary, the field has reached a research plateau.

We historical archaeologists seem to be writing for ourselves and talking to each other. We

FIGURE 1. Artifacts recovered from a Chinese laundry site in Stockton, California (Waghorn 2004:86). (Courtesy Anthropological Studies Center, Rohnert Park, CA.)

explore esoteric subjects and abstract theories that take the life from the same material novelists exploit to grab the public's imagination. We have gathered a mass of data. We have learned a lot. But to address Gordon Chang's simple charge to assess "what we do know" in relation to basic questions about the lives of Chinese railroad workers has proven difficult. Frankly, it has gone unanswered by more than one of the authors in this issue who has taken the usual paths through the archaeological, the esoteric, and the abstract. This is a harsh charge, and we (the writers) do not exclude ourselves from it.

Putting It Together: What We Know

Working from the articles in this issue and our own work, the authors make a preliminary attempt to piece together answers to the questions posed to the Archaeology Network. We believe that any story of Chinese railroad workers must include the Chinese settlements in cities, towns, and camps throughout the region, and span the generations. It is a story of connectedness that, of course, reaches to China and beyond. Those stories, however, are outside our reach just yet and are an important potential outcome of the larger CRWNAP.

Daily Experience

In the late 19th century, many Chinese immigrants divided their time between isolated job sites—railroad construction, mining, agriculture—and the familiar Chinatown environment. It is worth emphasizing those connections.

The frighteningly beautiful view from Donner Summit Camp and the deadly, inhospitable environment bore no resemblance to southern China. The workers found nothing familiar in these surroundings, except the presence of their countrymen and the Chinese goods shipped in for their use. Furnis and Maniery (this issue) provide much detail for the layout and operation of the railroad worker camp. Forty to seventy Chinese men may have lived at Lakeview Camp in the Carson Valley in 1872. They organized into two smaller groups centered on cooking and eating areas and slept nearby. Each group had a cook and received Chinese foodstuffs and supplies from outside. They made the best use of available resources, reusing and recycling mundane objects again and again. Structural lumber was burned for cooking; nails were employed for piercing metal fuel cans for use as strainers and rinsers; sheet metal was repurposed for funnels and patching; kerosene cans were refashioned as carriers for water or, perhaps, tea. The men used both Chinese and European American food, beverages, and tableware, but relied mainly on Chinese goods. They wore American clothing and engaged in Chinese versions of industrial workers' pastimes the world over: gambling, smoking opium, and drinking alcohol.

By the 1860s most sizable communities in California had a Chinese district, often adjacent to a creek or lake, that would have been quite exotic to the European American. Merchants and itinerant peddlers commonly displayed their wares in front of shops, exposing passersby to sights and smells of foods and other goods that would have been strange to the uninitiated. Street vendors carried their wares in baskets suspended on bamboo poles. Buildings sported cloth or paper banners in bright yellow, red, and gold, and signs painted with Chinese characters. Alleyways flanked with flimsy wooden shacks housed the poor. The distinctively Chinese landscape, defined by the built environment and its embellishments, created a social and cultural boundary with clear material indicators (Figure 2).

Archaeology provides prima facie evidence that Chinese immigrants brought with them diseases endemic to Asia and succumbed to new ones in the West. An archaeological site in Sacramento produced the earliest known evidence of the deadly Chinese liver fluke. Parasitologists also identified numerous ova from the human whipworm, a parasite common in warm-temperate, moist climates with poor sanitation. Heavy infections can produce a range of harmful symptoms in the digestive system (Hall 1982:113–120).

Heffner (this issue) summarizes the basic principles of Chinese medicine based on worldviews focused on restoring balance to a system, as opposed to contemporary Western practice that sought out miasmas and trauma. Traditionally, Chinese herbalists prescribed medicines with numerous ingredients specifically tailored to the patient's symptoms. These prescriptions were filled at an herbal shop and generally prepared at home. Chinese medicine bottles and homemade herbal remedies are commonly found on archaeological sites.

I STREET, "CHINADOM."

FIGURE 2. Sacramento's I Street, "Chinadom," in the mid-1850s (Barber and Baker 1855).

Yàojim—liquor, wine, or spirits in which medicinal ingredients have been steeped—is common in traditional Chinese medicine. These preparations were made by combining portions of birds, reptiles, and mammals with specific herbs to create remedies for a variety of ailments; these remedies were readily adapted to the West. Archaeologists found the remains of five American crows and assorted herbs (the flowers and bark of the mimosa tree [*Albizia julibrissin*], notopterygium root [*Notopterygium incisum*], and red sage) packed into a glass carboy at a Chinese site in Stockton, California (Figure 3). Chinese herbalists often also stocked a variety of both Chinese and Western patent medicines (Waghorn 2004:270–275). The familiar small glass vials are common on Chinese archaeological sites. Opium was an ingredient in both Chinese and Western medicines. While pharmacy bottles are common on European American sites, they are relatively rare on Chinese sites. Language, cultural, and economic barriers, as well as simple racism, discouraged Chinese American access to American medical

FIGURE 3. Large glass bottle that contained butchered remains of five crows and three identifiable herbs (Waghorn 2004:80–81). (Courtesy Anthropological Studies Center, Rohnert Park, CA.)

practitioners well into the 20th century (Massey et al. 2013:34), when Chinese American families began to encourage Western medical training for their sons and daughters.

Economics and Consumer Network

Chinese cooking distinctively combines multiple ingredients and flavors, the former cut up and mixed to form numerous dishes that vary in color, taste, texture, and smell. It is a very adaptable template, as ingredients can be added or subtracted depending on their availability. Chinese cooks in the West combined a wide range of fresh, preserved, local, and imported foods. The "kitchen-butchering" pattern of cuts and knife scars identified on pork bones by Sherri Gust (1982:87–112) documents an initial step in the preparation of these dishes that also included imported and locally grown Chinese vegetables (M. Praetzellis and A. Praetzellis 1982:158–159).

Pork was the most desired meat in southern China, and the evidence suggests that this preference traveled to the United States (Gust 1982:89). The IJ56 collection (from the Sacramento city block bounded by streets I, J, 5, and 6), associated with merchant households, was 95% pork measured by meat weight. Beef, however, provided the major meat source measured by weight at an adjacent Chinese boardinghouse on the city block bounded by streets H, I, 5, and 6 (Gust 1997). High- and moderate-priced cuts dominated the IJ56 collection, while moderate- to low-priced cuts dominated HI56. Here, very intensive kitchen butchering is evidenced on bones with low meat content, perhaps to maximize the value of meat purchases. These differences may reflect domestic vs. commercial living arrangements.

Dried fish was a staple part of the diet of poor Chinese in both South China and California. California fisheries caught some species (e.g., suckers and minnows) specifically for the Chinese market. By the mid-1850s, local Chinese fishermen caught and marketed fish to their compatriots. Fish remains from Gold Rush–era Chinese sites in Sacramento contain, almost exclusively, species listed in 19th-century accounts as eaten by the state's Chinese residents or imported dried from China in large brown-glazed stoneware containers. The yellow croaker fish was highly regarded in China when eaten fresh; however, the imported, dried yellow croaker fish-head soup eaten in 1850s Sacramento probably reflects "clay-pot" traditions of poor rural areas (Schulz 1982:83–85).

Consuming dog and cat meat was not uncommon in China. This practice continued to a limited extent in the West with the addition of local elk, deer, bobcat, jackrabbit, and wildfowl. Faunal remains reflect local conditions, as described by Kennedy (this issue). People feasted on traditional cuisine while staying in Chinatown and blended locally available ingredients into their cookery when away. Chinese cuisine's flexible list of ingredients adapted to scarcity and made the best of available resources.

Teardrop-shaped Chinese liquor bottles are ubiquitous on Chinese archaeological sites, sometimes numbering in the hundreds (Figure 4). Western alcohol bottles are also generally present, indicating the competing forces of tradition and innovation in daily life. Opium paraphernalia is generally present. American alcohol-laced bitters were another common element of after-hours relaxation and socializing.

Chinese communities have flourished for centuries throughout the world under the leadership of merchants skilled in creating overlapping business contacts and obligations. Known as *guanxi*, Chinese merchants developed long-lasting webs of reciprocity and trust based initially on kinship, locality, and personal recommendation, and reinforced through gifts, formal events, and favors. These merchants served as labor brokers and suppliers, moving workers and consumer goods where needed. Chinese merchants used American agents to supply those goods they could not obtain from China, from local Chinese suppliers, or from a limited number of non-Chinese businesses. These agents obtained lumber and building hardware; bulk foodstuffs, such as potatoes, onions, and salted fish shipped in barrels from the East Coast; as well as tools, equipment, and wagons (M. Praetzellis and A. Praetzellis 1997:287; Farkas 1998:48–49). The image of the isolated and autonomous Chinatown is a fantasy. These complex business relationships are evident in the spatial arrangement of Western goods at the Carson Valley railroad worker camp (Furnis and Maniery, this issue) and in the relationship

FIGURE 4. Chinese brown-glazed stoneware liquor bottles (whole bottles only—fragments not depicted) found behind a Chinese laundry in Stockton, California. (Photo by Ray Hellmann, 2004; courtesy Anthropological Studies Center, Rohnert Park, CA.)

between the Chinese and Virginia & Truckee Railroad investors (Sunseri, this issue).

Yee Ah Tye was a California Chinese merchant and labor broker whose family connections can be traced from the early Gold Rush to the present. Archaeologists have excavated materials associated with his family-association boardinghouse in Sacramento (M. Praetzellis and A. Praetzellis 1982, 1997) and his mining camp in Plumas County, California (A. Praetzellis and M. Praetzellis 1993). Perhaps his biggest success stems from the lineage that followed him—160 descendants in California through six generations, and counting (Farkas 1998:141; Praetzellis 2004:243).

Social Life

The late-19th-century anti-Chinese movement sparked vandalism and violence. In San Jose, California, arsonists destroyed the entire Chinese district in 1887 at the height of the anti-Chinese mania. The city newspaper proudly proclaimed: "Chinatown is dead. It is dead forever" (Yu 2001:30). The celebration was premature. Local businessman and German immigrant John Heinlen came forward and built a new Chinatown in brick—to avoid the fate of the earlier district—and with a fence around it to protect those on the inside. The new community called Heinlenville was a success and sheltered generations (M. Praetzellis and A. Praetzellis 2011).

Harrod and Crandall's (this issue) study of the remains of Chinese men buried in a railroad town in eastern Nevada also demonstrates the hard work and perhaps harder lives that faced these immigrants to the West. Skeletal remains showed evidence of muscle strain, poor health, and in at least two cases interpersonal violence that may have resulted in death. Archaeologists discovered the remains of an Asian man hidden in about 1900 under a house floor in West Oakland, California (Praetzellis 2004:247). The slim young man had worn Western-style clothes and carried a silver pocket watch and an expensive black silk handkerchief. The authors surmised that he had met with foul play.

Some Chinese hid their wealth rather than trust American banking institutions. As robbers targeted Chinese laundries, the cash drawers generally contained only small change for the day's use. Archaeologists found only a few small-denomination American and Chinese coins behind laundries in Stockton and Oakland, California. In Lovelock, Nevada, they found 24 small-denomination coins lost into the subfloor of a Chinese laundry, and a snuff jar with a Chinese brown-glazed lid containing $1,865 in gold coins buried in a pit beneath the cottage next door (Hattori 1979).

In the early decades, only wealthy Chinese could afford families in America. Many had wives in China to whom they hoped to return, but supported financially in the meantime. In western Nevada, some Chinese men married Paiute women, who brought with them knowledge of local foods and the use of obsidian tools (Sunseri, this issue).

Evidence of women and children is found in the archaeological record, although it is difficult to uncover in written documents. In Lovelock, archaeologists found two pieces of women's gold jewelry made by San Francisco Chinese goldsmiths (Wey 1979:544). Inexpensive jade-colored bracelets made of Peking glass (Tao Liao Ping) are commonly found on archaeological sites throughout the West. Women wore them, in part, to ward off evil spirits. A traditional Chinese belief holds that if a woman fell, the bracelet would break the fall and prevent her spirit from being broken (Hellmann and Yang 1997:201). In Los Angeles, archaeologists unearthed a small golden image of Shou-Xing, the god of longevity, that was once attached to the front of a child's hat (Figure 5) (Costello et al. 1999:236). Chinese characters stamped onto the piece identify the goldsmith as Chuen Chong, a San Francisco jeweler (Chinn 1989:appendix C).

Next Steps: Tracing Connections

Archaeologists resolved questions about the "ethnic markers" of American Chinese material culture years ago: it is well documented that Chinese immigrants brought with them distinctive ceramics and foodways. The important issue is not which goods they used, but how they used, reused, and adapted them, in what quantities, and for what outcomes in particular locations and contexts. How did individual Chinese households function within the wider community in which they settled, and how did this articulate with and contribute to the development of that community?

It is time to put these pieces together—people and places through time and across boundaries—to figure out how Chinese and Chinese American communities functioned. What kept them together, what pulled them apart? How did individuals/organizations/subgroups fit together, intersect/conflict? What elements of Chinese culture have adapted to meet the needs of the present?

Chinese districts disappeared from many towns in the early 20th century and only reappeared many decades later when favorable laws promoted new waves of immigration. It is important to reaffirm and celebrate the role of early Asian immigrants in the development of the West as a message to this group of new arrivals. We archaeologists must show how our results advance community building and a sense of place so that we have something of continuing significance to say.

The lives of Chinese railroad workers cannot be understood without reference to the Chinatowns that supplied them. These men were part of a complex system that provided labor for hire and supplied their needs through entrepreneurs like Yee Ah Tye. The system connected to China and outposts around the world, and functions to this day. The Chinese railroad workers who survived (and most did) went on to do other things. They had other life paths and left other markers.

Many basic questions that can be addressed by descriptive studies have been answered. We reiterate the observation by Voss and Allen (2008) that the future does not lie in creating more of the same. From our perspective, the next phase requires adjusting the scale of analysis to take advantage of archaeology's strengths as a place-based project. Reexamining the gray literature is a place to start. Studying orphaned collections, revisiting the population census to follow railroad workers and the merchants who controlled them, and connecting

FIGURE 5. Hammered gold ornament of the Chinese god of longevity that once adorned a child's hat (Costello et al. 1999:236–237). (Courtesy Anthropological Studies Center, Rohnert Park, California.)

with descendants and their contemporary Chinese relatives are all important. The Chinese Railroad Workers in North America Project has made strides in all these directions.

Archaeology outside the academy will not continue to be funded simply to enable archaeologists to pursue their personal quests supported by intellectual mystification and unsteady legal mandates. The descendent community must be involved, must support, and if necessary must demand the work. Without community support we predict that archaeological investigations prior to the development of heritage sites will become increasingly rare. Voss and Allen (2008) suggested that Chinese and Chinese American archaeology should be multistranded, multisited, multilingual, multiscalar, and multidisciplinary, while Paul Mullins (2008) calls for tackling the issues of power and race. We suggest that "imaginative and comprehensible" might be added to both mandates to humanize the process and to increase the involvement of non-academicians. How can that be done while also addressing the strategies suggested above? One approach is to reverse the usual process—by which archaeologists define important research issues and apply them to a data set—and to begin with the descendants. The authors do not suggest simply asking communities at large what they want to know about their history. Asking people to "represent" their community's interest in this way is unreasonable, and the research questions generated tend to be either materialistic (What did they eat?) or overly general (What was their way of life like?).

Instead, we suggest a method that might be called "descendant-generated." This approach involves working with descendants before, during, and after the excavation to develop the themes that are to be addressed in the report. It begins by interviewing individuals to determine the themes and values they believe are represented in the history of their community. These sessions are proposed as family history, in which naïve and generally fruitless questions like: "What would you like to find out about the history of these people?" are never explicitly asked. Instead, the values of families and the experience of communities reveal themselves in anecdotes that turn into the themes to be addressed by the archaeological report. The oral history of

the Lum family, for example, shows how the poor treatment of family members by white doctors led to a general distrust of the medical establishment. Hospitals were considered places to die, not to be healed. One oral account also claims that drinking winter-melon soup spared Chinatown from the effects of an influenza epidemic (Massey et al. 2013:83). In this way, historical experience led the family to rely on traditional and proprietary medicine.

These stories are apparently about family—that is certainly how they were told. Yet from them can be extracted research themes of the relationship between tradition, modernity, and self-sufficiency, as well as larger themes of race and power. Artifacts have a direct bearing on these tangled issues, although their meanings crosscut conventional groupings. Medicine bottles are not simply about "health," nor melon seeds about "food." While both are in some ways as political as an election button, they are also stories of families and places.

Archaeology is crucial because it is place-based. The events and processes that we archaeologists read about or are told about by elders happened right there at the places we call archaeological sites. These objects were witnesses to the past. More than just words about the place, they were actually present. And there lies their power to evoke a time and place. We believe that progress will only come from a vigorous application of imagination—both asking more interesting questions at a variety of scales and figuring out more effective ways of extracting meaning and presenting the results of our work. Our understanding of the people of the past can advance by both accumulating information and by coming up with innovative ways of reconsidering what we think we know. The most interesting questions have no definitive answers.

References

BARBER, EDMUND L., AND GEORGE H. BAKER
   1855 *Sacramento Illustrated.* Barber & Baker, Sacramento, CA.

BRIGGS, ALTON K.
   1974 The Archaeology of 1882 Labor Camps on the Southern Pacific Railroad, Val Verde County, Texas. Master's thesis, Graduate School, University of Texas, Austin.

CHINN, THOMAS W.
1989   *Bridging the Pacific: San Francisco Chinatown and Its People.* Chinese Historical Society of America, San Francisco, CA.

COSTELLO, JULIA G., ADRIAN PRAETZELLIS, MARY PRAETZELLIS, ERICA S. GIBSON, JUDITH MARVIN, MICHAEL D. MEYER, GRACE H. ZIESING, SHERRI M. GUST, MADELINE HIRN, BILL MASON, ELAINE-MARYSE SOLARI, AND SUZANNE B. STEWART
1999   Historical Archaeology at the Headquarters Facility Project Site, the Metropolitan Water District of Southern California, Vol. 2, Interpretive Report. Report to Metropolitan Water District of Southern California, Los Angeles, from Foothill Resources, Ltd., Mokelumne Hill, CA, Applied Earthworks, Inc., Fresno, CA, and Anthropological Studies Center, Rohnert Park, CA.

FARKAS, LANI AH TYE
1998   *Bury My Bones in America: The Saga of a Chinese Family in California, 1852–1996.* Carl Mautz, Nevada City, CA.

GUST, SHERRI M.
1982   Mammalian Remains. In *Archaeological and Historical Studies of the IJ56 Block: Early Chinese Merchant Community in Sacramento, California,* Mary Praetzellis and Adrian Praetzellis, editors, pp. 87–112. Anthropological Studies Center, Rohnert Park, CA. Sonoma State University <http://www.sonoma.edu/asc/publications/sac/ij56_block_sacramento_1982_part_1.pdf.> Accessed 26 May 2014.
1997   Analysis of Animal Bones. In *Historical Archaeology of an Overseas Chinese Community in Sacramento, California,* Mary Praetzellis and Adrian Praetzellis, editors, pp. 222–257. Anthropological Studies Center, Rohnert Park, CA. Sonoma State University <http://www.sonoma.edu/asc/publications/sac_hi56/index.html>. Accessed 26 May 2014.

HALL, H. J.
1982   Parasitological Analysis. In *Archaeological and Historical Studies of the IJ56 Block: Early Chinese Merchant Community in Sacramento, California,* Mary Praetzellis and Adrian Praetzellis, editors, pp. 113–120. Anthropological Studies Center, Rohnert Park, CA. Sonoma State University <http://www.sonoma.edu/asc/publications/sac/ij56_block_sacramento_1982_part_1.pdf>. Accessed 26 May 2014.

HATTORI, EUGENE
1979   Lovelock Coins. In *Archaeological and Historical Studies at Ninth and Amherst, Lovelock, Nevada,* E. Hattori, M. Rusco, and D. Tuohy, editors, pp. 410–435. Nevada State Museum, Nevada State Museum Archaeological Reports Series. Carson City.

HELLMANN, VIRGINIA R., AND JEANNIE K. YANG
1997   Special Studies. In *Historical Archaeology of an Overseas Chinese Community in Sacramento, California,* Mary Praetzellis and Adrian Praetzellis, editors, pp. 155–202. Anthropological Studies Center, Rohnert Park, CA. Sonoma State University <http://www.sonoma.edu/asc/publications/sac_hi56/index.html>. Accessed 26 May 2014.

MASSEY, SANDRA, DANA OGO SHEW, AND ADRIAN PRAETZELLIS
2013   Down to the Last Grain of Rice: Japantown Senior Apartments, San José Archaeological Investigations. Report to First Community Housing, San Jose, CA, from Anthropological Studies Center, Rohnert Park, CA.

MULLINS, PAUL
2008   The Strange and Unusual: Material and Social Dimensions of Chinese Identity. *Historical Archaeology* 42(3):152–157.

PRAETZELLIS, ADRIAN, AND MARY PRAETZELLIS
1993   Life and Work at the Cole and Nelson Sawmill, Sierra County California. Report to Tahoe National Forest, U.S. Forest Service, Nevada City, CA, from Anthropological Studies Center, Rohnert Park, CA.

PRAETZELLIS, MARY
2004   Chinese Oaklanders: Overcoming the Odds. In *Putting the "There" There: Historical Archaeologies of West Oakland,* Mary Praetzellis and Adrian Praetzellis, editors, pp. 237–259. Anthropological Studies Center, Rohnert Park, CA. Sonoma State University <http://www.sonoma.edu/asc/cypress/finalreport/index.htm>. Accessed 26 May 2014.

PRAETZELLIS, MARY, AND ADRIAN PRAETZELLIS
1982   *Archaeological and Historical Studies of the IJ56 Block: Early Chinese Merchant Community in Sacramento, California.* Anthropological Studies Center, Rohnert Park, CA. Sonoma State University <http://www.sonoma.edu/asc/publications/sac/ij56_block_sacramento_1982_part_1.pdf>. Accessed 26 May 2014.
1997   *Historical Archaeology of an Overseas Chinese Community in Sacramento, California.* Anthropological Studies Center, Rohnert Park, CA. Sonoma State University <http://www.sonoma.edu/asc/publications/sac_hi56/index.html>. Accessed 26 May 2014.
2011   Cultural Resource Management Archaeology and Heritage Values. In *Archaeologies of Engagement, Representation, and Identity,* Paul A. Shackel and David A. Gadsby, editors. Thematic issue, *Historical Archaeology* 45(1):86–100.

174

Schulz, Peter D.

1982 Fish, Reptile, and Cephalopod Remains. In *Archaeological and Historical Studies of the IJ56 Block: Early Chinese Merchant Community in Sacramento, California*, Mary Praetzellis and Adrian Praetzellis, editors, pp.74–86. Anthropological Studies Center, Rohnert Park, CA. Sonoma State University <http://www.sonoma.edu/asc/publications/sac/ij56_block_sacramento_1982_part_1.pdf>. Accessed 26 May 2014.

Voss, Barbara L., and Rebecca Allen

2008 Overseas Chinese Archaeology: Historical Foundations, Current Reflections, and New Directions. *Historical Archaeology* 42(3):5–28.

Waghorn, Annita

2004 Historic Archaeological Investigations of the City Center Cinemas Block Bounded by Miner Avenue and Hunter, El Dorado, and Channel Streets, Stockton, California. Report to Redevelopment Agency of the City of Stockton, CA, from Anthropological Studies Center, Rohnert Park, CA. City of Stockton <http://www.stocktongov.com/discover/history/mineLaundry.html>. Accessed 26 May 2014.

Wey, Nancy

1979 Chinese Written Material and Other Artifacts from Ninth and Amherst. In *Archaeological and Historical Studies at Ninth and Amherst, Lovelock, Nevada*, E. Hattori, M. Rusco, and D. Tuohy, editors, pp.539–548. Nevada State Museum Archaeological Reports Series. Carson City.

Yu, Connie Young

2001 *Chinatown San Jose, USA*, 3rd edition. History San Jose, San Jose, CA.

Mary Praetzellis
Anthropological Studies Center, Bldg. 29
Sonoma State University
Rohnert Park, CA 94928

Adrian Praetzellis
Department of Anthropology
Sonoma State University
Rohnert Park, CA 94928

Sue Fawn Chung (张素芳)

Forgotten Chinese Railroad Workers Remembered: Closing Commentary by an Historian
记住被遗忘的中国铁路工人：一个历史学家的总结陈词

ABSTRACT

In the concluding essay for this volume, Sue Fawn Chung (Zhang Sufang) briefly traces the development of historical and archaeological research in Chinese American studies that shows the new direction of multidisciplinary approach and multiethnic considerations. She has highlighted the contributions of the authors in this journal issue.

在本特辑的总结陈词中，张素芳教授简要地回顾了美国华人研究领域中历史学与考古学研究的发展。这些发展显示了跨学科方法与跨种族考量的新方向。她同时强调了本辑作者们的贡献。

In May 1969 the Golden Spike centenary was held to commemorate the completion of the first transcontinental railroad line. Although no Chinese American representatives were invited, the organizers of the train tour stopped and placed a plaque noting the 10 mi. (plus 58 ft., not noted) of track laid in one day (from 5 A.M. to 7 P.M.) on 28 April 1869, an unmatched feat. The teamwork of 1,400 Chinese workers and 8 Irish workers put into place 4,462,000 lb. of ties, rails, spikes, bolts, and other materials, allowing Charles Crocker of the Central Pacific Railroad (CPRR) to win the bet with E. P. Durant of the Union Pacific, on which crew could lay the most track in a day. Later the U.S. National Park Service allowed the Chinese Historical Society of America to place a bronze plaque about the Chinese railroad workers at Promontory, Utah, but the opening exhibit devoted little space to the Chinese. As a result, the Chinese were called "the forgotten railroad builders."

Little attention was paid to these men until the 1960s civil rights movement. The centrality of race relations in the West led to deeper studies about different racial groups, but many were based upon the assumptions that the white race was superior to all other races and that class conflicts and racism were inevitable. In the 1950s, historians turned their attention to the role of immigrants in North American history with the writings of Oscar Handlin, John Higham, and others. In the 1970s and 1980s, the "new social history" and "new western history" movements led to a focus on race, class, gender, science, ideologies, migration, diaspora, economics, art, and environment. Beginning in the 1980s, archaeologists followed this trend and paid more attention to Chinese immigrants. They began to interpret the material culture found at Chinese sites and gradually became more sophisticated at providing context. They understood that the Chinese were not homogeneous and unchanging as earlier scholars had assumed. Questions based on the theories of the 1920s Chicago school of sociology, such as why they did not assimilate, yielded to an acknowledgment of at least adaptation/acculturation to American society and a less-biased interpretation of their findings. In recent decades, Barbara Voss and others have advocated looking with an interdisciplinary (history, sociology, art, law, economics, and other disciplines) perspective at interethnic interaction, multiple scales of analysis, transnationalism, transculturalism, preservation of culture and adaptation to American culture, discoveries globally, and an understanding of the Chinese perspective. This journal issue exemplifies these trends in examining Chinese railroad workers in the field of archaeology.

Paul G. Chace and William S. Evans, Jr. pioneered the field with their 1969 study of a Chinese camp in the High Sierras. Later, R. Scott Baxter and Rebecca Allen investigated Summit Camp and gave the archaeological finds historical context and established the significance of this labor site. John Molenda dispelled the stereotype of the docile Chinese railroad workers as they participated in a

Historical Archaeology, 2015, 49(1):175–177.
Permission to reprint required.

strike reminiscent of the 1854 Chinese railroad workers' strike in Marysville, California, and raised an important concept: the differences between a Westerner's view of a "gentleman" and the Chinese view of a gentleman (*junzi*) that emphasized righteousness, benevolence, filial piety, education, and compromise. An old Chinese saying denotes the main qualities of a "gentleman": skill in calligraphy, poetry, and painting; in playing the qin (*gǔqín*), a seven-stringed instrument dating to the 5th century B.C.; and in the game of Go (*wéiqí*). How different this is from the American ideal of a gentleman!

At the end of the line, Michael Polk compared the Chinese workers' camp to white camps. The 1870 census manuscript listed 440 Chinese still working in the area around Promontory, while others traveled back to Nevada towns along or near the CPRR line and to California, as well as eastward. Lynn Furnis and Mary L. Maniery used a method of investigating horizontal deposits across the Virginia & Truckee Railroad (V&TRR) Chinese work camp at Lakeview, Nevada (on the western margin of Little Ranch), which was occupied from 1861 to 1905, instead of employing more traditional vertical excavation methods. This resulted in finding architectural, domestic, food, industrial, personal, transportation, and other types of surface artifacts. Putting the finds in context, they conclude that Lakeview Camp was occupied in the 1870s by a series of Chinese workers in two major crews, and project what everyday life for them was like.

Charlotte Sunseri's ethnography covers what happened to some of the former CPRR workers. When the CPRR reached Reno, Nevada, in early 1868, only 5,000 workers were retained, while several hundred went to work in building the V&TRR, Carson & Colorado Railroad, and Bodie & Benton Railroad, as well as other lines. At the same time, men went into logging for the Carson & Tahoe Lumber & Fluming Company and other newly established lumber companies. Tim Urbaniak and Kelly Dixon also study the period after the CPRR, analyzing rock inscriptions. Chinese railroad workers were hired by mines and other industries after the rails were built, and they left their mark on the landscape near Roundup, Montana.

Later, with the growing restriction on Chinese immigration, railroads hired maintenance crews from other ethnic groups, including Japanese, English, and Norwegian immigrants.

Daily life is explored in several works. Marjorie Akin, James Bard, and Gary Weisz provide cultural context to a frequently found artifact on almost all 19th-century Chinese sites: Asian coins. Based on the work of J. Ryan Kennedy, it becomes obvious that the Chinese consumed lots of pork, fish if available, and local animals. Different foods were evident at different sites. One wonders if one additional factor to the environmental availability of foodstuffs was the eating habits of the immigrants based on those of their home villages, so that Zhongshan immigrants, having lived near the South China Sea, were more partial to seafood. Medical care was of great concern to these immigrants, who were familiar with practices over 2,000 years old. Sarah Heffner examined health-care practices that included the incorporation of more readily available Western medicines and traditional herbal remedies. Chinese workers were practical people who used whatever medicine was available. Many contract laborers insisted upon the presence of a Chinese practitioner hired by the regional or family association, so in 1870 in Elko and Winnemucca, two railroad towns, for example, there was at least one physician. Finally, Ryan Harrod and John Crandall examined the bones of men buried in the Chinese cemetery of Carlin, a railroad town that began in 1869 and was the home of many Chinese railroad workers and their supporters, including Chinese farmers providing produce for the cooks who served food to the passengers and crewmen 24 hours a day. All of the 13 male skeletal remains revealed poor health and hard work, and showed signs of stress and strain on their bones. They truly led hard lives.

This important issue brings together information about these railroad builders so that they are not forgotten. Although these Chinese left no written records, archaeologists have uncovered artifacts that have shown aspects of daily life, racism and discrimination, health, culture, perspectives, and accomplishments. By bringing together scholars from several disciplines interested in the subject of Chinese railroad workers, greater knowledge and understanding has been gained, and new research questions have been posed. These studies have opened the door to a greater understanding of material culture and the lives and experiences of late-19th-century Chinese railroad workers.

SUE FAWN CHUNG
DEPARTMENT OF HISTORY
UNIVERSITY OF NEVADA, LAS VEGAS
4505 MARYLAND PARKWAY
BOX 5020
LAS VEGAS, NV 89154-5020

Go Online at <http://www.sha.org> for SHA Publications

Search *Historical Archaeology* articles with an author, title, and subject keyword-searchable directory, or browse the journal by volume and issue.

Consider **Reviews**. SHA publishes its reviews on books, films, exhibits, and websites online twice annually.

Hone your skills with *Technical Briefs in Historical Archaeology*. These specialized technical papers in historical archaeology, maritime archaeology, material culture technology, and materials conservation are published annually. Titles include:

- Using Ground-Penetrating Radar to Map the Historic Pottersville Kiln, Edgefield, South Carolina
- A Critique of the Fundamentals of the "Commercial Salvage" Model of the Excavation of Historic Shipwrecks
- Virtual Artifact Curation of the Historical Past and the Next Engine Desktop 3D Scanner
- Three-Dimensional Models of Archaeological Objects: From Laser Scanners to Interactive PDF Documents
- Vase Rollout Photography Using Digital Reflex Cameras
- Evidence of Use and Reuse of a Dog Collar from the Sloop of War HMS *Swift* (1770)
- Use of Remote Surveillance Motion-Activated Cameras for Monitoring Rural Archaeological Sites
- Metallographic Analysis of a Spearhead Found near Fortlet Miñana, Argentina
- Forensic Hair and Fiber Examinations in Archaeology
- Telling Time for the Electrified: An Introduction to Porcelain Insulators and the Electrification of the American Home
- Delineation and Resolution of Cemetery Graves Using a Conductivity Meter and GPR

Catch up on society news and events. The *SHA Newsletter*, a quarterly publication, contains news, a range of topical columns, a current research section featuring historical archaeology news from around the world, announcements, and a calendar of events. SHA newsletters from 1999–2007 are posted in the Newsletter Archive.

Download the **SHA Style Guide** to learn how to prepare articles for submission to the journal.

Visit **SHA Online** to purchase publications on historical archaeology, including recent editions of *Historical Archaeology*. Other titles now available through our Print On Demand bookstore, <http://www.lulu.com /spotlight/shabookstore>, include:

- *Ceramic Identification in Historical Archaeology: The View from California 1822–1940*, edited by Rebecca Allen, Julia E. Huddleson, Kimberly J. Wooten, and Glenn J. Farris (2014).
- *Perspectives from Historical Archaeology and ACUA Proceedings: Maritime Archaeology*, compiled by Ben Ford and Wendy van Duivenoorde (2013).
- *Historical Archaeology in Central Europe*, edited by Natasha Mehler (2013).
- *Historical Archaeology and the Importance of Material Things II*, edited by Julie Schablitsky and Mark Leone (2012).
- *Perspectives from Historical Archaeology: The Archaeology of Spanish Missions and Colonies in the New World*, compiled by Steve Tomka and Timothy Perttula (2011).
- *Perspectives from Historical Archaeology: Revealing Landscapes*, compiled by Christopher Fennell (2011).
- *Perspectives from Historical Archaeology: Mortuary and Religious Sites*, compiled by Richard Veit and Alasdair Brooks (2011).
- *Perspectives from Historical Archaeology: The Archaeology of Native American–European Contact*, compiled by Timothy Perttula (2010).
- *Perspectives from Historical Archaeology: The Archaeology of Plantation Life*, compiled by Nicholas Honerkamp (2009).
- *Archaeology of Early Colonial Settlement in the Emerging Atlantic World*, edited by William Kelso (2009).
- *Historical Archaeology and the Importance of Material Things*, edited by Leland G. Ferguson (2012 reprint).

**Members have access to all *Historical Archaeology* journal articles online.
Nonmembers have access to articles published prior to 2009.**

www.ingramcontent.com/pod-product-compliance
Lightning Source LLC
Chambersburg PA
CBHW041115120626
46547CB00019B/2714